'FLATTIE'

'FLATTIE'

MEMORIES OF A RELUCTANT TRAVELLER

JEAN STIRLING

Matador
Unit E2 Airfield Business Park,
Harrison Road, Market Harborough,
Leicestershire. LE16 7UL
Tel: 0116 279 2299
Email: books@troubador.co.uk
Web: www.troubador.co.uk/matador
Twitter: @matadorbooks

ISBN 978 180313 625 7
British Library Cataloguing in Publication Data.
A catalogue record for this book is available from the British Library.

Typeset in 11pt Minion Pro by Troubador Publishing Ltd, Leicester, UK

Matador is an imprint of Troubador Publishing Ltd

Dedicated – with great love –
to 'our Mam'...

always the wind beneath our wings.

ACKNOWLEDGEMENTS

My grateful thanks to:

Professor Vanessa Toulmin, Founder of the National Fairground Archive, University of Sheffield, for allowing me to refer to her book *Pleasurelands*.

Thomas McCann, Parkhead Historical Society, for the Vinegarhill article.

Brian McGinlay, John Sinclair, BP, Cinema Treasures, and various family members, for their kind permissions to use photographs.

Members of the Tyne and Esk writers' group (Penicuik branch) for their interest and patience.

All illustrations are mine. Some additional photographs have been obtained via the internet when stated as 'copyright free', and while I have been unable to trace the original source for these, I will be happy to delete them, if requested, from any future prints.

FOREWORD

As youngsters my brothers and I were fascinated by Mam's account of her life and how she met Dad. Always good with words, her stories painted pictures for us that we felt should be captured somehow and kept as a permanent reminder of our 'roots.'

Time passed, lives moved on and for Mam, reminiscing was something she preferred to avoid. I sensed that a whole chapter of 'our' story would be lost unless someone took over as historian, and in the absence of anyone else, I duly undertook the task.

To say it has been cathartic is an understatement. I realised when writing this that much of my own early life experience is enmeshed throughout the account; therefore I make no apology for some nostalgic self-indulgence.

It is also an acknowledgement of a lifestyle long gone and a special group of people, almost like a 'lost tribe' – the 'travellers' – who were so much part of my formative years.

To any fellow travellers of my time who might perhaps take issue with some of the detail – please remember that we may have taken the same journey... but by different roads. This was my family's journey, and these are my memories. I hope that some of these accounts will resonate with you, albeit that your own experiences were not quite the same.

Jean Stirling

ONE

'So, Mrs Stirling, tell us about your life with the Carnie.'

It was 1988 and Mam, Dad and I were in Dallas, visiting my younger brother David who was completing his PostDoc at Texas University. As we were nearing the end of the holiday and being wined and dined by David's colleagues, the host, much to Mam's embarrassment, made this request.

At first she misunderstood the term, then realised this was the Americanism for *Carnival.* There was silence around the table, all eyes on Mam... apart from Dad's; he didn't know *where* to look. I wondered momentarily how this chapter in our lives had become common knowledge, then realised that David must have been the mole.

'Well...' She shifted uncomfortably in her seat and for a moment I thought she was for once going to tell her story. She looked at David, who was grinning sheepishly, and continued, 'That's a closed book now and I won't bore you with the details.' She smiled apologetically, cheeks just a little flushed, and our host very graciously changed the subject.

We enjoyed the meal and the remainder of the evening but for Mam, everything had changed, and I could see she was distracted and thoughtful. I understood what was happening. Two worlds had collided – worlds that she had tried so hard to keep apart. The first, which in its twenty years she had never accepted and had tried so hard to leave, and the second – *her* world of mainstream society, conformity, acceptance and stability.

To discover that strangers were not only aware of our history but were *interested* had thrown her. She wanted to hold fast to this second life we had all created and to lock the past away, almost as a guilty secret never to be shared.

On reflection, I realised that I had also observed this privacy 'rule' and had never discussed my early or teenage years with friends. The lifestyle would have seemed totally alien to them, *my* experiences would be so different from *theirs* and I had no wish to be viewed as some strange curiosity.

David, on the other hand, seemed to have no such qualms and had obviously shared some of the story with his American friends, who were now clearly disappointed that they would not receive their after-dinner talk.

Talking this over with Mam later, when we were home, she agreed that our earlier life, while different and certainly hard, was nothing to be ashamed of, and in fact was something we should really be proud of in terms of our social mobility and who we now were.

But where did it start and why, even after so many years, did Mam still feel unable to talk openly about 'that life,' as she called it?

TWO

In normal circumstances, the chances of our parents ever meeting, let alone marrying, was unlikely.

Our mam Winifred (Winnie) was born in 1921 in Newcastle and lived with her parents and older brother Leslie in Gateshead, which she described as 'a posher part of Newcastle'! Our dad, Richard, born in 1920 in a caravan in St Cuthbert's stable yard in Edinburgh, was one of a family of ten children, his parents Scottish Travelling Show people.

In short, Mam and Dad were geographically, sociologically and culturally poles apart! The catalyst was, as with most of that generation, World War 2. Times were anything but normal, throwing people together from all walks of life, and such it was for my parents.

Dad's regiment, the Cameronians, was based in Alnwick and the soldiers often attended dances in Newcastle. Mam was reluctantly talked into attending one of these by Freda, her workmate.

Freda was a bit of a free spirit; she loved an exciting social life and had been 'seeing' a soldier – who was married – from the regiment. Freda needed Mam as an alibi in case the soldier's wife found out. Her idea being that, if confronted by the man's wife, she could explain away any notion of improper liaison by claiming she was chummed to the dance by Mam, not the soldier. The soldier, using similar logic, coerced Dad into going with him, figuring there was safety in numbers! Without realising it, Mam and Dad would be on a blind date.

The dance hall was noisy, smoke-filled, hot and overcrowded, and Mam's first instinct was to escape. Just as she was about to devise her strategy, Freda charged through the melee, reappearing with the two soldiers in tow.

Hurried introductions done, Freda dragged her partner onto the dance floor, waved to Mam, then was swallowed up in the hordes of swirling bodies dancing to the local band's attempts at Glenn Miller music.

Mam was mortified, realising she was now 'stuck' with this young soldier who scarcely seemed able to string two words together. Common decency dictated that she could not just abandon him and, all things considered, where was the harm, she thought, in staying just for an hour? After all, the chap was quite good-looking – a little like Robert Taylor, the film star she had a bit of a crush on – and so smart in his uniform.

He seemed painfully shy, but she noticed his foot tapping in time to the music so as an ice-breaker she made the first move and asked if he would like to dance.

Dad couldn't believe his luck. His blind date was quite a looker. Long shiny dark hair, a Hollywood smile, and slender legs that seemed to go on forever! He was so in awe of her he could hardly speak.

Three hours later they were still in the dance hall, Freda and her partner long gone, and Mam and Dad now lost in each other's company.

During the intervals when the hall was slightly quieter they talked, discovering a shared love of music, animals, country walks, quiet times. Mam described her family, her job, her likes and dislikes, and Dad listened attentively.

Mam (Winnie) and Dad (Dickie)

It never occurred to her that this young man, whose company she was now enjoying, seemed reluctant to describe *his* background, beyond saying he was from a large family and they lived in Glasgow.

Mam had no steady boyfriend. She enjoyed a social life that centred around her membership of the YWCA. Her few dates with male companions she described as either 'dull as dishwater,' or 'hands-everywhere types' that she had to 'slap down'! Dad fell into neither of these categories. She found his quiet manner and initial shyness attractive and even felt a little sorry for him.

He walked her to the tram stop and after a very chaste kiss, she agreed to meet him again.

Their first 'proper' date was to a local cinema. The couple were gradually relaxing in each other's company; Dad was less tongue–tied, Mam discovering that he was fun to be with and, importantly, 'really gentlemanly' (i.e. did not take 'liberties'!).

He was beginning to share a little of his background. She learned that though he was named Richard, everyone called him Dick, and he had three sisters – Becky, Lizzy, and Rosie – and five brothers – Harry, Edward, Tommy, John, and the youngest, Walter.

Mam found it so funny that three brothers could be called Tom, Dick and Harry. Tommy had been called up at the same time as Dad and was serving with one of the Highland regiments. John, despite wanting to follow his brothers into the army, was conscripted as a 'Bevin Boy' (this was a very crude, numbers out of a hat selection process to ensure coal mines would always have the essential pit workers).

John found himself reluctantly working at the coal face, and with no uniform to 'prove' he was *also* doing his duty. For the Bevin Boys this was a problem. Many conscientious objectors had been assigned to work in the mines and 'legitimate conscripts' were often confused with the 'conchies' and abused by ill-informed members of the public who accused them of cowardice and dodging military service.

Dad's sister Rosie was a munitions worker (unmarried 'mobile' women were given the choice of conscription to the forces or working in essential industries). He wasn't sure why Rosie opted for industry but was aware that she earned good money in munitions. The work was dangerous, and the pay reflected the hazards to which they were exposed.

Women on the munitions production line during WW2

Mam continued to press Dad for more information, intrigued by his slowly unfolding story, yet finding him still reluctant to discuss what his parents did, or where they lived. Dad was equally fascinated in Mam's lifestyle and background but wondered why she lived with two aunts rather than at her parental home. He thought that perhaps her family had met some misfortune and he was reluctant to broach the subject, fearing it might be painful to her. However, on one of their dates she willingly described her childhood and upbringing, Dad listening intently as she explained the circumstances that had led to her living with her aunts Hilda and Edith.

THREE

Mam's early years had been traumatic. Her own mum, Jane, died in 1930 when Mam was just nine. Jane had suffered for years from what she dismissed as 'just bilious attacks' but was eventually diagnosed as inoperable cancer.

Mam was inconsolable. This beloved person, Jane, her mother, was gone and nothing could ever replace her. Jane had been the centre of everything important in her life. The one who taught her the Charleston dance and had entered her, aged just three, in a local talent show, which she nearly won. Jane encouraged her to have piano lessons, taking pride in her progression through the various exams.

She was full of fun, neighbours always popping in to have their teacups read – Jane pretending she had the 'gift' of fortune telling, making up stories and the people believing her! She had a strong social conscience – it wasn't the first time Mam returned home from school to find a gypsy or some homeless person sitting at the kitchen table enjoying a meal, invited in by Jane, who felt sorry for them.

Mam remembered as a six-year-old being sent with a bundle of clothes she had outgrown to a nearby family and being horrified at the impoverished state of the home. They were living in one room with no floorboards, just an earth floor, and the children, while clean, were sparsely clothed, barefoot, and looked malnourished. (This was not uncommon in the 1920s – social welfare was not easily obtained, and families often survived on charity.) Mam noted the proud bearing and dignity of the woman, who offered her a glass of water with all the aplomb of the lady of the manor, and her gratitude when receiving the clothes.

Returning home, she recounted what she had seen and how 'awful' the place was, only to be reproached by Jane, who told her how wrong it was to judge people, explaining there was 'no man in the house' and the mother was trying hard in very difficult circumstances to make the best of what she had.

During very cold winters, Jane gently chided Mam for making ice slides on the road, telling her it was dangerous for old people and that the milkman's horse would slip. Jane fed the horse daily, much to the irritation of the milkman; the horse stopped at the house every morning even when there was no delivery and refused to budge until Jane came out with its carrot.

Jane was the one who provided the love in the house, who cuddled her children, who sang, danced and did daft things just for the fun of it. She could rattle out a tune or two on their old piano, albeit she was self-taught, and was in great demand at their parties. She filled the house with her presence. Home *was* Jane and now she was gone.

The house, once full of laughter, seemed hollow, empty – no longer home – and the world was now a frightening, lonely place. Mam's father Jack, who worked shifts as a railwayman, could not take time off work to look after his two children so hired a live-in housekeeper.

The woman, an Irish lady, had previously been a cook at Durham prison and required lodgings. Her culinary skills were basic and she was kindly – but was no mother figure and Mam became a quiet, lost child, seeking solace in touching the clothes and belongings, not yet removed, that still held the memory of Jane's fragrance.

One comfort for her was the school janitor's dog Jess, a golden Labrador bitch, which decided to 'adopt' her. It was as though the dog recognised a lost hurting soul and it accompanied her everywhere, even hopping on trams to the shops with her.

And so time passed, weeks turned to sad, empty months, and slowly some semblance of routine evolved. Then, one weekend, she overheard a conversation the housekeeper was having with a visiting friend as they sipped tea from Jane's best china cups, unaware that Mam – who sat in the corner with a book – was listening.

'So,' asked the friend, elbows propped on the table, cigarette clamped between nicotine-stained fingers, leaning forward as though some secret was about to be shared, 'I hear you will be looking for new lodgings soon?'

'Aye,' sighed the housekeeper, adding, 'The boss got married this weekend, so I'll not be needed when he brings the new wife back.'

The two women continued to talk, completely oblivious to the child, now white-faced and shaken in the corner, trying desperately to make sense of what she had just heard. *Surely* they were mistaken. She was not aware that her dad was even seeing anyone, let alone *marrying* them.

She vaguely remembered being taken to Saltwell Park one afternoon and meeting an awkward, gangly woman whom he introduced as a friend, which she had thought no more of. Now, listening to this conversation, she realised that the 'friend' was to become her dad's new wife and she felt sick with apprehension and foreboding.

Who was this woman – this stranger who would be invading their home? Why hadn't her dad talked about any such arrangement with them? How *could* he so easily just dismiss her mum's memory and allow this to happen? She felt lost and betrayed.

Mam now eleven years old, and two years after the death of her mother, this new person – Janet – moved into the family home.

The stepmother made it abundantly clear that she did not like the girl, probably seeing her as a constant and irritating reminder of the woman she was replacing.

She removed all trace of Jane's home and memory – carpets, furniture, little ornaments Jane had cherished, claiming they just gathered dust. The one thing she could not get rid of was the other woman's daughter and she dedicated herself to making life as miserable as possible for the child.

It soon became clear to mam that this woman Janet was 'not quite right' (or, as my dad put it later, 'a nutcase!') She was obsessed to the point of fanaticism with germs and anything that might harbour these was thrown out. All carpets were removed, leaving cold bare linoleum. The few remaining pieces of furniture were covered over with assorted dust sheets. She would only touch door handles using a cloth. She emptied Mam's room of everything previously loved and treasured – little dressing table ornaments, things bought by Jane to make the room cosy, pictures, pretty eiderdown, and curtains. Even the lampshade was removed, leaving an exposed bulb and Mam's room almost like a cell.

Her dad Jack seemed detached from everything, either oblivious to what was happening or afraid to confront the madness of the woman who was now his wife. He was able to escape back to the comfort of his own familiar world of work.

The stepmother refused to allow Mam to practice the piano – saying 'the thumping gave her a headache' – and cancelled her lessons, claiming 'it was a waste of money.' Her brother Leslie, being older, was able to confront and challenge many of the stepmother's idiosyncrasies but this failed to stop her targeting Mam at every opportunity.

The cruelty was never physical but sometimes Mam wished it *had* been; then she would at least have proof, something to evidence the misery she was being subjected to. The only time she could remember the woman ever touching her was when she decided that Mam 'probably had nits because all children her age had them'! She made her strip down to her vest and pants and stand on a newspaper that was placed on the cold scullery floor, then proceeded to pour a paraffin liquid all over Mam's head. She forced her to stand there for an hour, then grabbed her and produced a steel comb, which she dragged unmercifully through her hair. She examined the comb with each 'trawl' – like a huntress desperate for her prey – and seemed almost disappointed not to have caught anything. Mam was cold, upset and started to cry, only to be scolded for being 'such a stupid big baby.' The child vowed in that miserable moment, that she would never *ever* again give this heartless woman the satisfaction of seeing her cry.

The stepmother, within just weeks of arrival, demanded Mam's house key, saying she did not want her poking around when she was out – and this was most days. Neighbours became aware of the child sitting on the doorstep for hours after school – sometimes with arms wrapped for comfort around the dog Jess, often in the foulest of weather, cold, wet, and waiting for someone to come home and let her in.

One neighbour, incensed by this and knowing that one of Mam's aunts worked in a large department store in town, went to see her to advise her of the situation, stating her concerns and that – in her view – this was child neglect.

Mam was never too sure what happened thereafter but suspected that her aunts called a summit meeting with their brother Jack and trusted him to sort things out. One positive outcome from this was that she was encouraged to visit and often stay for weekends with the aunts at their house in Pelaw.

Happier times with Mam's beloved mum Jane, brother Leslie and dad Jack

The stepmother suspected this was some form of monitoring by the aunts and interrogated her after each visit, furious when she refused to cooperate but powerless to do anything about it.

A type of 'cold war' relationship developed. Mam, now a young teenager and at senior school, was enjoying new friends but never able to invite any of them home. Instead she accepted *their* invitations to parties, sleepovers, outings… anything that removed her from the toxic environment of her own home.

Then one morning she woke from a restless sleep, in desperate pain and terribly ill. With each spasm, she cried out, writhing in agony, only to hear the stepmother shouting from another room that she should 'stop that bellowing!,' telling her dad to, 'Take no notice – it's just attention seeking; she's just bilious and likely been eating rubbish again.'

For once, her dad ignored Janet and on seeing Mam's distress sent Leslie to the nearest phone box to call for help. The doctor attended, an ambulance was called and Mam was rushed to hospital with a burst appendix and peritonitis.

Mam knew that she would have died had she been alone in the house with the stepmother… and *so did her dad.*

Requiring post-operative recovery and care, the aunts insisted that she was to be discharged to their home. This suited the stepmother since the prospect of an invalid in her house was abhorrent to her. Mam was delighted. The Pelaw house felt like sanctuary and as she drifted in and out of a medicated

Mam's granda's kingdom

sleep, she remembered the many happy times spent there when her mother was alive.

They had been regular visitors, the aunts enjoying Jane's company while Mam pottered around her granda's allotment opposite the house. She had no memory of her grandma, who died when Mam was only two, but was devoted to her granda and followed him around like a little puppy. He was a railway signalman. The signal box was not too far from the house and she remembered visiting him at work, being helped up the steep stairs into the box and instructed not to touch anything. She loved the sight of all the highly polished levers and the view of the rail track, bending like a silver ribbon into the distance.

Mam's granda was a meticulously clean man – always with starched white collar, suit and waistcoat, shoes gleaming. He was also extremely well read; the house contained a library of his favourite authors and was where Mam's love of Dickens developed. His allotment provided all the vegetables needed for the aunts' kitchen; his chickens laid fresh eggs almost on demand.

Lying in bed, Mam could shut her eyes and picture her aunts – Hilda and Edith – bustling around the kitchen downstairs, the range fired up, the aroma of roasts or home baking drifting up to her bedroom; and her Uncle Fred, always full of banter, insisting on serenading everyone with his attempts at Gilbert and Sullivan. This was a happy place, somewhere to recover, be protected and loved.

The aunts fussed over her, taking turns to carry trays up to her room, encouraging and helping her to eat and assisting her to bathe and toilet. 'En suite' consisted of a potty under the bed, which the aunts emptied in the outside toilet.

They devoted themselves to the task of her recovery without complaint and soon she was able to be helped downstairs, where they had made up a day bed, allowing her to enjoy and be included in the happy banter and interaction of her relatives.

Mam's beloved granda enjoying a book

Her Dad, Jack, visited occasionally to check her progress; his wife chose not to come. On one of these visits the aunts suggested that it would be better if Mam just stayed with them, making the excuse that they still needed to keep an eye on her, but the real reason was Janet – the stepmother. The aunts were not prepared to expose their niece to any further neglect and abuse at the hands of this woman. Jack obviously understood the hidden agenda and agreed, returning a few days later with the few possessions from Mam's old room.

This was to be the start of a new chapter for Mam, a time of happy family life in the house at Pelaw with her granda, aunts Hilda and Edith, and Uncle Fred.

She was fourteen, it was 1934 and life felt good again.

FOUR

Her granda sat in his favourite chair, newspaper on his lap, and looked up as Mam pranced around the room, showing off her latest dress, preparing to meet friends.

'Aye lass… you enjoy yourself while ye can because there'll soon be another war.'

'Aw Granda – don't be such a misery,' she laughed and ruffled his hair, disturbing the comb-over he carefully brushed each day to conceal his balding crown.

'I'm telling you, lass, it might not be in my time, but all the signs are there and it's going to happen again.' He pointed to his newspaper – the headline in bold black letters stating that Hitler had announced conscription and Germany was engaged in rearmament.

Her grandfather remembered the horror of the First World War. Too old to enlist but still working as a railway signalman, he remembered the young men in his area being called to arms, the death toll, the maimed, the stories of men being gassed. It was to be the 'war to end all wars' yet, just twenty years on, Germany was sabre-rattling again and her grandfather recognised all the signs.

Mam's head was full of other things. She was loving her new job as a typist with the Deaf and Dumb Society in Newcastle (this was the politically correct term at that time) and enjoying a social life, much of which centred around her membership of the YWCA. She had no interest in politics and Germany could be the other side of the moon for all she cared.

In April 1939, her much loved granda died and five months later, just as he'd predicted, war was declared.

'Where's the shelter?!'

The Pelaw household was now all-female. Her granda was gone and Uncle Fred, in a reserved occupation as a manager with the oil company Shellmex/BP, was having to work in various parts of the country – sometimes driving the company tankers.The aunts were unsure what *they* should be doing. They had received their gas masks (thirty-eight million of these had been distributed to every household in Britain) and were aware of war preparations around them, including their next-door neighbour being the designated air-raid warden. All cinemas, dance halls and places of large public gatherings were closed by Government order for fear of bombings and mass casualties. (This was rescinded two weeks later, officials aware of the need to maintain 'morale' but also bowing to public pressure.)

The neighbourhood warden gave the aunts advice on blackout and applying sticky tape to windows in case of blast damage. They busied themselves with this but much later, to the warden's surprise, he heard furious, panicked knocking on his front door and opened it to the spectacle of Aunt Hilda, resplendent in gas mask, like some alien creature, demanding to know where the shelter was, unaware that the air raid warning siren was just being tested.

Mam found this extremely funny but also realised that the war was real – not some movie – and that the sound of the air raid siren would become a familiar and terrifying part of the life she had just begun to enjoy.

The aunts still tried to maintain some semblance of normal routine –

Edith working in the haberdashery department of the department store, Hilda running the house and maintaining the allotment, and Mam continuing to work as office typist with the Deaf Society. The YWCA provided a sort of reassurance for her, a comfort in the familiar busyness; there were activities to be organised and the amateur dramatic plays in which she had leading roles (including Malvolio in 'The Merchant of Venice' and the Ghost of Christmas Present in 'A Christmas Carol').

And so it continued, the logistics and mechanisms of war being implemented across Britain. All men aged between eighteen and forty-one were conscripted. (Dad was called up on 13th June 1940. He was twenty years old.)

The gas attacks everyone had feared did not happen, but people still automatically carried their gas masks around in the little cardboard boxes provided – some fashion houses even produced 'designer' bags for the masks. Anderson air-raid shelters were quickly installed in gardens and back yards in preparation for German bombardment.

Newcastle was a prime target, and everyone dreaded clear moonlit nights that illuminated the Tyne and provided a route to strategic target areas for the bombers.

'The balloons are up again tonight.' This became part of everyday small talk. Barrage balloons were attached by cables to lorries and winched up when enemy aircraft raids were expected. The main deterrent was the cable, destroying immediately any plane that touched it and forcing aircraft to fly higher and lose bombing accuracy as a result.

For Mam, it was almost akin to checking the weather forecast before going out and, while not blasé about potential risks, she always felt reassured if no balloons were up. The air-raid sirens became a feature of everyone's lives.

In October 1939, the first warning sounded over Tyneside and the 'all clear' siren was not set off for nearly two hours, until defences were sure there would be no enemy action. People huddled in shelters, terrified of the anticipated onslaught, listening for every sound that might be enemy bombers – parents hugging frightened children tightly to them, some people quietly praying, others cursing… everyone hoping they would be safe in the shelters.

For about eight months after this, many more warnings and 'all clears' were sounded, to the point where people were beginning to find it a nuisance, often ignoring warnings to go to the shelters. However, on 2nd July 1940, a major air raid took place in the late afternoon; enemy bombers tried to destroy the High

Level Bridge, missed their target, and destroyed the Spillers factory. Thirteen people were killed and 123 injured.

Bombing raids were increasing in intensity but often planes were flying over Newcastle to target other cities – Clydebank suffering huge losses in March 1941.

Mam had adapted to a sort of wartime 'norm.' Like everyone else, she still went to work, and she became used to the food rationing, the queues for things, the warning notices flashed on cinema screens to advise audiences of impending raids. She followed the aunts out to the shelter, hating the night-time sirens that dragged them from warm beds out to the cold, damp corrugated shelters.

She listened on the aunts' wireless, to the 'fire in the belly' speeches by Winston Churchill, trusting his assurances that Britain would survive.

Then, in April 1941, Newcastle was again a target, with more than fifty bombers causing widespread damage. Mam decided to ignore the siren, exhausted from night after night without sleep and reluctant to face another session in the Anderson. Her aunts had already left the house – complete with their blankets, vacuum flasks and anything else they could think of to provide some comfort in the shelter – assuming she was following them.

Just as she was about to climb into bed, Mam decided to look out the window and was horrified to see an enemy bomber caught in the cross of the searchlights and being targeted by the ack-ack (anti-aircraft) guns. She flew down the stairs and out the back door, heart pounding, hearing things peppering the ground around her like hailstones as she ran to the shelter.

The next morning they emerged, bleary eyed, to discover the 'hailstones' she had been dodging were just a bit more dangerous – the whole area was covered in pieces of shrapnel. Between July and December 1941, the German Luftwaffe, using high explosive bombs, incendiaries and parachute mines, continued to target Newcastle. With a death toll of over 400, whole streets destroyed and entire families wiped out, the need to maintain morale was important.

The King and Queen, the Princess Royal, Winston Churchill, and even the entertainer Gracie Fields, visited during this period. The 'Newcastle Blitz' was happening, yet the Tynesiders still carried on with life, picking their way through the bomb-damaged streets to get to work… glad to have survived another day.

FIVE

In all this madness – the last thing on Mam's mind was a boyfriend.

The aunts had previously attempted some matchmaking, introducing her to the son of family friends. The young chap was a university graduate and had been working his way up the promotion ladder of the banking industry prior to being commissioned in the army.

Her aunts were impressed by him. They saw him as a good prospect – he ticked all their boxes in terms of 'suitability' – and they were at a loss to understand why Mam did not share this view. What she didn't tell them was that on her first (and only) 'date' with him, his hands were everywhere, and it was like trying to dance with an octopus.

The 'blind date' with dad was so different for her. This was someone who ticked *her* boxes, and as the weeks and months progressed, she realised that at some point she would have to introduce him to her aunts.

Aware that this chap, whoever he was, had caught their niece's eye, the aunts saw it as their duty to check his suitability, so they suggested he attend one afternoon for tea.

Aunt Hilda prepared a feast of home baking and Mam duly arrived with a terrified Dad in tow. His uniform was immaculate, the crease of his tartan trews razor sharp, boots polished to a standard even her granda would have approved of.

The aunts were introduced, Dad shuffling his feet – clearly wishing he could be anywhere but here and in awe of these two ladies who featured so prominently in Mam's life.

Shy and awkward in new company, he had difficulty conversing, leaving Mam to fill in the silences. A type of interrogation took place, the aunts determined to find out more about this young man – Dad appearing 'shifty' by avoiding anything about his background and family beyond what he had already told Mam. The aunts decided between themselves that he was the wrong 'type' for their niece.

They saw him as gauche and ill-equipped to engage in normal conversation. On the few occasions he did speak, he mumbled, and his accent was hard to follow. He lacked refinement and culture. This was just not what they had in mind for Mam.

However, realising that she was keen on him, they decided to pass no comment beyond telling her he seemed *quite nice*. They assumed that if they just let things run their natural course, the relationship would eventually just 'fizzle out.' On the few occasions she mentioned Dad, they quickly changed the subject, choosing instead to talk about rationing constraints and how beneficial the allotment continued to be. Mam was in her own happy world, failing to notice that her aunts never spoke of or enquired after the young Scottish soldier their niece was seeing.

Aunt Hilda (right) showing a visitor round the allotment

Happily oblivious to the aunts' disapproval, Mam and Dad continued to meet, albeit these liaisons were quite haphazard and dependent on where Dad was based, how much leave he could arrange, and whether he could make it back to barracks by the required time.

Several times he didn't

manage this, resulting in 'jankers' (punishments) ranging from being confined to barracks or having extra parade duties. For one punishment he was ordered to clean the windows of the Grand Hotel in Scarborough, part of this hotel being used by RAF officers and cadets. He later told Mam that he'd cleaned 'every single window in the hotel.' Knowing the size of the building, she suspected this was a slight exaggeration but allowed him the drama of the story without contradiction.

The courtship continued, the couple meeting at every opportunity, even if that meant another encounter with her aunts. On one of these visits, much to his dismay, she announced that she had to go down to the little church at Pelaw. The organist had been conscripted and a replacement was required urgently. The aunts had 'volunteered' her services, despite her protests since it meant much practice and preparation ahead of each service. Dad, not wishing to be left alone with the aunts, offered to go with her.

The church was quiet, the atmosphere solemn, the only sound the rustle of papers as she looked through the order of service and hymns.

Dad was impressed that she could read music and the church organ fascinated him. It was obvious that he was keen to have a shot, reminding her that he had taught himself to play the piano accordion and knew his way around a keyboard.

To her horror, he asked her if she could play 'In the Mood,' a popular Glenn Miller tune and part of dad's 'repertoire' on the accordion. Realising that he had no sense of decorum, she pretended not to hear and suggested he might like to help by operating the bellows at the back of the organ.

She sorted through the sheet music and started to play the first hymn. The old organ began to creak and groan in protest. She wondered whether damp or perhaps mice had caused a problem and continued playing, but with each key touched, the noise increased to an alarming pitch. Fearing the poor old thing might explode, she stopped and looked behind the organ to find a very red-faced and out-of-breath Dad pumping enough air into the organ to raise a barrage balloon!

Finding the whole experience very funny, she innocently relayed the story to her aunts when he had gone, thinking they would enjoy the humour and not realising this just served to reinforce their view that he was virtually a heathen.

They became quieter and even more tight-lipped whenever his name was mentioned, still hoping the novelty of this young Scottish soldier would wear off and their niece would come to her senses.

Mam, Edith and Hilda were sitting round the kitchen table, Hilda trimming the pastry round the edges of a plate pie, Edith listening to the wireless and quietly sewing. Mam had chosen this moment carefully.

'Dick has a weekend pass and he's invited me up to Scotland,' she announced, in what she hoped was a matter-of-fact voice.

The aunts looked up – horrified.

'It's alright,' Mam laughed, knowing how prudish the aunts could be. 'It's perfectly respectable; I'll be staying with his parents.' She scanned their faces, looking for some sign of approval.

Hilda put the pie down, wiped the flour from her hands and brushed the front of her apron. Edith turned off the wireless and placed her sewing on the table. They were going to face this situation 'full on' and Mam realised her news had not been well received.

'And *where* exactly do his parents stay?' asked Hilda, a harsh edge to her voice.

'It's somewhere in Glasgow,' Mam replied, a little shaken by the hostility she was experiencing. 'Dick said he'll meet me at Queen Street Station and take me there.'

'Somewhere in Glasgow?' Hilda repeated. 'That's just not good enough, Winnie. You don't *know* these people or *where* they live, yet you plan to just jaunt off on the say-so of this soldier? Anything could happen to you, and we wouldn't know how to find you.' Hilda turned to Edith for confirmation.

Edith took Mam's hand. 'It's your life, lass, and we do not want to seem to be interfering, but Hilda's right – you do not know what you might be walking into.'

They waited for her answer.

'Oh, you both worry too much,' she laughed. 'I'll be alright.'

As she left the room, the aunts sighed and shook their heads.

The station was crowded, people jostling, pushing to get either on or off the different train platforms, some waving goodbye; others waiting, craning necks, searching for whoever they were meeting.

Her senses were assaulted by the noise and the smell – from the trains of coal smoke and oil, and of tobacco smoke mingling with perfume from women as they brushed past. She began to feel nauseous and was worried that she would never find dad in the chaos.

This wasn't how she'd pictured their meeting. Ever the romantic, she'd imagined a quiet rendezvous, perhaps under the station clock – just like Robert Taylor in the movies – her beau so smart in his uniform, waiting to greet her, possibly with flowers.

'Winnie... Winnie… over here!' She turned and there he was, red-faced and flustered, waving frantically as he pushed through the crowds to reach her.

Just for a second she didn't recognise him. He was in 'mufti;' it was the first time she had seen him out of uniform. The suit he wore was ill-fitting, his shirt not exactly pristine, and his shoes were muddy. No flowers, no lingering embrace… nothing like Robert Taylor. Just a muttered 'Hiya … you made it then' as he grabbed her arm and propelled her unceremoniously out of the station, saying they had to hurry to catch a bus.

They sat upstairs, Dad smoking and Mam gazing out at the black city buildings, noting the orange trams, the low bridges they passed under, the many cobbled streets. She asked him where in Glasgow his parents lived – was it far, what sort of house, did they have a garden and so on. She wondered why he was smiling as he answered.

'You'll see when we get there.'

She became aware that the scenery was changing as they travelled; there were not so many houses. They held hands, chatting happily, Mam still asking questions, Dad avoiding answers. An hour later they arrived… in Kilmarnock.

'Hi Dickie!' The man waved cheerily as they got off the bus.

'Who is that?' she asked.

'Oh… just a fella I know,' he replied and quickened his step, making it quite clear he did not wish to stop and talk. These rather strange encounters happened again as they walked – Dad being greeted by various people who obviously knew him – yet he made no attempt at explanations or introductions.

She began to think perhaps he was embarrassed by her. She'd often been told of the so-called animosity between Scotland and England and wondered whether her English accent might be the problem.

Beginning to tire, and feet hurting now in the high heels she'd thought so smart – but not designed for a route march – she asked him, 'Are we nearly there?' and was relieved to hear it was 'just round this corner'.

Granny's wagon

She was dying for a cup of tea, thinking wistfully of the welcome always offered by her aunts, and hoping for something similar at his parents' home.

And then she saw it. At first she was unable to understand what she was looking at – or why he had brought her to what, at first glance, looked like a scrap yard.

On closer scrutiny, she realised that it was a fairground, with lorries and caravans everywhere and the stalls and rides half assembled.

Without any explanation or preamble, he propelled her up the wooden steps of a wagon, and past a multitude of children who were tumbling out in all directions to the sound of a woman yelling, 'Get out of here ye wee buggers, before I tan yer bleddy jacksies!'

This was Mam's first introduction to Granny Stirling – Dad's mother.

The interior of the wagon was dark, not helped by the very dark brown, almost black, wood panelling, and it was a few seconds before Mam's eyes adjusted to what might be inside.

Immediately in front of her as she stood in the doorway was Granny, a homely plump lady, white hair pulled back and secured with combs, her clothing almost in the style of an Eastern European peasant, a voluminous ankle-length black skirt covered by an equally large grey apron with huge pockets, thick black stockings and a black cardigan. Were it not for her rosy cheeks and blue eyes, she would have been monochrome.

Seated in the corner was Grandad Stirling, introduced as 'Old Teddy,' a thin, surly-looking individual who muttered a brief hello in her direction before leaving the wagon, making it obvious that he was not interested in entertaining company.

Granny poured water from a large metal can into a huge copper kettle and placed it on the hob of the stove, which took pride of place opposite the door. The stove was black enamel with chrome fittings and was highly polished.

She then pulled open the drawer-like coal box just below the oven and scooped out a shovel full to add to the fire and boost the heat under the kettle.

Above the stove was a large mirror and just beneath this, a mantelpiece with a clock at the centre and on either side, two large, gilded ornaments of Grecian-style ladies holding the reins of horses. They looked valuable – probably antique – and Mam wondered whether they might have been wedding presents from years ago.

She tried not to appear to be gawping but was struggling to cope with such a different environment. She was tongue-tied and felt desperately out of her comfort zone.

A stove almost identical to Granny's

The next few hours were just a blur for her – people coming and going, introductions, names and faces just not registering with her as she tried to grapple with this new scenario. Her only experience of fairgrounds had been a visit to the Town Moor Carnival as a child. Now she found herself behind the scenes, sitting in a wagon with Dad, who was happily oblivious to her discomfort. He had chosen to keep this part of his life a secret from her and was now back in his own familiar environment and almost forgetting she was there.

The wagon seemed to be everyone's meeting place. Cigarettes were being passed round, travellers were smoking; they were talking so fast and their voices were so loud she could hardly follow them.

The room quickly filled with tobacco smoke and Granny instructed one of the men to open the '*malacrofts*' – which turned out to be the hopper-type windows in the roof. This was Granny's mispronunciation of 'Mollycroft,' that being the name of this style of wagon.

The men laughed and joked with Dad, taking delight in embarrassing him in front of his girlfriend. They kept calling him 'Pearl,' much to his annoyance, and explained to Mam that when he was eleven, Dad was asked to help in one of the sideshows. The owner's assistant was ill and couldn't appear in the show – which was called 'Pearl, the real live Mermaid.' (Sideshows such as these were commonplace, the successful art of illusion depending on the props and trickery used. Losing a prop meant no show and no income.) The owner had done a quick trawl of all the traveller kids to see if any would fit into the mermaid's costume and – unfortunately for Dad – it was him. He had spent all day sitting in a glass tank, resplendent in fishtail, coconut shell bra and long wig, being ogled at by the punters and ridiculed by his siblings. The owner was grateful, however, reminding dad that without him, the show would not have

A typical Mollycroft wagon

opened. The payment of five bob made up for the embarrassment of the day, but not the label 'Pearl,' which stuck into adulthood.

Another story they told was about Dad – afraid of the dark as a youngster – being sent out for some coal. His sister Rosie decided to dress as a ghost, covering herself in a white sheet, and jump out from the darkness to scare him. Unfortunately, she wasn't prepared for his reaction, which was to smack her over the head with the coal shovel, sending her flying.

Mam was beginning to warm to these people and enjoy the humour, often quite ribald and specifically at Dad's expense. They told her of his love of animals, that he'd bred budgerigars and cried if any died; and that he'd taught himself the accordion, shutting himself away for hours in the lorry, practising… being berated by Old Teddy for not doing his chores.

The areas of his life he'd been so reluctant to share with Mam were now quite openly being discussed and she was enjoying his discomfiture.

Sometime later, realising that she hadn't been to the bathroom for several hours, Mam leaned across to granny, trying to ask quietly and discreetly, 'Could I use your toilet, Mrs Stirling?' She then realised from the expression on the woman's face that this might be a problem.

'We don't actually have any facilities in here,' whispered Dad, adding, 'I'll walk you round to the toilet' – whereupon she found herself being escorted to the public toilets two streets away, accompanied by a procession of traveller children, and given a penny by Dad to unlock the lavatory door.

Walking back, they were still followed by the children, who were giggling and chanting, 'Dickie's caught a flattie... Dickie's caught a flattie!'

Mam asked him what a 'flattie' was, and he explained the term related to anyone not born into the 'business' – a non-traveller, someone who lived in a house or flat. She asked him why he hadn't told her about his family and lifestyle before this.

He admitted that he was afraid she 'might have gone off him,' hurriedly adding that he intended to settle down and get a job after the war.

'So, when you settle down will *you* become a 'flattie'?' she asked, and noticed that he didn't answer, pretending instead to joke with and chase the children.

She wondered whether he hadn't heard her but thought no more of it. The night was drawing in; she was tired and beginning to feel cold. It had been a long day and with the prospect of another bus and train journey back to Newcastle the following morning, she just wanted to rest.

When they returned to the wagon all the visitors had gone, and Granny was pouring hot steaming tea into huge breakfast cups, beckoning her to sit down. The seat was a little locker fixed to the wall and topped by a square cushion covered in maroon Rexine (an artificial fabric made to look like leather). The locker was attached side-on to a little table with a flap that folded over, supported by two wooden pegs. She marvelled at the efficient use of space. Everything was tucked away in various recesses, ready to be pulled out or opened up when needed.

Buttered slices of bread, processed cheese and a pot of jam were on the table, and she was invited to tuck in. Mam thanked Granny for her kindness and as they sat drinking the tea, she gazed around the wagon, wondering what the sleeping arrangements were to be.

To her right and just beyond a partition, she could only see a double bed, which she presumed was for Dad's parents. Granny must have read her thoughts so explained, 'Our Rosie's working this weekend, so you'll have her bed and Dick will sleep in the wee wagon.'

As Mam was curious to know what the 'wee wagon' was, Dad told her it was just a cubicle with a bed, behind the cab of their lorry. Realising that she still could not work out where Rosie's bed was, he pointed to the opposite end of the wagon, where there were two cupboard doors, the front of each covered with an ornamental mirror etched with birds, grape vines and flowers.

He slid the doors open to reveal a single bed. It was spotlessly clean, the candy-striped flannelette sheets and pillowslips freshly laundered in preparation for the visitor, yet that night Mam hardly slept. She tossed and turned – the strange bed, the excitement of the day's events, and a bit of anxiety about how she would explain the visit to her aunts keeping her awake.

And then there was the itching. All through the night something was causing her to scratch. The following morning as she dressed, she noticed large red spots on her arms and legs and pointed these out to Granny, who said it was just the 'different water,' hurriedly changing the subject while trying to coax some life into the stove with sticks and paraffin.

The weather had deteriorated. It was raining heavily, the sky an unbroken miserable grey and puddles quickly forming outside. The wagon was cold and its old roof not coping with the deluge; various pans and basins placed strategically by Granny gave a melodic plink-plonk as they caught the drips.

Old Teddy was still in bed and his snores could be heard through the partition. Clearly, he did not see fire lighting or flood prevention as *his* job and Mam wondered what he actually *did* apart from scolding his family and smoking Woodbine.

Dad came into the wagon and announced that they had the offer of a lift into Glasgow, and to hurry. With a quick thanks to Granny for her hospitality, Mam grabbed her bag and coat and followed Dad down the steps and across the – now very muddy –ground to their 'lift'... an old lorry.

He hoisted her up into the cab with a brief introduction to the driver, who said that he was going to buy some 'swag' and would be passing the station en route. As Dad explained to her that fairground prizes were referred to as 'swag,' she began to realise that 'flattie', 'Mollycroft,' 'wee wagon' and now 'swag' were part of the travellers' normal vocabulary, and she wondered how many more of these unfamiliar terms she might encounter.

During this very brief visit she had observed the social interaction and the respect afforded to the old people – the travellers, children *and* adults, referring to parents as 'Mammy' and 'Daddy.' Everyone, young and old, had a part to play in running the travelling fairs and she was beginning to realise that this was not just a business, but rather a lifestyle and culture that was quite unique.

She listened to Dad as he talked to the driver, both men happily discussing the fair, the price of swag, the next 'gaff' (fair), the efficiency or otherwise of the lorry and so on. She wondered how difficult it might be for any traveller to settle down and whether Dad had genuinely considered this.

While she appreciated the lift, the journey had not been comfortable. The cab was cramped and cold, and by the time they arrived at the station it was full of cigarette smoke, which billowed out into the Glasgow air as Dad helped Mam to climb out.

There was no lingering embrace or fond farewell – just a brief hug from Dad and a 'see you soon' comment as he climbed back into the cab and drove away. Mam was viewed with disdain by passers-by as she stood outside Queen Street Station waving off the lorry.

The morning train was busy but she managed to find a seat in a non-smoking carriage, acutely aware that she still smelled of the cigarette smoke from earlier.

The train had corridor coaches that meant that passengers could walk the length of the train, and more importantly, each coach had a toilet. (If the train did not have a corridor, passengers were stuck in their coach compartments until the end of their journey!)

Realising she must look a mess – her shoes and legs still splattered with mud from the ground, clothes crumpled – she made her way to the small toilet and tried to make herself presentable for the return to Newcastle and her aunts' scrutiny.

She arrived back home to the expected 'friendly interrogation' by the aunts. Deciding that it would be pointless avoiding the subject, especially when she would still be seeing him, she described the visit and told them that Dad's family were Travelling Show people. She 'sanitised' her account a little, avoiding any detail that might not meet her aunts' standards of acceptability.

Their reaction was not what she expected, and she was pleasantly surprised. They seemed genuinely interested, asking her about the accommodation, the people she met, the family. What she didn't realise was that they were actually relieved, convinced that Mam, who loved her home comforts, would quickly tire of such a rough and ready existence. They had decided not to show any disapproval and to continue playing a waiting game, convinced that she would eventually see sense, dump Dad, and find some nice 'conventional' man.

Besides, they had other worries. It was 1942 and the war situation was becoming even more critical. Their brother Fred was seldom home, his job with the petroleum company exempting him from military service but not removing him from dangerous situations. He always told them he was quite safe, but they were aware that he was driving tankers, often to areas that were targets for bombers.

In the wider scheme of things, their niece and her choice of boyfriend seemed less important… just an awkward event that would sort itself out, given time.

SEVEN

'I've been called up,' she announced proudly to her office colleagues. (By 1942, all men between the ages of eighteen and fifty-one years and women between twenty and thirty years were conscripted. Married women with babies were exempt.)

This trawl included Mam and, while not relishing being a conscript, she quite enjoyed the office banter and jokes about square bashing etc. She was no stranger to these stories since Dad was always regaling her with the larger-than-life descriptions of *his* experiences. She wondered how he would take the news but since his next pass was not for a few weeks, she thought it best to wait until she knew where she might be posted.

The aunts were pleased at this development and reminded her that she would be in good company, since Elizabeth the Princess Royal was also now in the forces. They didn't add that military service would hopefully put paid to Mam's romance.

She attended for her initial medical on the required day, only to be given the lowest grading on health grounds and turned down. Returning to her office, she was greeted by colleagues singing 'You're in the Army Now' and she burst into tears, explaining she'd been rejected.

She was so devastated by this that her Aunt Hilda took her to their family doctor, who explained that the army medic had discovered a slight heart murmur and could not risk recommending her for service. Had she signed up and the condition deteriorated, the army might have been liable to pay a pension.

Mam was shocked, never aware of any heart problem, but – reassured by the doctor that she was not about to expire – she gradually shrugged off the experience and continued working and adjusting, if that was possible, to the wartime world.

Her consolation was the few hours she could spend with Dad when his leave allowed. He was delighted that she had been turned down, explaining that some women in the forces had quite a 'bad' reputation. She was puzzled by this strange attitude and the fact that he seemed more concerned about her 'moral welfare' than her health!

On his next leave mid-summer, Dad invited her to visit his folks again, saying they were now opening at Broughty Ferry, almost on the beach, and good weather was expected. Again, the aunts received the news with tuts, tight lips, and suggestions that she would be far safer staying at home. Her Uncle Fred, home on leave and fully updated by his sisters, was curious about the rules and regulations required of the travelling fairs during wartime.

Mam tried to remember Dad's stories and did her best to describe the rudiments of how travellers managed. She explained that the fairs were given special dispensation by the Government since they were seen to be a crucial element in maintaining the nation's morale. This included Travellers' Ration Cards and Showmen's Vehicle Fuel Ration Cards, which could be used countrywide. Some fairground equipment had 'blackout' shutters and could still operate their lighting systems at night.

Spitfire 'The Fun of The Fair,' donated to the nation by the Showmen's Guild of Great Britain

She felt a need to emphasise their patriotism, describing articles she'd read in 'The World's Fair' (the fairs' trade newspaper), which not only listed the many casualties but also the young travellers who had received service bravery awards. Included in the paper was an article describing fund-raising efforts by the showfolk nationwide, which paid for a Spitfire, aptly named 'The Fun of The Fair.'

Her uncle Fred, while still fascinated by her description of the travellers, also knew that his two sisters were not happy with the situation and expected him to be the voice of reason.

'Well, Winnie,' he started, 'you're a young lass with a lot of life ahead of you and this lad you've met sounds a decent enough chap…' Fred paused, his voice faltering, realising that this was unfamiliar territory to him. Uncomfortable with the role of family sage, he added, 'And with this damned war, you should just enjoy things while you can.'

She was delighted that her uncle seemed to approve and left the room to pack a small bag for the trip to Broughty Ferry. Fred was left to face the wrath of the aunts, aware that he had not adhered to the role of 'disapproving elder.' The berating he had anticipated did not happen and instead, Edith and Hilda just shook their heads then set about the task of preparing dinner.

He could hear Mam upstairs, drawers and cupboard doors being noisily

Fred enjoying club life

Fred with 'hiking equipment'

opened and closed as she prepared for her weekend. In the kitchen pots rattled, and the aroma of food cooking drifted through to the living room as he turned his attention to winding the old grandfather clock. It had never kept proper time since his father died – the care and maintenance no longer regularly offered. Other things took precedence: the war, family issues, just living and coping.

He recalled his own social life pre-war. He was a member of countless clubs – cycling, rambling, tennis, even cricket, albeit he hated the game. He was ambitious and recognised the importance of networking and 'connections.'

He was hardly ever home and never as involved in his niece's earlier traumatic years. He realised that he had been quite selfish, being fussed over by his sisters, leaving them to care for all the home and family needs while he was free to enjoy a career and lifestyle just as he pleased.

He had been aware of Mam's treatment at the hands of her stepmother and could never understand why his brother had not intervened. Jack surely must have known what was happening yet had remained loyal to the second wife Janet, despite her 'peculiarities,' and this had caused a rift in the family. Hilda and Edith's role of informal guardians had been essential and they were to be commended for the job they'd done. Winnie was now a well-educated, sensible young woman who was growing in confidence, but Fred was concerned that

During WW2, all oil companies merged and traded under the brand name 'Pool' – this would be the type of tanker driven by Fred

his sisters were becoming overprotective. However, he did not feel it was his place to lecture Mam on who she should be seeing. He enjoyed the avuncular relationship he had with his niece and had no wish to become the heavy-handed patriarch of the family.

He thought about the choices *he* had made, the career he was forging within the management structure of a major oil company… a job which exempted him from military service yet did not remove him from danger. Along with other colleagues, he had to assist with fuel deliveries, driving tankers in often difficult situations, looking for safe spots during air raids, often sleeping in the cab when lodgings weren't available.

He chose not to tell this to his sisters, knowing they would worry, assuring them that he was office-bound and safe – not realising that they were already aware of the risks he ran.

He was sure that, given time – and the freedom to make her own choices *and* mistakes – his young niece would be alright.

EIGHT

As promised, the fair was next to the beach and the weather was hot. Dad carried Mam's little suitcase, having met her at the bus stop, and as they reached the ground and walked past the lorries and wagons, she could hear women talking.

'So, is that your Dickie home on leave again?' said one.

'Aye, 'n he's brought his English fanny with him,' said the other in a sarcastic voice.

Mam realised that this referred to *her* and felt an instant hostility towards this person.

As they approached Granny's wagon she came face to face with her nemesis. Dad took Mam's hand, knowing she must have heard the conversation.

'Winnie, *this*… is Rosie.' He glared at his sister, his expression making it quite clear that she'd been overheard, his terse introduction and emphasis on 'this' a warning to Rosie that he was angry with her. The other women, although curious to learn more about Mam, melted discreetly into the background, not wishing any involvement in the awkwardness of the situation.

Rosie must only have been in her mid-thirties but seemed to Mam to be much older. Her figure was angular and shapeless; her hair was frizzy with no style and already turning grey, resembling a mop of steel wool. She was washing clothes, a tub of hot soapy water and a rubbing board receiving vigorous attention, while an almost full-length orange rubber apron tied with string provided protection from the suds, which seemed to splash everywhere. An old pair of wellington boots, the tops rolled down to her ankles, completed the ensemble.

Mam was aware of the contrast in their appearances and felt embarrassingly overdressed, aware that she was being scrutinised from head to toe by this woman.

A nod of her head and gruff '*hello*' was grudgingly offered by Rosie before she rejoined the other women who were still hovering in the background, keen to be appraised of this newcomer and Rosie's opinion.

The next few hours were awkward. Rosie had to give up her bed to Mam and made her displeasure known. It soon became clear that Rosie liked to think she ruled the roost, and her aspirations for her brothers did not include courting flatties – especially not English flatties. Mam was a 'loser' on both counts!

Another uncomfortable night in bed, constant itching, and the same familiar spots in the morning did nothing to assuage her concern that the weekend was going badly.

Left to her own devices while Dad and his younger brother Walter were building up the stalls, she needed to avoid another encounter with Rosie so decided to venture out. The sea looked tempting, and she longed to take a dip. No one was in the wagon and a brief moment of privacy allowed her to change into the swimsuit bought especially for the trip. The costume was of a modest design and with a small skirt, yet she still felt self-conscious and hoped she could make her way to the beach without being seen.

Clutching a large towel, she appeared at the doorway, not realising that Old Teddy was sitting on the steps enjoying a cigarette. She paused, wondering whether to retreat, but the sun on her skin and the prospect of the beach was too tempting.

She smiled at him as she squeezed past and headed down the steps to the water. Old Teddy had possibly never seen so much bare feminine flesh at close quarters.

He coughed and spluttered, nearly choking on his Woodbine at the apparition as she passed, before exclaiming to no one in particular, 'Bloody hell! Did yees see THAT?'

The heat of the day was becoming quite fierce, and many people were now in the water. Mam, although not a swimmer, enjoyed splashing and paddling in the shallow waves and wished Dad could have been with her instead of working.

As she sat on the beach drying off and trying to dress under the towel, which didn't quite accommodate her modesty, she was aware of a commotion at the water's edge.

Someone shouted, 'Help, an old man is drowning!' A few young travellers ran to help and Mam watched as the 'victim' was dragged protesting from the water – coughing, spluttering, and uttering every imaginable oath, insisting he was just wanting a swim.

His 'rescuers' realised that it was just Old Teddy. Tempted by the water but not owning a swimsuit, he had improvised by taking a dip wearing his dungarees, which ballooned in air pockets, giving the impression of a floating body!

Curious to discover what had happened, Mam finished dressing and followed the ever-growing procession of laughing youngsters who were escorting him home.

Back in the wagon, the story of his 'rescue' was shared, the humour of the event increasing with each retelling. Dad and his siblings had all now gathered in the wagon, abandoning their various tasks to enjoy their father's discomfiture.

Old Teddy – a humourless man at the best of times – stood dripping in the middle of floor, thoroughly disgruntled at being the object of everyone's hilarity and even more annoyed to realise his forgotten packet of Woodbines was now a soggy mess in his bib pocket! His humour was not assuaged by Granny who was berating him, calling him 'a silly old bugger' as she threw him a towel, commenting that this was the first time he'd ever been clean and he should have taken a bar of soap with him and done a proper job.

Mam watched the family interaction, seeing that for all their 'rough and readiness,' there was real affection. The event had been an ice breaker and even Rosie was laughing.

The weekend had become quite enjoyable, but Mam would be glad to return home to 'normality' again. Sitting with this family, she realised that their lifestyle was alien to her, and she smiled at Dad, so glad that he had told her of his intention to 'settle down.'

A few weeks after this visit, Dad proposed to Mam as they casually window-shopped and meandered along the streets in Newcastle. Mam stopped in her tracks, not prepared for this. He gazed at her, searching her face for some sign of assent, afraid that he'd not used the 'right' words and she might turn him down.

Despite having fallen for him, she was also concerned for any future they might have post-war. She explained that while she had every respect for his family and their way of life, it just wasn't for her. She needed stability and the security of a settled home.

Dad promised faithfully that he did plan to settle down and get a job, maybe as a driver or even a mechanic. He emphasised the fact that he'd been away from 'the business' for two years now, thanks to the war, and was quite conditioned to a flattie's life. He was imploring her to accept, describing the life they could have – a nice little house somewhere, a pretty garden, a dog... maybe children at some point later.

She trusted him implicitly and accepted his proposal, gasping in protest as he grabbed her without warning and lifted her off her feet in a huge bear hug, to the amusement of passers-by.

Afraid that she might change her mind, he insisted that they shop for an engagement ring. He had prepared for the moment and brought money he had saved for the event, telling her that she could pick whatever she liked, and after gazing in the windows of several jewellers they chose the ring.

It was platinum with a tiny claw-set single diamond and the band had the Newcastle assay mark. (This ring was to feature in our lives many years later.) The jeweller assured them that platinum was better value than yellow gold and a bargain at the price he was asking. To Mam it just looked like silver, but it was within Dad's price range and the ring fitted her slim finger.

They celebrated their engagement that day with a meal at one of the ration-free British Restaurants then went to a nearby cinema to see 'Gone with The Wind,' which had been newly released.

The epic film – which lasted four hours – and late return to Pelaw meant she had to save the news for her aunts until the next day.

She hardly slept, bursting with excitement, replaying the day, anticipating the future – desperate to tell everyone and show off her ring.

NINE

'You've done WHAT?!!' Aunt Hilda's voice seemed to rattle around the kitchen.

'Dick and I got engaged last night,' Mam repeated, not expecting such a negative reaction. Her aunt thumped the breakfast dishes down on the table.

'Are you pregnant? Is this a hurry-up job?' Hilda demanded to know, completely ignoring Mam's attempts to show her the ring.

'Of course not... How could you think such a thing?' she replied, her voice now quavering with disappointment and alarm.

Edith came into the kitchen, curious to know why there were raised voices. Hilda turned to her, hands outstretched in despair, realising now that their 'waiting game' had backfired and looking to Edith for support.

'What do you think of this bombshell then?' she asked. 'She's just told me she got engaged to that... that... that...' (Hilda could not find a sufficiently derogatory word) '*SCOTSMAN!*'

The aunts, Edith and Hilda

Mam, never particularly good at confrontation, shook her head and stood up from the table. 'I'm really sorry you feel this way. I thought you liked him. I have to get to work now but we'll talk about this tonight.' She turned away from them, gulping back tears.

'Too true we will, m'lady,' said Hilda, a sharpness to her voice as Mam left the room. The day Mam had relished the thought of had turned into a nightmare.

At work she confided in Freda, who was always very streetwise and down to earth. She admired the ring, adding, 'Now look here, hinny, just you enjoy the day, and don't you worry about those two old biddies. You mark my words – given a few hours to think about things and cool down, they'll be fine.'

Freda managed to make her laugh, reminding her of the blind date that had resulted in Mam and Dad meeting. 'There you were, so reluctant to go to that dance, me setting you up with the chap that you end up falling for, and me being dumped by my date! By my reckoning, since I was the matchmaker, I'm claiming the role of bridesmaid!'

Freda had managed to reassure her and at the end of that working day, Mam felt positive again, convinced by now that the aunts would surely see reason and give their blessing.

The usual welcoming aroma of dinner cooking was absent when she opened the door. The house was quiet – no wireless playing, no sound of the aunts' happy chatter – just a worrying stillness. She hung her coat in the hall, checked her appearance in the mirror and tried to control the panic she was beginning to feel as her breathing quickened.

They both sat in the living room waiting for her and she realised that they had probably spent most of the day rehearsing their argument and preparing for battle. The next few hours were traumatic for her *and* the aunts. Logic and calm debate sacrificed to emotion as they tried to reason with Mam.

'Winnie, you are not thinking things through properly,' Hilda insisted. 'This is just you getting caught up in 'war fever'... everyone living each day as though it were their last.'

'You know we only have your best interests at heart,' Edith added. 'Can't you see that this is all happening too quickly?'

Mam tried to counter every argument, telling them she loved Dad and they were planning their future after the war. 'You don't understand,' she pleaded. 'He's no longer a traveller – he will be settling down after the war and getting a job. There will be plenty of work when the war's over, and with the army gratuity he'll receive when he's discharged plus our wages, we'll be able to afford a house somewhere.'

The aunts shook their heads in disbelief. Hilda looked at Edith then turned to Mam. 'You are living in fool's paradise. He'll never settle down and you will never change him. He will always be a traveller, it's in his blood. You have not been brought up in, and have no experience of, that lifestyle and no matter what you think, this engagement just can't happen… *surely* you see that?'

Mam was now weeping, never good at arguing. All she could think to say was, 'But we love each other, and we *will* be happy.'

Realising they were getting nowhere, her aunts pulled out their final piece of ammunition, convinced that the shock of this would bring her to her senses. They both stood up, as if to add extra weight to what was about to be said. Hilda cleared her throat and stared at her niece who sat, head bowed – and momentarily Hilda felt pained to speak. She had never previously been required to scold or discipline this young woman, but for her own good, it had to be done.

'Well m'lass, we've said our piece and you know how we feel. We don't agree to this… you are about to make the biggest mistake of your life and we have to put an end to this nonsense. You either tell him the engagement is off – or you don't come back here!'

They left the room, Mam heartbroken and shocked by the ultimatum. She looked around her, seeing all the familiar trappings of the home she had loved since childhood. The longcase clock so meticulously maintained by her late granda, which had seemed to go into a decline after he died; the many books she had read still sitting in the bookshelves, waiting like old friends to be revisited and enjoyed again; the many happy memories of her beloved aunts who had been like parents, rescuing her from the neglect of her stepmother and providing the love and security she longed for; her granda's allotment opposite the house where as children she and her brother Leslie used to raid the rhubarb patch and enjoyed eating the pink stalks dipped in sugar begged from their aunts; her uncle Fred, larger than life and full of fun, always pulling her leg and telling her stories of his 'adventures' with his various clubs.

She wished he was here to take her side now as he always had a way of winning the aunts round and might have made them see reason. His job meant that he was very seldom home so she could not call on his advocacy role at short notice.

There was a noise in the hall, and she hoped for a moment that her aunts were returning. Perhaps they had reconsidered? They were fair-minded people after all and ultimatums were just not in their nature. She waited, listening… then was disappointed to realise from the clink of glass that one of them was just putting clean bottles out on the doorstep for collection by the milkman.

She thought of Dad, the love they shared and the future they had hoped to share. She cried. A decision had to be made and whatever it was, she would be hurting someone.

Sleep was impossible that night, her mind in a turmoil. She had not bothered to undress, alternating between lying on top of her bed and getting up, pacing the floor, sobs racking her exhausted body in uncontrollable spasms.

She gazed out the bedroom window, the street deserted apart from a cat prowling in the allotments opposite. She looked at her watch, shocked to see how quickly time had passed. It was now 4am and in a few hours the aunts would be awake. Torn with the guilt of what she was about to do and also her cowardice in not facing them, she packed just enough clothes to last a couple of days. She then unzipped a little writing case, selecting plain paper rather than the pretty floral notelets, which seemed too frivolous and inappropriate under the circumstances.

Those few lines were the hardest she'd ever written; several attempts were torn up and thrown into her litter basket. No words could adequately express the pain she was feeling or the grief she knew she was causing her aunts.

She wrote that they had forced her to make an impossible choice, but that her decision was to remain engaged and ultimately marry Dad. She told them she loved them dearly and was sorry things had gone this way. She assured them that she would be alright, and she would send her new address once settled.

Taking one last look around her room, she opened the door, tiptoeing out onto the landing and down the stairs, alarmed at how loudly the door hinge squeaked and the floorboards creaked – sounds she hadn't previously noticed. Even the old grandfather clock, which had not kept time for years, was now coming to life, the chains and weights in the wooden case rattling a warning of imminent and inaccurate chimes.

She imagined the house was trying to betray her departure.

Propping her letter against the toast rack, she noted the kitchen table set ready for breakfast and her throat constricted as she realised there were still three place settings. Clearly, the aunts expected her to be there that morning.

Carrying her small case and trying not to bump into anything in the dark hallway as she left, she closed the front door behind her and popped her key through the letterbox, glad now that the old clock was still chiming, disguising any noise made as the key and fob hit the floor.

Returning the key was throwing away a lifeline and she had a moment of panic, knowing she was turning her back on everything she had needed in life – safety, security, a loving family. She had chosen the opposite of these, and now everything familiar, cherished, and safe – her world – was locked behind that door.

She checked her watch. It was still just 6am and they would not be up yet. Maybe she could sneak back, tear up the note, make up with them, let things cool down for a bit? Then she remembered the surrendering of the door key and sighed.

On the doorstep, careful not to knock over the two empty milk bottles, she was joined by the neighbourhood cat, now bored with its forage in the allotments, wrapping itself round her legs and demanding attention. The warmth of its little body and the caress of its fur against her bare skin was strangely comforting. As she bent to pat it, the early morning sun caught facets of the tiny diamond in her engagement ring. It glinted and sparkled – a sign, she thought, that she should walk on, albeit to an uncertain future, but one to be shared with the man she'd chosen to marry. She picked up her case and with one final look back at the house, set off down the street, with only the cat to notice her departure.

At work that morning, Freda noticed Mam's bag in the staff room and that she was red-eyed. Mam explained what had happened and Freda was horrified, feeling partly responsible for events, having been the catalyst to Mam meeting Dad.

'Haway hinny,' she said in her best Geordie voice, an arm solicitously round Mam's shoulders. 'Ye can doss at mine 'til ye find a place. C'mon now, naebody's deid!'

The days spent with Freda allowed space and thinking time, and Mam's first task was to find alternative accommodation. She managed to rent a room

Two Ball Lonnen in the late 1930s, probably as it was when Mam boarded with the Wilkies

from a couple who had converted one of their larger upstairs bedrooms into a bedsit. The room was freshly decorated, furnished adequately and the couple – Mr and Mrs Wilkie – were not asking much for the rent.

The house was in Two Ball Lonnen in Fenham, and she warmed to the couple instantly. They were already fussing around her as though she was a visiting relative.

(When Mam told this story I always thought the house number was 2 and the street name was 'Ball Lonnen'. I discovered later that 'Lonnen' was 'Lane' in the old Geordie dialect and the two balls were quite literally that – i.e. the entrance to the original old lane was flanked by two pillars with large stone balls on top!)

Mam wrote to her aunts, giving her new address, willing them to reply.

They never did. She contacted her father Jack, explaining the situation and asking if he could act as intermediary. He returned from Pelaw with her belongings and the message from them that if she wished to 'come home' she could, but only if she dropped any 'silly idea' of marriage to Dad.

The old 'Lonnen'

Mam resigned herself to this dreadful impasse sadly, not knowing it would be over twenty years before she would have any contact with them again.

Dad was never a great letter writer but replied to Mam's note to him by return, telling her how sorry he was to have caused so much grief and suggesting that they just go ahead and get married now since any prolonged engagement seemed pointless.

There was a sense of urgency with everything. Dad's regiment was being prepared for something and he felt they were going to be shipped abroad again soon.

On 30th January 1943, they married at a little church in Fenham. It was a quiet affair, Mam's father giving her away, Freda acting as bridesmaid and one of Dad's army pals being best man. The aunts did not acknowledge the event.

Clothing rations did not allow for bridal wear, so Freda decided to 'glam' Mam up by lending her a fox-fur stole and wide-brimmed hat. Mrs Wilkie made a corsage and between them, they reckoned they had made a rather good job of the outfit.

The task of the groom was easier – the uniform, suitably pressed, did the job.

'Job done!' – Dad posing, ring on view

Mr and Mrs Wilkie insisted on a small reception at their house and laid on some refreshments, including a sponge cake baked by Mrs Wilkie, over which was placed a fake cover made of cardboard to look like an iced wedding cake.

The honeymoon was a short event, Dad having to report back to barracks within two days, so they travelled to Perth to visit his family then spent the night at a hotel, not realising it was a temperance establishment (alcohol-free) and both dying for a drink!

And so began this new chapter in their lives, each hoping that fortune would favour the brave and that together they would overcome any obstacles.

TEN

ealistically, my parents were aware that these were increasingly dangerous times.

America was now at war with Japan following the Japanese bombing of Pearl Harbour, and German U-boats were targeting any supply ships heading for the UK, adding that the USA would be punished should they interfere.

Rationing of food and clothing continued; queues formed outside any shop that might have a delivery of any scarce item. Imaginative alternatives were created – for example, powdered eggs.

Dad worried that Mam might be lonely while he was away and, knowing how much she loved animals, bought her a dog – a beautiful little Pomeranian. Unfortunately, he had not thought this through properly. She worked full-time, which meant the dog would be left far too long in the bedsit. He didn't think to check that the Wilkies would be alright with a dog in the house.

Several days later, after many puddles on the floor and a huge hole chewed through the seat of a chair in the room, the little dog had to be rehomed. Dad's parents agreed to take it but unfortunately the animal was not streetwise and when allowed to roam free with the rest of the travellers' dogs it was run over.

Mam was terribly upset at this outcome and, while appreciating that he had only her best interests at heart, she was beginning to realise that Dad could act on impulse without considering consequences.

She was gradually getting to know Dad's family. His brothers, John and Tommy, both still single, visited her and she was escorted to various events by them when they were on leave. They danced to well-known bands, including

Geraldo, Joe Loss, Edmundo Ross etc. Even her 'nemesis' – Rosie – visited and Mam began to wonder whether Dad had told them all to keep an eye on her.

Rosie, having been presented with *fait accompli*, had resigned herself to the fact that her brother was now married to an English flattie and used her visits to 'remind' Mam, during conversations, of the family pecking order and that they deferred to *her* in all things.

Mam was slightly intimidated by her and decided that the most prudent tactic would be to acquiesce and not challenge Rosie on anything unless she felt absolutely confident to do so. Unfortunately, this subservience would later have a consequence for Mam, affecting her future hopes and aspirations, and contributing to the unique life experience of her children.

Mam was slowly adjusting to life in the bedsit and developed a real affection for her landlords. Mrs Wilkie advised her on the bureaucratic requirements of wartime – the various ration books and which shops to register these with. Mr Wilkie was the handyman of the house and was always available for any odd jobs needed in the bedsit. Dad visited whenever leave allowed and the Wilkies enjoyed his company. Resigned now to being estranged from her family, Mam tried to concentrate on whatever the future held.

Dad's regiment was being prepared for combat and he warned her that he would not be able to tell her when this might be. Several battalions of the Cameronians had already seen battle in France and Belgium (in 1940, after taking part in some of the heaviest fighting in the Dunkirk campaign, fragments of the 2nd, 6th, and 7th Battalions were evacuated from the Dunkirk beaches).

Dad's section of the 7th was the Bren Gun Carrier platoon and he trained as a Bren Gun Carrier driver, giving his vehicle the nickname Angus.

In April 1944, Dad's leave was cancelled and shortly after this, Mam received a very brief note from him that announced that 'Angus gets his new raincoat next week'. (All mail was heavily censored to ensure that no sensitive military information was revealed.) This message was Dad's quite imaginative way of telling her the Bren Gun Carrier was being waterproofed, and they were about to be sent overseas.

His battalion set sail for France in June 1944 as part of the Normandy landings, disembarking at Arromanches on 23rd June, capturing its first objective – the village of Haut Du Bosq – and proceeding to Caen, where battle had been raging since 6th June.

'Angus' – Dad's Bren Gun Carrier

A brief respite for the battle-weary at Caen

'My God – they're getting slaughtered over there!' exclaimed Mr Wilkie. He sat at the kitchen table, newspaper spread out and puffing furiously on his pipe as he read the casualty lists. He felt it his duty to keep giving his wife and lodger running commentaries on the progress of the war. Mam wished he would stop, aware that Dad was somewhere on the front line, and she dreaded each rattle of the letterbox that might announce the worst possible news. She had already witnessed some of this – a neighbour of the Wilkies losing her son at sea, and an office colleague of Mam's being told his RAF son was 'missing – presumed dead.'

And then... on 27th July 1944 – 'Winnie... Winnie... Are you up, love? There's a letter here for you.'

Mrs Wilkie didn't normally come up to Mam's room to announce post. She kept any mail on the little hall table for her to collect on her way out.

Mam's throat constricted and her legs turned to jelly, every possible scenario racing through her head as she threw on her dressing gown. She opened her room door, took the letter from an anxious Mrs Wilkie and gazed at it – reluctant to open the envelope, fearful of its contents.

Hands trembling, she read the very brief missive from the M.O.D. with a tick in the relevant box – 'wounded.' There was no detail about the extent of the injuries or whether they might be life-threatening... just the stark word 'wounded' and details of which hospital to contact. Mam burst into tears, fearing the worst.

'Now c'mon, lass. He'll be ok,' said Mrs Wilkie, trying to sound confident, holding Mam's arm as they made their way downstairs. They sat in the kitchen, Mam oblivious to the fact that she was still in her nightie and dressing gown, hands shaking as she sipped the tot of brandy Mr Wilkie had given her for 'medicinal' purposes. The liquid burned her throat but helped calm her a little as she watched the Wilkies check the timetable of trains to Liverpool, where Dad had been repatriated.

The train seemed to take forever and with each stop she became more agitated. She tried not to make eye contact with other passengers in the carriage, fearing she would dissolve into tears if someone spoke to her.

Gazing out the carriage window she began to see evidence of the 1941 firestorm blitz on Liverpool. Huge areas of the city had been destroyed; skeletal blackened remains of buildings still stood defiantly, almost challenging the enemy to try again. The horrific loss of life in Liverpool (over 4,000 people) was second only to London.

She had not been prepared for the scenes at the station when she arrived.

Injured servicemen were being tended to, stretchers gently lowered from the train onto the station platforms, nurses and doctors working along the rows of casualties – tending to the most urgent cases, trying to reassure others. Volunteers were busy offering tea, cigarettes, helping hands wherever they could. Everywhere there was a sense of urgency, but also care and compassion. Policemen were trying to hurry the civilian passengers out of the station, but it was impossible for them not to see some of the dreadful injuries.

Neither had Mam realised that blood has a quite distinctive, sickly aroma – and mingled with the soiled clothing and dressings of the casualties, the smell was overpowering. This was the reality of war – not the gung-ho propaganda movies being shown in the cinemas. There were no tough-guy stereotype film heroes here, just severely damaged men lying on stretchers, some moaning in pain, some crying, one calling for his mother, and some ominously still and quiet, a sheet soon to be pulled gently over their faces.

These terrible images haunted her as – in a daze – she found her way to the hospital, dreading what she would find when she arrived and fearing the worst.

'Hiya. You made it then?'

Mam was momentarily stunned. This was the same familiar greeting she had heard when he had met her in Glasgow and for a moment, she thought she was hallucinating. Dad was standing at the door of the ward smoking a cigarette, smiling at her – and apart from a bandage around his left leg, he seemed to be alright. She was so relieved she could have slapped him.

He gave no detail of what he or his battalion had gone through, just telling her that he had been caught in sniper fire and that the bullet was still in his leg. Compared to the other casualties he was not considered high priority for surgery, being categorised as 'walking wounded,' and had been told he would be sent to a hospital in Wrexham to have the bullet removed. He told her not to worry and that he would let her know when he was being transferred. Reassured, she returned to Fenham and to the Wilkies, who were waiting anxiously for news. Life restarted.

There was a delay in Dad being sent to Wales and this resulted in the bullet shifting and the wound becoming badly infected. By the time he was moved to

Wrexham, he had high fever and blood poisoning and there was the possibility that he might lose the leg. Mam visited as often as she could and was relieved when the surgeon advised her that the crisis was over and her husband would be returned intact.

Dad had to remain at the Wrexham hospital for a few weeks' convalescence and because of the distance and problems of wartime transport, he told her not to keep visiting, promising to write daily with updates.

Two weeks passed and no letters were received so Mam decided to pay a surprise visit. On arrival she could not see him in the ward and another patient, looking a little embarrassed, informed her that Dad was taking a walk in the hospital grounds.

Mam looked out the window and spotted him strolling along the path, accompanied by a pretty little nurse… the twosome seeming just a bit too friendly for her liking.

She sat in the chair by his bedside and waited. He eventually arrived – nurse still in tow – and seemed less than pleased to see Mam. The nurse, without any introduction, quickly disappeared, leaving Dad to bluster that she was 'just helping his mobility.'

Mam – in the space of seconds – experienced almost every imaginable emotion. She was hurt by the cool reception, angry at this possible dalliance, hated the nurse without having even spoken to her, and was furious with dad, who looked like a naughty schoolboy who had been caught out. She remembered her Aunt Hilda's warning that she 'didn't really know this man' and realised there might be aspects to his character she had not anticipated. After a brief and very icy visit, she left.

Back at work she shared her concerns with 'worldly wise' Freda, who told her, 'All men's heid's are turned by nurses' and that she shouldn't think that he had 'shifted his affections.'

Dad started writing as promised and Wales was never mentioned again!

Now fully recovered and promoted to Corporal, he was returned to active service. Unfortunately this was not a reunion with his comrades, since the Normandy landings had decimated his battalion's numbers and the few remaining men were reallocated to other units. He was assigned to a transport section, never again to be reunited with 'Angus.'

The war continued, Germany attacking Britain with V1 rockets, the first on 13th June 1944 – targeting London in a 'revenge attack' one week after the Allied landings in Europe. The rockets – known as flying bombs or 'doodlebugs' – were fired from sites along the French and Dutch coasts, reaching areas primarily in southeast England. They had limited range, although this was not known initially and people countrywide dreaded being the target.

Mr Wilkie sat at the kitchen table, paper spread out as usual, chewing on the stem of his pipe as he scanned each page. Mrs Wilkie stood at the sink, peeling potatoes as Mam tried to shift Mr Wilkie in order to set the table for their dinner.

'It says here,' he announced, 'that as long as we can hear these doodlebugs' engines we'll be ok, but if the engines cut out, that's a sign that the bomb's going to drop.' He looked up from his paper for signs of appreciation for his advice.

Mrs Wilkie thumped a potato into the basin, splashing water everywhere, and turned to face him. 'For goodness' sake man, can you not find anything cheerful to read out from that damned paper? What do you expect us to do if we hear one of those things, write back to the paper and tell them the bugger missed us?'

Mam smiled at Mrs Wilkie, realising that the woman was genuinely afraid and Mr Wilkie's war updates were not helping.

The death toll was horrific. By August 1944 there were 6,000 dead, 17,000 injured and massive destruction of buildings. These were fearful times, but the Allies were gaining ground in Europe, culminating in a final offensive in December known as 'The Battle of the Bulge.'

Little did she know it then, but Mam would soon be fighting her own Battle of the Bulge! Germany surrendered on 18th May 1945, and two months later… I was about to appear.

City hospitals were still coping with civilian and military war casualties and any imminent maternity cases were moved to outlying areas considered to be safe.

Mam was advised that she had been allocated to a facility in Cumbria with the grand name of the Gilsland Hotel, and she sent Dad a very brief note with directions.

She packed a small bag and, with Mrs Wilkie's help, made her way to the station with a mix of excitement and apprehension, being waved off by her tearful landlady as the train left.

The Gilsland Hotel (now refurbished)

ELEVEN

The Gilsland Hotel, at one time a convalescent home for WW1 servicemen, had been unused for many years and had fallen into disrepair, then hurriedly been brought back into service during WW2 as a temporary maternity hospital.

It was arranged for Mam, along with ten other pregnant women, to be admitted to the Gilsland and she was entrusted with all the files/case notes to be handed to Matron on arrival.

The train journey from Newcastle to Gilsland was enjoyable, the women split between two carriages – six in one carriage, Mam and the other four, chatting and sharing the 'joys' and otherwise of their pregnancies, in the other carriage. They did not notice until it was too late that they had missed their stop. The six women in the first carriage had alighted, and the train was now travelling to the next stop, several miles further on.

A very bemused porter found himself surrounded by five heavily pregnant women, all asking where to get a bus to Gilsland. They became extremely agitated when he told them there was not a bus due for hours, and he feared he might witness some premature deliveries. He offered to call a local farmer who had an old van converted to take passengers, saying this was sometimes used as a taxi.

They were already extremely late by the time the farmer arrived and he looked in horror from his potential passengers to his incredibly old van and debated whether the springs could cope.

The women all squeezed in, grateful for any mode of transport and leaving him with no choice but to accept the 'fare,' the farmer glaring at the porter for calling him out.

The journey was agonisingly slow, the women's bladders complaining as the driver carefully negotiated the bends and bumps in the country road, one hill almost bringing his van to a standstill. Mam asked jokingly if they should get out and push.

On arrival the driver refused to take their fare, saying he'd 'just done his bit for the war' – secretly relieved that he hadn't been required to deliver 'extra' passengers – and drove off, smoke billowing from the old 'taxi' as it rattled back down the hill.

They were met by a very agitated Matron who dashed out and grabbed the files from Mam, not being able to arrange admissions until she had these and seeing her as an irresponsible courier and probable cause of all the administrative problems.

The hotel, for all its grand position high above the Cumbrian countryside, had obviously seen better days. In many of the rooms fungus was growing out of the walls and the smell of damp was everywhere. For a brief moment she thought they might all be safer exposed to German bombardment than to any of the spores flying around the building.

She wrote to Dad (postal services were incredibly efficient, with deliveries three times a day!) and he managed to visit once, assuring her that he would be given a pass once the baby was born, and that the Matron had his contact details.

Her travel companions were gradually giving birth and leaving with their little bundles. I, on the other hand, seemed reluctant to make an appearance, and the nursing staff were taking bets on which shift would see me make my debut.

Wearying now, Mam spent her days wandering around or sitting at the front of the building, the view no longer a novelty and the hot July weather a misery to her. When things eventually 'began to happen,' she had to suffer five agonising shift changes before I condescended to arrive!

Uncle John, Dad's brother, was her first visitor following the birth, his posting in one of the Durham mines making access to Cumbria fairly easy. Dad arrived at Gilsland one hour later, just a little annoyed to discover that his brother had beaten him to it and the nurses had mistaken John as the father.

Mam and Uncle John thought this was very funny, but Dad was not amused, and Mam noticed that he was quiet until his brother left.

Dad gave Mam a gold locket to mark the occasion. (When cutting my first tooth I bit into the locket, leaving *my* mark – a permanent indentation that, she assured me in later years, made it all the more precious to her.)

As promised, Dad visited regularly and was besotted with this new addition to the Stirling clan.

Although from a large family and surely familiar with his siblings as babies, Mam sensed that he was uncomfortable during feeding times, always making the excuse to go out for a smoke when she prepared to breastfeed me. On one occasion he noted at her bedside a trumpet-shaped glass instrument with a rubber bulb and asked jokingly whether she used that to call for a nurse. He was horrified to be told that it was a breast pump, and that she was donating breast milk to other mothers who were having difficulty feeding their babies. He could scarcely conceal his embarrassment and distaste at the idea.

This 'naïve prudishness' bothered her for a moment, then she dismissed the notion, now with thoughts only of going home.

The Wilkies welcomed Mam and baby back as though *they* were the proud grandparents. There was no acknowledgement from either Mam's dad or the aunts. Freda, her bridesmaid, was now heavily involved with an American G.I. but sent a note and a little gift for the new arrival.

The Wilkies had found a pram, a beautiful Churchill coach-built high pram complete with sunshade. Mam was at first reluctant to take a second-hand pram but when she saw the vehicle, she immediately fell in love with it and wheeled me out and about at every opportunity, enjoying the attention of passers-by and neighbours.

The summer was hot, I was thriving, and Mam was loving life again.

TWELVE

The war in Europe had ended but the British Government delayed discharging its military personnel while hostilities continued with Japan. Dad was required to remain with his battalion but being home-based he was able to arrange leave fairly easily.

The couple – with me now in tow – visited Dad's parents whenever possible. Sleeping arrangements were still not ideal, Dad back in the 'wee wagon' with his brother Walter, and Mam now sharing the small recess bed top to tail with Rosie. A makeshift bed was made for me in a large drawer lined with pillows.

On one of these visits I became ill. Mam was distraught, knowing a doctor should attend but not sure how to arrange this in a strange town. She asked Rosie for advice and also – in deference to the fact that this was someone else's home – for 'permission' to call in a doctor. Rosie told her it was 'probably just a chill' and that I would be alright the next day. Mam became desperately worried as my temperature rose. Dad was unaware of all this, having gone away earlier with his brother to look at a lorry, and she felt completely helpless.

Harriet – one of Mam's sisters-in-law – came into the wagon to ask how the baby was. Mam, knowing Rosie was in the bedroom having a wash, whispered, 'She's really ill and I wanted to get a doctor, but Rosie said not to bother.'

Rosie had been listening and came charging out of the room wild-eyed and raging, every word she uttered emphasised with a stabbing finger as she shouted, 'I said no such thing… she's *your child* and if *you* want a doctor, *you* get one!'

She stormed out of the wagon, leaving Mam in tears and Harriet trying to console her, telling her to ignore Rosie, that it was 'just her way.'

Becky, another of the sisters-in-law, came into the wagon, witnessed the aftermath of Rosie's wrath and completely misinterpreted the situation, thinking Dad had assaulted Mam.

'Where is he, the bugger? Did he hit you? I'll sort him out,' she promised.

Becky was a big lady, clearly well able to 'sort out' any miscreant and quite disappointed to be set straight, missing a chance to chastise her younger brother.

By now, everyone (apart from Rosie, who was still noticeable by her absence) was agreeing that a doctor should attend but it was past surgery hours and too late for a home visit. Granny came to the rescue, her 'remedy' a home-made poultice that she applied to my front and back, swaddling me tightly and taking turns with Mam to sit in front of the fire with me during that night.

Old Teddy was in bed and could be heard snoring on the other side of the partition, the 'crisis' of no interest to him. Granny talked quietly to Mam as they tended to me. 'Now I know this looks bad, lass, but you mustn't worry,' she assured her. 'I've nursed many a child through these illnesses and they've all recovered.'

She told Mam that she had suffered miscarriages and had lost one son in his early teens. The boy was disabled and needed to be pushed around by his siblings in a bathchair. Granny sighed wistfully, poking more life into the fire as she talked. 'He was a lovely singer… the voice of an angel. His favourite tune was Danny Boy' (Londonderry Air) 'and when he died, I couldn't stand to hear that song. I made it a family rule that no-one ever played, sang or whistled it ever again.'

As she listened, Mam felt a great respect for this woman. She had reared ten children, lost one and suffered miscarriages, all in the most difficult of living conditions.

Old Teddy seemed devoid of any affection, albeit he was evidently able to procreate quite successfully, and it was left to the daughters – Lizzie, Becky and Rosie – to help Granny. Lizzie and Becky eventually married, and Rosie was then the only female left at home to help. Rosie took her role of remaining 'big sister' very seriously, her bossiness and possessiveness of her brothers spilling over into the running of the home, requiring Granny to remind her periodically who was the matriarch.

'I wonder sometimes whether we expected too much of Rosie,' Granny mused. 'She never made time for dances or men… not like her sisters. She worked alongside the boys, building up and pulling down the joints' (stalls) 'and would have driven the lorries given half a chance. We just took her for granted, I suppose.

'She never talked about her work in munitions, but I think it must have been hard. She wasn't used to being away from home and missed the freedom of life as a traveller. I don't know why she dislikes the English so much. A lot of the factory women were English… maybe some gave her a bad time.'

Aunty Rosie years later (around 1998)

Mam felt that Granny was trying to explain Rosie's abrasiveness and to an extent understood, but she still viewed the sister-in-law as cold, without empathy – and a potential adversary.

The following morning a doctor attended and was not sure what had ailed me, but praised granny's remedy, saying she had managed to break a fever and I was 'on the mend' – with the help of an antibiotic.

Granny went outside to tell everyone that I had survived and Old Teddy, now awake and dressed, joined her – with no acknowledgement of the night's events or how I was.

The crisis over and the wagon now quiet, the doctor asked Mam if anything else might be bothering her, noticing her scratching the spots that were quite visible on her arms and neck. She told him that they only appeared when she stayed in the wagon and Granny's explanation was that it was 'the change of water.'

He looked around the wagon, asked her what the sleeping arrangements were, and whether the itching bothered her more when in bed. The doctor, an elderly man who had tended to families in the poorest and most squalid of living conditions, had seen these spots many times before. Mam pointed to the bed, still unmade from the previous evening, and he examined the bedding, pointing to some tiny dots on the sheet.

'See there… and there? Just as I thought... they're blood spots! Well, m'dear, it looks like the bed bugs are makin' a meal o' ye.'

She was mortified. How could this be? The bedclothes were clean… the nice freshly laundered sheets. Surely he was mistaken? The doctor explained that the bugs lived in mattresses and cracks in woodwork etc and came out at night to feed.

He patted her hand reassuringly and as he left, she looked round the old wagon – seeing it for the first time as a hazard. The dark wood panelling, clothing just rammed into cupboards, the mattress on Rosie's bed, which was probably ancient – everything harbouring these nocturnal predators.

She gazed at her precious baby, now sound asleep, and was thankful that they would soon be leaving the wagon… *and* the lifestyle. The little bedsit and the Wilkies felt like home and she longed to get back safely.

The train to Newcastle was quiet and they had a carriage to themselves. Dad stood outside in the corridor smoking a cigarette and Mam, having nursed me to sleep, picked up a newspaper left by an earlier passenger.

She thumbed idly through the pages, just enjoying the respite, and not particularly interested in the local Scottish news items until she came to the property page.

'Look, Dick.' She beckoned to Dad as he came back into the carriage. 'The prices of houses are quite reasonable. We could just about afford a rental until we've saved enough as a deposit to buy one. What do you think?'

She tried to show him the paper and was a little disappointed at his apparent lack of enthusiasm as he gave the briefest of glances then changed the subject.

She wondered whether he was really thinking ahead, then reasoned to herself that the war probably still preoccupied his thoughts. Rationing and shortages of certain foods and commodities were continuing to present difficulties.

And yet here she was, with a young husband who loved her and a baby they both adored – the ingredients for a life ahead that could surely promise only good things. She put down the paper and smiled at the thought.

THIRTEEN

The next few months seemed to fly by. Mam was totally absorbed with her baby (me) and planning for a proper married life with Dad when he was discharged from the army. She was reluctant to continue the visits to his parents, explaining to Dad that she worried about the unsanitary conditions (no toilets or running water) and the baby's welfare.

He understood and agreed to split any remaining leave between his two families, staying first with Mam then going on to wherever his folks happened to be. Tommy and John had not yet been fully discharged and with only his young brother Walter and Rosie left to help run the business, Dad – along with the other married brothers (Harry and Edward) – pitched in where they could.

In June 1946 Dad was given his discharge papers, his conduct described as exemplary.

The summer season was well underway for the travellers and Dad helped his parents out at every opportunity, justifying the trips now as 'earning a bob or two.'

Knowing that they would need some capital when they set up home, Mam did not mind these absences, her time consumed with her baby – now eleven months old. When spending his time in Newcastle with Mam, she talked excitedly about their future, imagining their home and how it would be furnished, telling him she wouldn't mind if he preferred that they settled in Scotland.

She worked out their finances, figuring that with the small amount she had saved plus his army gratuity they could afford to rent a nice little house

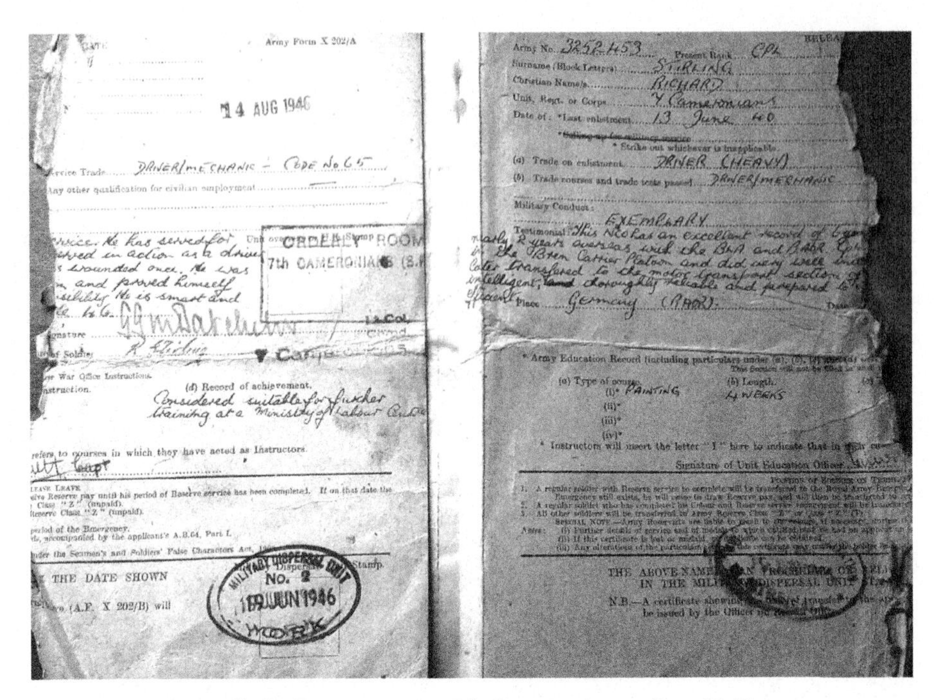

Army Form X 202/A

14 AUG 1946

Service Trade DRIVER/MECHANIC – CODE No 65

Any other qualification for civilian employment

He has served for ... served in action as a driver ... wounded once. He was ... and proved himself ... He is smart and ...

ORDERLY ROOM
7th CAMERONIANS

Signature

of Soldier R. Stirling

War Office Instructions.

(d) Record of achievement.
Considered suitable for further training at a Ministry of Labour Centre

refers to courses in which they have acted as Instructors.

period of the Emergency.

under the Seamen's and Soldiers' False Characters Act,

THE DATE SHOWN

(A.F. X 202/B) will

MILITARY DISPERSAL UNIT
No. 2
19 JUN 1946
YORK

Army No. 3252453 Present Rank CPL
Surname (Block Letters) STIRLING
Christian Name/s RICHARD
Unit, Regt. or Corps 7 Cameronians
Date of: *Last enlistment 13 June 40

* Strike out whichever is inapplicable.

(a) Trade on enlistment DRIVER (HEAVY)
(b) Trade courses and trade tests passed DRIVER/MECHANIC

Military Conduct: EXEMPLARY

Testimonial: This NCO has an excellent record of ... nearly 2 years overseas with the BNA and BAOR ... in the Bren Carrier Platoon and did very well ... later transferred to the motor transport section ... intelligent, thoroughly reliable and prepared to ... efficient.

Place Germany (BAOR)

* Army Education Record (including particulars under (a), (b), ...

(a) Type of course (i)* PAINTING (ii)* (iii)* (iv)*
(b) Length. 4 WEEKS

* Instructors will insert the letter "I" here to indicate that in ...

Signature of Unit Education Officer

THE ABOVE-NAMED ... IN THE MILITARY DISPERSAL UNIT ...

N.B.—A certificate showing ... be issued by the Officer ...

Dad's discharge papers – 7th Cameronians – June 1946

somewhere and manage until he found work. She failed to notice that he didn't seem to share her enthusiasm, avoiding any discussion by playing with – and talking 'gobbledygook' baby talk to me.

They sat in the little bedsit, Dad chain-smoking and looking nervous, Mam wondering what on earth he was about to tell her. He had arrived back from one of the trips to his parents' and before she could ask how everyone was, he interrupted, saying he had some news.

'Rosie said it would be a good idea for me to give travelling a year... just to get it out of my system and help me to settle.' He blurted this out at rapid speed, hardly taking a breath, and looked for some reaction from her.

She couldn't quite work out what he meant. Did he intend on leaving her and the baby in Newcastle while he travelled for a year? The idea certainly did not appeal to her but, she thought, would it be so different from his time in the army when she was alone for long periods?

Before she was able to react, he took her hand and continued, 'And Rosie knows where there's a lorry and also joints' (stalls) 'for sale.'

She was aghast. This had a feeling of permanency and she needed to nip things in the bud quickly. Her young husband could be impulsive – the incident previously of the little dog he had bought her being one example of his best intentions going horribly wrong. Not wishing to dampen his enthusiasm for the idea, she tried to apply some logic.

'But Dick, think this through – jobs are being snapped up quickly now by all the returning servicemen and if you delay things by a year there will be nothing left. You *know* that we need to save, and every penny counts.'

Dad was becoming even more agitated, face turning red as he interjected. 'But Rosie has already paid for the stuff.'

Mam was astounded. Rosie certainly earned good money as a munitions worker but she had never seemed to Mam to be the altruistic type. Why on earth would she spend her money to indulge her brother for a year? The question had to be asked.

'So where did Rosie get the money to pay for all this?'

Dad gulped, drew heavily on his cigarette and turned away from her as he muttered, 'Well… she took charge of my gratuity pay and that's what she used.'

There was an uncanny stillness in the room. Dad now standing at the window, his back to Mam, waiting for her reaction and not relishing the thought of her response.

She gazed at him, desperately trying to make sense of what she had just heard. This seemed to be *fait accompli*; the future she'd dreamed of was about to be snatched from her without discussion.

She felt betrayed. The man she had trusted implicitly had set his own needs above those of his family. This was akin to the childhood memory of her father not telling her he had remarried, and all the feelings of hurt and abandonment she'd felt as a child resurfaced. She was so angry, needing to lash out at someone – anyone who had been party to this 'conspiracy.' She wanted to scream at him, throw something, but the baby was sleeping, and also she was aware that Mrs Wilkie was downstairs and might hear.

'So *this* is what you were doing when you were 'helping' your folks? Everything all nicely arranged… *you* just handing over your gratuity to 'big sister' Rosie. *That* was supposed to go towards our deposit for a house – our first home – and you've allowed it to be spent on a load of junk that, by the way, I haven't even seen. How *could* you?'

He struggled to find words that might justify his actions and also serve to reassure his young wife, who was now sitting on the edge of their bed weeping.

'It'll be alright… you'll see. We can live quite comfortably in the lorry. It's been fitted out with a double bed and a cot for the baby. There's a dressing table for you with mirrors… we got it cheap at the Barras.' (The Barras was a flea market in Glasgow.) 'There's even a wee stove just like the one in the wagon.'

His words were having no effect on her and he was shocked to see her so distressed. He wanted to comfort her and continued, 'Just give me a year. I promise we'll settle down after that, but there's a real chance to make a bit of money this year. Now that the war's over, punters are spending at the shows and there are a few really good gaffs' (fairgrounds) 'to be had. We could double – even treble – my gratuity in a year and afford a better home.'

Mam, always the realist, gazed at him in disbelief. He actually expected her and the baby to live in an old lorry and be shunted around Scotland like cattle, exposed to every imaginable hazard.

She was now really worried, haunted by her aunts' parting statement that she 'would never change him… travelling was in his blood.'

She saw Rosie as the chief architect of this plan and hated her for meddling. She pictured the scenario – Rosie chipping away at him with each of his 'helping' visits, using her monopoly of his time to remind him of his 'roots' and the money to be made when he returned. *How could he be so easily beguiled?* she thought.

Yet, here he was, arm reassuringly around her – reiterating that it would only be short term, that he still intended on looking for a job afterwards and settling down as promised. He told her that it would be good for the baby, the fresh air and outdoor life far better than the noise and clamour of the city. His abundance of relatives would mean that there would be a whole network of people around to support her. His promises were unending, as were his declarations of absolute love and devotion for her and the baby.

As the night wore on, whether from sheer exhaustion or just her awareness that she had burnt her bridges and had no escape route, she reluctantly agreed to 'give it a try,' reasoning to herself that after all, it would only be for a year.

FOURTEEN

'Here ye are then…wha' d'ye think?' Dad led Mam towards an old Albion lorry that looked as though it had been a furniture van in its heyday. It was parked next to Granny's wagon, and it seemed that just about every traveller on the ground had turned out, curious to witness the 'grand unveiling' and Mam's reaction.

The left side of the Albion had been fitted with a door and two small windows, and just below the door was a set of wooden steps.

Uncle Harry (Wilmot), Dad's brother-in-law, appeared at the door. He was a skilled carpenter and had been overseeing the 'fitting out' of the lorry. He beckoned Mam to come and see what they had done and helped her and the baby up the steps.

Inside, facing her, were cupboards, a mirror, and a small blue hostess stove similar to Granny's. Below the first window was a table with extending flap and under this, some drawers. A locker seat was fixed either side of the table.

A wooden partition separated this section from the 'bedroom,' which had just enough space for a double bed, a cot and the little dressing table, resplendent with its central and hinged side mirrors. Hardboard panelling, which lined the walls, had been painted a sickly pink colour and fumes from the paint were still strong, requiring dad to open the window. The floor was covered in a patterned Congoleum, which was a cheap form of linoleum. The joints (stalls) were stored behind a partition at the back and also tied up on the roof of the Albion.

There was no toilet – everyone 'just used buckets,' advised one helpful

There are no photos of the Albion so this is my illustration

onlooker, adding that water had to be carried in cans from wherever a tap could be found. Mam noted the two old, dented water cans that had been painted orange, alongside a chipped white enamel pail placed next to the steps. She wondered how on earth anyone could carry those cans when full; they would be so heavy.

All eyes were on Mam. She knew how much it meant to Dad that she 'approved' of what they'd done to make the lorry habitable. He stood with his entourage, gazing proudly at their creation, seeing an acceptable showman's home.

'Better-off' travellers had stainless steel water cans such as these

All *she* could see was a box on wheels.

She noticed Rosie standing at the door of Granny's wagon – her arms folded, probably watching for any adverse reaction that would confirm her view that this English flattie – now her brother's wife – would never make it as a traveller.

Aware that a response was needed, Mam thanked everyone for their help and complemented them on their workmanship, all the while thinking to herself that it would only be for a year, and she could survive these living conditions short-term. After all, the aunts' house in Newcastle had an outside toilet, and the nocturnal use of a 'po' was not so unusual. Not having a supply of water might be a problem, especially with a baby, but she reasoned to herself that if Granny Stirling had managed with ten children then surely *she* could cope safely with one?

Their few belongings from the bedsit had been transported in a borrowed van and everyone was now unpacking these and loading them into the Albion. She knew they only meant to be helpful, but their actions left her feeling disempowered. Children were running in and out, shouting at each other excitedly and being cursed by various adults, who were also adding to the melee in their attempts either to help or spectate.

The Albion – despite its uniqueness – was to be their first family home, something she had wanted to set up privately, and just with her husband. She felt exhausted, overwhelmed, and that she was being rushed into this strange new environment with hardly any time to think. Clutching her baby tightly, she looked pleadingly to Dad.

Sensing her distress and realising how alien everything must have seemed to her, he asked everyone to leave, saying that the baby needed to be settled.

'This'll do us for a wee while,' he reassured her, his statement almost confirming to her that it *was* a temporary arrangement.

Yes, she thought, *I can survive a year.*

Before going to bed that night, mindful of her earlier experience in Granny's wagon with the nocturnal 'vampires,' she checked the bedding, and was relieved to find that everything was new – mattress, pillows, sheets and blankets all unwrapped and the bed made up ready to welcome its exhausted occupants. Baby was already snuggled down and cosy in the new cot, happily oblivious to this new environment.

Waking with a start, disorientated, unsure of the time and momentarily forgetting where she was, Mam turned on her side to enjoy a soft breeze from the window, which was still slightly open in order to ventilate any lingering paint fumes. The Albion felt warm, and the walls were not quite the sickly pink she'd thought previously. It was daylight and looking out of the window, she noticed for the first time that they were parked in a grassy field surrounded by trees. The various lorries and wagons were arranged in a large semi-circle, the fair not yet built up.

The grass had been cut at some point prior to the fair's arrival and the sweet smell of the clippings drifted through the open window. The sun was shining, birds were singing, and she could hear voices and laughter drifting out from a few of the wagons. Baby was awake and gurgling happily in the cot, blanket kicked to one side by chubby little legs. She could hear Dad trying to make breakfast, dishes rattling and kettle whistling on the stove.

She realised that they had all slept really well despite the excitement and upheaval of the previous day. She felt fully rested and much more optimistic. For the year she had promised, she would do her best to support him. This was *his* world and there was much she still had to learn about her young husband, his family, and the unique lifestyle to which she was being introduced. But.., she reasoned, it was just a break from the 'norm' before they set up their 'proper' home.

She sat at the small table and sipped her first cup of tea in their new 'temporary' home as Dad tried to describe to her the complexities of showbusiness.

He explained that the war years brought an unexpected prosperity to the fairgrounds. The drive to boost morale meant that many more towns and villages were encouraging fairs to open. Parks, village greens and areas of common land were made available, and several local authorities even waived rental fees in order to attract the fairs.

A few sites were potentially more lucrative than others and there was a need to stake claims to grounds quickly. Fortunately this process was carefully controlled. Fairground operators now had to be members of, and adhere to the rules of, the Showmen's Guild (the trade organisation for travelling funfairs) in order to avoid any territorial clashes.

In earlier years, showmen had been known to battle for pitches and to race from fair to fair in order to obtain the best position. Now there were specific rules – allocations controlled by 'lessees,' these commonly being the owners of one or more of the large rides (waltzers, dodgems etc).

It was the responsibility of lessees to liaise with the various local authorities, and arrange dates and times of the fair's arriving, opening and departing and where water could be sourced. Lessees set the rents for the fairs; charges were based on the size per foot of each pitch.

Dad's family already had an established round of fairs but were tempted by the thought of adding new and more lucrative grounds. They very quickly learned where there might be new fairs, which lessee might be opening these and staking their 'claim.' Mam discovered that Dad had been acquiring pitches during the visits to his parents that summer. Some of these were older 'tired' grounds passed on to him as starters by his parents and a few others were new fairs he had successfully negotiated with the various lessees.

She looked out the window, aware of a group of men gathering nearby. Dad noted her curiosity, telling her that this was the start of the process of setting out the ground, pointing out the lessee – tape measure in hand, carefully checking a list to see how much footage could be placed where.

The traveller men – and she noticed that no women were taking part – followed the lessee, agreeing or disagreeing with their allocation. Dad explained that this was a new ground and these allocations, once recorded by the lessee, became permanent 'tenancies,' the specific measured position and ground space reserved as a right for that showman every year thereafter.

The pitch location was crucial. Too close to the fair's entrance then it was

Typical fairground layout of the time

likely that the 'punters' (paying public) would walk past the first few stalls, impatient to see what was ahead; too far round the other side of the ground and chances were that the crowds had already spent their money and were heading home.

There was a traditional layout for the fairgrounds, the large rides (waltzers, dodgems etc) being in the centre, circling these the round stalls and smaller children's rides, then the outer circle of stalls and sideshows.

Hidden behind these were the wagons, lorries and paraphernalia of the travellers – this area being their private living space, albeit short-term and not for the general public.

Dad explained that the joint (stall) he bought only measured fifteen feet, but he intended on extending it and had claimed thirty feet with lessees at other grounds. Only half listening now, Mam struggled to digest everything he was telling her. The secretive, almost cavalier way he had organised things still bothered her, and mindful of his 'promise,' she couldn't resist asking, 'But what will you do with all of this at the end of the year?'

Scarcely pausing to catch breath, he replied, 'Don't worry, I can resell the joints and also my 'rights' to the grounds I've reserved. We will make a bob or two, you'll see… We will be alright.'

Later that day, all 'pitches' agreed – including the space for Dad's joint – the build-up began. Lorries were being shunted around, ploughing furrows in the soft grass as they were repositioned and then unloaded.

While this was happening, Mam decided to go with Granny to the local shops. The weather that summer had not been particularly good but for a week now there had been respite from the rain. The June sun was hot that afternoon, the sunshades of most shops unrolled and extended for the first time in weeks, bringing welcome relief to the queues waiting outside. Shopping was an uncomfortable experience for Mam, not being registered with any of the stores and embarrassed at the extra scrutiny paid by many assistants to her new ration books, which now declared her as an itinerant customer.

All books were colour-coded – buff for adults and green for babies. The green book gave the parent first choice of milk and any available fruit, and a double supply of eggs. (The egg allowance was only one per adult.) She felt so guilty when buying an orange!

Granny was shopping for her family, and had ration books for herself, Old

Teddy, Rosie, Walter, and also John and Tommy, who had now been demobbed and were back home. The queues behind them seemed to grow at every shop as Granny produced all six books and the harassed shopkeepers tried to sort and stamp her purchases.

At various shops, Granny advised Mam on the best buys – food that would 'keep,' and also a rubbing board for the washing, a bar of Sunlight soap – which would 'do for the dishes as well as the washing'. She added, 'And you'd better take a couple of these Dolly bags. They're good for bites and stings.'

This puzzled Mam. She was familiar with the 'blue bags,' as her aunts called them, which were little cloth parcels tied around a tiny wooden peg and added to the final rinse on laundry days; the aunts explained that they made the clothes whiter. She never considered them as a medication and wondered whether she had misheard Granny until the shopkeeper added, 'Yes, that's right. They contain baking soda and soothe the skin if you have a rash or any bites. You just dip the bag in water and dab it on the sore bit.'

Mam was grateful for the information but secretly wished she had known of this remedy earlier, thinking back to the consequence of her first overnight stay in Granny's old wagon.

Having worked their way from shop to shop, Granny's huge bag was now so heavy that Mam insisted she put it in the pram, carrying me while Granny enjoyed pushing the magnificent 'Silver Cross shopping trolley' as they made their way back to the ground.

They had been away less than two hours, yet Mam was amazed at the transformation. Shutters and poles had been bolted together, forming the framework for the stalls, the wagons and lorries gradually being hidden from view as these were built up. Local children were running around, scarcely able to contain their excitement as they saw the rides being assembled and annoying the men who were trying to unload the heavier machinery for the dodgem.

The afternoon sun brought a beautiful dazzling brightness to the ground, illuminating the vibrant colours of the painted, gilded and highly varnished artwork of the fair's equipment, which stood on the grass like jewels placed on a green velvet cushion.

It was a few moments before she could reorientate herself and locate their 'pitch' – and then she saw it. An assortment of poles and wood propped against the Albion, not yet assembled or resembling anything like a stall. Dad and his brothers Tommy and John were standing – hands nonchalantly in dungaree pockets – watching Rosie, who was kneeling on the ground examining an old tarpaulin that had been rolled out for inspection.

Granny hauled out the heavy message bag and I was comfortably resettled in the pram, surrounded by children all asking Mam if they could push me.

Old Teddy sat on the wagon steps, smoking his Woodbine and cursing the various grandchildren who were jumping on and off the platform, being teased by his youngest son Walter. He made no attempt to help his wife as she struggled past him with her bag, his only comment to her being a resentful 'You took yer time, didn't ye? Are we getting any dinner today?'

Dad turned, noting Mam's bemused expression, and realised that her first impressions of the joint were not favourable. His brothers tried to ease the situation.

John joked, 'We're just trying to work out which bits fit where and if anything's missing.'

Tommy added, 'We've got the hammer and nails ready for you.' This did not help.

She looked from the beautifully maintained stalls that were being built up around them to the dirty, cobweb-covered jumble of debris propped against the Albion and her heart sank.

What on earth possessed him to invest in such a pile of junk? she thought, then remembered him telling her that Rosie had been the broker. She felt resentment at this woman's interference in their lives rising like a bile in her stomach.

As though reading her mind, Rosie sensed that some defence was needed, explaining, 'The stuff belonged to an old fella who stopped travelling years ago. He kept it all dismantled in a yard and didn't bother painting it or anything… just covered it over with a tilt. That's how we got it so cheap. Once it's tidied up a bit and set out with swag' (prizes) 'it'll be fine.'

Getting up from her knees, the inspection of the tilt over, she added, 'By the way, there's are a couple of rips there that'll need patching.' At which point she left them and followed Granny into the wagon, leaving Mam to gaze at the old mildew-covered canvas in disbelief.

'Don't worry about that,' Dad reassured her. 'I have another one in a better condition. This one will come in handy because the joint doesn't have any side or back panels, so I will just use this old tilt until I can get some wood and do proper job.'

A little relieved now that she did not have to be a seamstress, she asked him, 'So… what sort of stall will it be?'

His family had a rifle range, a darts stall, a round stall and also a kiddie's roundabout. Did he have something similar in mind? He grinned and, taking her arm, led her to the back of the Albion, where he slid out a tea chest, the contents rattling as it bumped to the ground.

'Go on – take a look,' he urged and, not sure what to expect, she gazed inside the chest, discovering nothing more exciting than a load of empty soup or bean cans, the labels removed, and the cans painted. There was also a hessian bag containing dozens of ping pong-sized wooden balls. She still could not imagine how this would become a fairground attraction.

She looked again at the ramshackle joint that Tommy and John had started building up, and back at the contents of the tea chest. How could this rag and bone conglomeration earn them any money? she wondered.

Dad's enthusiasm was almost palpable as he explained that he had painted the tins in sets of three, each set a different colour. They would be stacked on a shelf and the game was to knock a complete set off the shelf to win, using only three wooden balls. He continued, 'I know we'll be competing with other travellers for the punters' attention, so I've got a sheet of tin to hang behind the cans. The noise of the wooden balls hitting the tin should do the trick.'

He seemed so sure that this would actually work. Mam trusted his judgement and in the following few days, she helped him to set out the few bits of swag (prizes) comprising mainly of coconuts and a few bits of glassware (vases, salad bowls and beer mugs). While not the prettiest of attractions, their 'can joint' was ready to make its debut.

Opening night was the success Dad had predicted. The noise, plus the activity of hurling the balls at the cans, drew the crowds (and also the attention of other travellers, curious to know how he was managing to pull the punters!).

Mam helped where she could, aware that all the other traveller women were working the stalls. Various cousins were babysitting, but she still felt anxious, leaving Dad every five minutes to check that I was alright.

This was her baptism as a traveller's wife, and she was not enjoying the experience. She was trying to restack the cans as they were demolished, often colliding with Dad as he handed out balls. She was shouted at by drunks who claimed she had deflected their aim and every so often she was struck by a ball, sometimes accidentally but occasionally on purpose.

They had been open since 1.30pm and eventually closed at 11.30pm and she was exhausted. They sat that night at the small table in the Albion, cups of tea steaming, and counted their takings. Coins stacked in little piles – coppers dirtying their fingers and leaving a metallic smell, a couple of crumpled, pink ten-shilling notes, the aroma of tobacco from previous owners still clinging to the paper… and best of all, two £5 notes. (This seemed a fortune considering an average weekly wage at the time was around £3 to £4.)

'You see… I told you we'd do ok,' Dad announced triumphantly after finally working out what they had spent on diesel, swag and rent that week. They had made a small profit.

She was too tired to point out that he had not included the cost of buying the Albion and the joint. He was already describing the next fair they would be moving on to. It was considered a good gaff, and in his view, success was guaranteed.

FIFTEEN

Travelling to the ground – a journey of around thirty miles – was a salutary lesson for Mam. This was to be her first trip in the Albion, and she had not realised that the small living area would also have to provide temporary extra storage space. As well as the pram, which was quite large, she watched as the water cans and bucket, a box containing electric lightbulbs for the joint, and breakable swag was loaded.

Neither had it dawned on her that cupboard doors should be secured for the journey. The baby was her priority and the main focus of her attention, and Dad just took it for granted that she would know.

The old Albion did not offer a comfortable ride, every bump and bend of the country road ricocheting and jarring through the lorry's framework. Mam sat gazing out the side window at the passing countryside, unaware of water slopping out of the cans.

One huge jolt resulted in the cupboard doors bursting open. Dishes and foodstuffs slid off shelves onto the now-wet floor and Mam tried to keep her balance as she tried desperately to save things. Dad, ensconced in the cab and lost in his own thoughts, drove on, unaware of the chaos unfolding behind him. I continued to sleep happily, my cot in the bedroom area and fortunately not near anything calamitous.

When they arrived at the ground, Dad jumped out of the cab, stretched, lit a cigarette, then walked round to the Albion's living area to check on his young family. From his initial shock as he opened the door, he could scarcely contain his laughter as he realised what had happened at the sight that met him.

Mam was covered in every ingredient she'd tried to save as they had tumbled from the cupboards. Flour, rice, salt, milk, even the one precious egg, had all ended up on the floor, the Congoleum becoming a skating rink as she slipped and slithered across it.

Dad was joined by John and Tommy, who on seeing the flour-covered state of Mam, jokingly asked her when the cake would be ready. There was an ominous silence. The three brothers stood, watching her, waiting for a backlash or tears. Instead, catching sight of herself in the mirror, she burst out laughing, as much from relief that the journey was over as the vision before her.

They started to clear up and the pram, relatively unscathed, was unloaded along with the other items of extra storage – and then they began to assess the damage. Scarcely a dish remained intact, plates were cracked or broken, and of the only four teacups they possessed, only two remained intact but were now minus their handles.

They salvaged the few remaining dishes. John examined the cups and debated whether the handles could be glued back on. Dad reassured Mam that they would get replacements at the Barras. He secured the cupboard doors with snibs as Harriet, his sister-in-law, helped Mam wash the sticky liquid off the Congoleum.

Harriet was from the Codona family, travellers of years standing, and she was well-versed in the tips and tricks of safe transportation.

'You should stand the milk bottles in a pan on the floor then if they spill, it just goes into the pan. Use your towels to wrap round the dishes, don't leave cups hanging from the hooks, and remember to tie the door handles together in case those snibs don't hold.'

Harriet looked round the Albion, still sparsely furnished. 'And if you get any ornaments, just put them on the bed.' As she mopped the floor, she added, 'And make sure the water cans aren't full when they are lifted in. Oh, and by the way, you should take down the Tilley lamp mantles and sit them in a cup or something. If they break, it is hard to get replacements in some of the places we go to.'

(The mantles were fragile affairs, delicate little gauze nets that were fastened to the lamp via a little clay ring. Initially flat when bought, they puffed up in the flame and glowed, giving a bright light. They damaged easily – the slightest

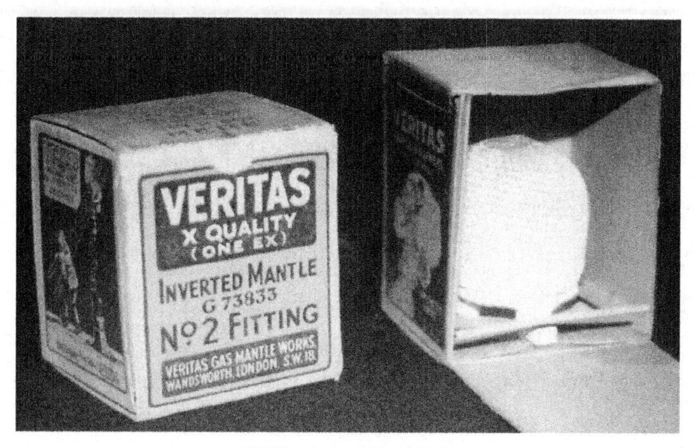

'Tilley' gas mantles

touch and the gauze powdered away, the lamp's flame flaring out of the hole and making a 'put-put' noise as it escaped.)

Mam listened to Harriet as they worked, appreciating the advice but also realising that she should just have used basic common sense and a bit of foresight.

And so they travelled across Scotland, every week in a different town or village, the fairs opening at Highland Games, gala days and sometimes just in little hamlets where the 'shows' were the only event that week.

Mam quickly became adept at 'packing up' and there were no further breakages. She also realised within those first few weeks that there was no room for passengers in show-business and that everyone, regardless of age, was required to work. The women dealt with all the homemaking and domestic requirements, and quite commonly the book-keeping and budgeting, but also helped their menfolk with the heavy manual tasks associated with building up and pulling down. Children carried water and went on errands. Girls looked after younger siblings, while boys learned at the men's shoulders how to run a fair. This included tinkering with engines and also manoeuvring lorries.

Mam noted that very few of the children attended school with any regularity, especially not the boys. If they could manage the three Rs they were considered sufficiently well-educated. It seemed that if they could drive lorries, repair things and count money, this was all that was expected.

The old people travelled with their families and those still fit enough for the task took their turn at 'minding the stuff,' as did the children, many often still of primary school age. The elderly show-people held status within their community and younger travellers respected their wisdom and knowledge.

Mam was slowly becoming familiar with the routines of travelling – the building up and pulling down, helping Dad with the heavy lifts (shutters and boxes that required two people to handle), planning meals around opening times, minding the joint, and tending to me.

She was reluctant to admit it, but just as Dad had predicted, I was thriving. The summer was warm; I was outdoors most days and brown as a berry. I was being constantly fussed over by my various cousins, all vying for the right to push the pram. The boys had a vested interest in the pram, seeing the possibility of the chrome wheels from the Silver Cross eventually being the pride of the next 'guider' (barrow) they would build!

SIXTEEN

The joint continued to earn just enough to provide an income week by week and, while not amassing fortune, they were getting by, Dad always assuring Mam that 'the next ground' would bring in the money.

Mam liked the continual contact and involvement with Dad, the lifestyle dictating that they were never apart, but such closeness meant she was now noticing traits in her young husband's character that previously she hadn't been aware of. He hated being the butt of anyone's jokes or being placed in any situation that made him look foolish, even by proxy, once telling her she was 'making a fool of herself' when seeing her attempting to teach his young brother Walter the steps of a popular dance. He avoided any friendships and if he noticed her talking to anyone beyond his own family circle, he needed to know who they were and what they wanted. There were also occasions when, for no apparent reason, he sank into black moods that could last for hours, then – inexplicably – he snapped out of them again. The first couple of times this happened, she wondered whether she had unintentionally done something to upset him. She remembered Granny telling her that he had been a sulky child who 'couldn't take a joke against himself.'

She tried not to let any of this bother her, reckoning that he was still settling into married life and assuming that this was just the normal growth and development stage of their relationship. The concept of coercive control was not commonly discussed or even acknowledged in the 1940s/50s. Women just put up with things.

She was beginning to enjoy the ever-growing extended family, each ground they travelled to resulting in yet more aunts, uncles, cousins – first, second, third generation – being introduced. Even those who were not blood relatives were referred to as 'aunty' or 'uncle.' While all just a bit confusing, she was always warmly welcomed and felt that she had been truly accepted when they stopped introducing her as 'Dickie's wife' and instead referred to her as 'our Winnie.'

Despite this, she still missed the familiarity of her own small family in Newcastle. There had been no contact from her aunts, and she was forced now to accept that they really had disowned her. Leslie, her brother, was married – and with three small children and a demanding job, he had little time to worry about his nomadic sister.

In 1942 her Uncle Fred had married a widow with a young son. The boy was proving difficult, not relating well to his stepfather, and was about to be packed off to boarding school, so Fred was also wrapped up in his own concerns.

She wrote every few weeks to her father, trying to keep him up to date with my progress and to assure him that all was well. While living at the Wilkies' bedsit in Fenham it had been a two-way process, the beautiful copperplate written replies from her dad arriving almost by return. This was now a problem since she could not provide an address, every week being a different location.

On one occasion she tried forwarding the number of a local telephone box, saying she would be there at a specific time for him to ring. She stood outside the box for nearly an hour, anxiously waiting as other people used the phone, worrying that he had been unable to get through. No call came.

She tried to reason why. Perhaps the box near him was out of order? Or, she feared, he might be ill. But then more probably, the stepmother had made it impossible for him to leave the house. After all, he had indicated in his last letter that Janet was 'a little unwell.' Mam realised that her father was probably facing the reality of his wife's mental instability. She wondered as she walked back to the ground whether he now understood the misery this woman had caused his young daughter.

She vowed never to allow her own child to experience such unhappiness and that no matter what their circumstances, their home would always be a place of love and protection.

Back at the Albion, sipping the hot tea Dad had poured, she described her

Vinegarhill (843 Gallowgate, Glasgow)

unsuccessful vigil at the phone box. She tried to make light of the situation, but Dad could see that she was upset and offered a solution.

'Next time you write, why don't you give him Becky's address at Vinegarhill?' (Dad's sister Becky no longer travelled and lived with her family on a ground in Glasgow called Vinegarhill. The actual address was 843 Gallowgate, Glasgow, and it had been a permanent site and also showmen's winter ground for years.)

'She can hold on to your dad's letters until we get to Glasgow… or even get Jim to bring them out when they visit.' Jim (Becky's husband) had a car and regularly took trips out to the various grounds; Becky always knew which weeks and towns their relatives would be opening. Mam cheered up immediately, delighted that a problem she had considered insurmountable had been solved by her young husband.

Becky agreed to being the convenience address, and the system – although a little more protracted – worked. The letters from her dad resumed, allowing her to feel once more in touch with her 'old world' of Newcastle.

SEVENTEEN

The season was to finish at what the travellers referred to as the 'back end' – i.e. late September/October. Dad had been adventurous here, crossing the border and reserving pitches on the Cumberland run, which covered, among others, areas such as Gretna, Whitehaven, Aspatria, Morpeth, Millom and Parton.

They met, departed and met up again with dad's family, depending on who had pitches at which fair. Mam enjoyed the reunions; there was a feeling of security when surrounded by her new relatives and a strange loneliness when they all moved to different events.

It was at one of these grounds that luck ran out. The can joint was attracting the usual interest, pitch after pitch gathering to watch, enjoying the noise – Dad giving the spiel and Mam, by now an expert at re-stacking the cans, helping.

The takings were slowly mounting as the day progressed. In the absence of a cash box, Dad used one of the glass prizes, a large beer mug that he hid behind a shelf at the back of the joint. The takings were added to this until early evening when the crowds began to drift away.

It had been a long day, but they were pleased to have made some money. Having opened at lunchtime and not closed until midnight when the last of any potential punters had gone, they were both exhausted, but reckoned it was worth it. Mam collected me, still tucked up and sleeping, from a woman who had been minding various children in her wagon during the day and returned to the joint. She expected to see Dad shutting the stall down but instead found him white-faced and frantically searching for something.

'We've been robbed! All the takings are gone. I don't know how that could have happened.' His voice faltered, disbelief and shock evident. 'We were here the whole time. We would have seen if somebody had come in.'

By now, other travellers had joined them having noticed that something unusual was happening. Mam wished her brothers-in-law were there. They always brought a sense of security and safety. Instead, this group of men, travellers she had only met that week, were gathering – almost like the punters they had been serving all day, she felt – to observe the spectacle. She wished they would go away. This was a private misfortune that only she and Dad should deal with and not for public entertainment.

'The BASTARDS! Dickie… come here and look at this.'

Angry voices in the darkness called Dad to the back of the joint, where the men pointed to the temporary tarpaulin walling, which had been cut, the slit large enough for the opportunist's arm to reach through and steal the beer mug without being noticed. The mug and a few coppers lay on the ground, all that was left of their day's work.

Dad was distraught, blaming himself for naively thinking the canvas would suffice until he could get around to building proper wooden panels. He had been thinking only of the joint being made temporarily weatherproof – not thief-proof.

Mam tried to console him, saying it was also her fault for unwittingly advertising where they were putting the takings. They had obviously been watched and the thief had waited until it was dark – and also for the cash to build up – before sneaking round the back of the joint, slicing the canvas and grabbing the glass mug.

This was a catastrophe. They had no financial reserve and had been living week by week on the takings from each ground. By the time diesel, swag and rent was paid –plus the costs of daily living – they were only just getting by. They now only had the few coins left in their pockets, and no way to buy the next day's provisions or to pay the lessee his ground rent.

'You'd better grab those two rozzers and report it,' volunteered one of the men, pointing to the policemen patrolling the ground, which was now almost cleared of punters.

The officers reluctantly took note of Dad's complaint. Their task that night had only been to ensure the fair closed at the prescribed time – not to chase criminals. They wanted to finish their shift and go home. Dad realised that they were just paying lip-service to logging the crime, especially when one of them asked for a coconut as they were leaving.

'Well... Egremont's our chance to earn a bob or two again. We'll be ok after that. It's a good gaff and the people are great.'

It was Sunday afternoon. The various stalls and machines were now dismantled and loaded in readiness for moving to their various next fairs. Mam and Dad had spent most of the night trying to work out the logistics of just surviving until they had some money. The theft had shaken Mam, and this rather strange nomadic world she was sharing with her young husband now felt suddenly hostile. She sat, a cup of tea on the little table next to her untouched and now cold, rocking baby (me) on her knee as Dad tried to take her mind off the theft by describing the next fair.

Looking out the window as he talked, Dad's heart sank as he saw the lessee approaching, obviously en route to collect the rent. The man came into the Albion, accepted the lukewarm tea poured by Mam and sat politely sipping it, watched by the anxious couple. He was a jovial chap, remarking how comfortable the Albion was, making a fuss of the baby, sympathising over the theft and assuring Mam that this was not the norm in fairgrounds. The couple waited anxiously for the punchline – the request for the ground rent; after all, the man would be unaware that they were now penniless. Instead, he thanked Mam for the tea, patted her hand – telling her everything would work out alright – then turned to Dad and whispered discreetly that he was waiving the rent. He started to chuckle – he had a story he really had to share with them.

'By the way, I heard that the local minister gave his congregation hell this morning. He heard about the theft and was so furious; his sermon was full of fire and brimstone. He was almost pointing the finger of guilt at every parishioner and had them wriggling in their seats. It did nothing for the collection plate, but it made the minister feel a bit better!'

The lessee was still laughing as he turned and made his way down the steps. Now the ground was slowly starting to clear, the travellers moving on to their various next fairs.

Over at least one financial hurdle, Dad reckoned there was just enough diesel to get them to Egremont, and there was still a small amount of swag left that would allow them to open the can joint. However, they still had to survive until then. Fairs only opened on Fridays and Saturdays, which meant they would have no income for nearly a week.

There was a quiet, almost apologetic knock on the door and a traveller woman –who declined to be invited in – handed Mam a bag of vegetables. The woman, not wanting to embarrass the young couple with an act of charity, claimed it was just a few extras she didn't need before hurrying off. This was repeated by other travellers with shy excuses of surplus foods that 'would just go off.' From one, a loaf of bread; from another, a bottle of milk and two precious eggs; a tin of spam and packet of lard was handed in by someone else along with some cigarettes for Dad. Small offerings given freely to this young family were enough to allow them to survive the week.

Mam was overwhelmed by the kindness of the travellers and the concern shown. She realised that this was a community with a tradition of kinship and support for each other. For the first time she began to understand why Dad was drawn back into the lifestyle.

They continued travelling the Cumberland area trying to recoup their losses, but at the end of 1946 there was a flu epidemic in England. Thought to have originated in prisoner of war camps, it quickly spread. All schools were shut, and children and the elderly were especially vulnerable. The fair, which was now in Millom, remained closed as townspeople and travellers became infected.

Mam dreaded venturing out as there seemed to be a funeral car on every street. On the fairground one little boy was so ill his father gave him his Christmas presents early, fearing the boy would not survive until then.

My parents fretted over me, taking turns each night to sit with me as I slept, anxiously watching for any sign of cough or fever. Fortunately, I was a robust baby and kept well, as did Mam and Dad. Granny was not so fortunate and succumbed to the virus, Mam having to care for her in the absence of Rosie – who, according to Old Teddy – had 'buggered off to Glasgow on business.' Mam felt sure this was just Rosie's excuse in order to escape any nursing tasks and possible infection.

Dad came into the wagon and sat next to Mam, who was trying to coax Granny to sip some soup she'd made. Her three brothers-in-law, Tommy, John, and young Walter, had been fed and were visiting friends in another wagon. Outside, it was cold and raining, adding to everyone's misery. Dad spoke quietly.

'I've been talking to the other men and we have all decided to pack up and go. It's too risky to open here while this flu is raging, and in any case, no-one is going to chance coming to the shows. People are scared and only going out for essential things. Most of the loads are heading back to Glasgow and the lessee here has a pitch for his dodgem at the Kelvin Hall.'

Realising that Mam had never heard of the Kelvin Hall, he explained that this was a traditional winter indoor fair and a huge attraction in Glasgow with many shows and often a circus.

'The lessee says me and some of the lads can help with the build-up, and he might keep a few of us on when it opens, to mind the stuff. It won't be much money, but it can keep us going for a while.' As he talked, he became more enthusiastic, almost designing his ideas for their future as they came to him.

Mam helped Granny back to bed. Old Teddy, having enjoyed the lunch Mam had made for him, was outside enjoying a smoke. She noted that there was no offer of thanks from him, either for the care of Granny or the meals she'd cooked for him and his sons. It just seemed to be taken for granted that she would do it.

Dad continued, 'It will give me a chance to pick up some wood and fix up the joint. John and Tommy said they would help. I'll extend it to thirty feet because that's what I've reserved for our grounds next year. It means we will have twice the earning power because we will have another joint... maybe make it a darts joint.'

Mam's heart sank as she listened to him, realising that nothing in his plan included leaving the business. He was talking about another year travelling. While not wanting to seem a killjoy, she desperately needed to remind him of his promise.

'But you said this would only be for a year to get things out of your system. You *did* say that we would be settling down after that.'

She was aware of her voice, which seemed to be detached from her body, sounding peevish – like a fractious child not getting the anticipated treat – but she was exhausted and could only see further worry.

Dad thought for a moment, preparing his response. 'Ah – but don't forget, we only started mid-summer, half-way through the season and less than four months ago, not a year. Just give me a bit more time. We'll get the winter over, start out in the spring with everyone else and do the full run of all the grounds

I've booked. We'll make up the money we lost and not only get our wee nest egg back but add more. Honestly... it *will* be better next year, I promise.'

His voice was conciliatory, his logic and conviction hard to dispute, and Mam realised that her only choice was to trust his judgement and hope he would be proved right.

EIGHTEEN

The trip to Glasgow from Cumbria was monotonously slow. They were travelling in convoy, Granny's wagon being towed by an old, long-nosed Scammell lorry that kept breaking down, forcing everyone following to stop. Dad and Uncle Tommy were good with engines – skills they'd learned during their six years in the forces – and they somehow managed to get the Scammell going each time.

It was almost dark by the time they reached Glasgow. Streetlights illuminated tenement buildings and people going about their business – stopping briefly to gaze curiously as the strange convoy passed.

The 'yard' Dad said they would stay on turned out to be Vinegarhill – the repository for Mam's letters from her father. She had always been curious about the place, knowing that Dad's sister Becky and oldest brother Harry now lived there with their own families.

Harry had married a traveller, Harriet, who was descended from a long line of show-people, but Becky had chosen to marry a flattie – Jim. The irony of this did not escape Mam when thinking of Rosie's coolness to her and the double standards she evidenced. She had obviously accepted Jim into the fold without demur – he was a Scotsman, and male. Mam, on the other hand, was female – a threat to Rosie's power over her brothers – and worse than this, an English flattie!

Still thinking about this, she was aware of the Albion slowing down and turning from the main road into a narrow lane flanked by derelict buildings. Looking out, she could just see in the gloom that they were passing under a rusting arch, its broken lettering presumably once displaying the name of a previous landowner.

She recalled the saying from Dante – 'Abandon hope all ye who enter here', with reference to the entrance to Hell – then dismissed the notion. She was over-tired and her imagination was working overtime.

Everyone parked wherever there was space, the men jumping out of their lorries and in the darkness gathering round the remains of a bonfire to share cigarettes and discuss the various trials and tribulations of the journey.

There was a knock on the Albion door and Mam opened it to find her sisters-in-law Harriet and Rosie there.

'I've made a few sandwiches and the kettle's on,' Harriet stated, continuing before Mam could say anything, 'You won't feel much like cooking after that trip. C'mon into the wagon, it's warm inside. Bring the baby. The men will just appear when it suits them.'

Rosie, who had not enquired after her mother's health, was instructed by Harriet to go and see how Granny was and whether she needed anything. Mam warmed to Harriet, who was obviously a match for Rosie, and accepted the hot tea and sandwiches gratefully, not realising until then how hungry she had become.

As she ate and Harriet made a fuss of the baby, Mam looked round the wagon. It was spotlessly clean. Anything that could be polished was burnished to a high standard. Various pans simmered on the stove and there was a wonderful aroma of mince and onions cooking. Washing had been done and was ironed, neatly folded and waiting to be put away.

'Oh how I envy you that,' Mam blurted out, pointing to the clean clothes. 'It's so hard trying to do the washing. We have to borrow a boiler – that's when we have enough water to fill it – then I am constantly interrupting Dick when he's busy, to put up a clothes line.'

Harriet chuckled. 'Problem solved – I'll take you to the wash-house tomorrow!'

The following morning Mam opened the door, hoping to venture out with the baby, and recoiled. The air was putrid, polluted with something, causing her to gasp in horror.

'My God, Dick – what on earth is that?' She slammed the door quickly in an attempt to barricade their home against the horrific stench.

'Oh, it's from the gut factory round the corner. I forgot to mention that to you. Everybody here is used to the smell; it's been around for so long I don't think they even notice it now… It won't do you any harm; it's almost a Vinegarhill trademark,' he joked.

It's not something I will ever get used to, Mam thought as Dad helped her down the steps with the pram. She looked about, trying to find something positive but just seeing the rusting remains of old lorries and a couple of derelict wagons – their owners possibly deceased long ago, their homes abandoned. Wagons and living vans of all sizes and descriptions were parked, some permanently, others just there short term.

Around her was blackness. Old, blackened buildings surrounded them on all sides, factory chimney stacks emitting God knows what; even the ground was black, human and animal detritus of years soaked into the earth.

Memories of some of the grounds they had been to that summer – the green fields, wildflowers, trees and birdsong – and windows opened to the sweet smell of freshly cut grass were all a bitter contrast to this place.

She looked across to Harriet's wagon and saw her outside, cleaning the windows – a woman so house-proud, successfully raising her own children and clearly at home in this environment. She thought back to her childhood and the experience of taking the alms to the impoverished family in Newcastle. She remembered her mum's gentle rebuke – telling her not to judge, and saying 'there but for the grace of God', and she felt ashamed. Bouncing the pram across the ground, she walked over to Harriet and asked, 'Right – when are you taking me to this wonderful wash-house?'

Over the next few weeks she adjusted to the environment but never the smell – a constant, repugnant presence that seemed to seep everywhere. The trips to the wash-house became a regular outing, Dad looking after me while Mam loaded my pram with the bath of clothes, rubbing board etc and hurried along Gallowgate with her sister-in-law to get the best booth and drier before it got busy.

Aunty Harriet was proud of this local wash-house, explaining that Whitehill was different from other 'steamies' in Glasgow, having a gymnasium, swimming pool, Turkish baths and over sixty booths for the washing.

Mam's first trip there had been a bit intimidating. Two women had been arguing and almost coming to blows over ownership of the hottest drier. Others were helping each other to fold newly dried sheets and blankets, clearly enjoying the drama. Harriet, ignoring the scenario as though it was an everyday occurrence, shepherded Mam to their allocated booths and proceeded to instruct her.

'Mind and separate the whites from the coloureds… be careful with that boiler… watch your fingers in the spinner, it's lethal… don't let that wee bugger over there mooch your soap powder – she never brings it back… I'm in the next booth if you need anything.'

Harriet was enjoying the mentorship of her novice, and Mam, while appreciating the advice, just relished the luxury of constant hot water. After a few weeks she was well acquainted with the 'steamie' and began to recognise the regulars, enjoying the banter and camaraderie.

There was a sense of huge satisfaction in wheeling the bath of clean sweet-smelling washing back to Vinegarhill. She felt a little victory had been won briefly against the all-pervading smell of the gut factory.

NINETEEN

That winter of 1946/47 was recorded as the snowiest of the twentieth century and at a time when Britain had still not recovered from the war.

There seemed to be nothing to cheer the mood that year, not even the prospect of the royal wedding of Elizabeth and Phillip. The country was in a state of depression, the euphoria of peacetime quickly evaporating as the reality of the war's legacy hit home. There was a lack of everything – food, adequate housing, money, and prospects.

Rationing continued. Meat allowance was reduced to one shilling's worth per week. Even worse, potatoes – a staple diet for the impoverished – were placed on the restricted list. The list of items rationed was endless and there was no sign that the situation would improve. As Mam had predicted, demobbed servicemen were pushed to the back of the queue for jobs, overtaken by those who had missed the fighting. This was despite assurances of full employment being promised to servicemen by politicians such as Ernest Bevin.

Dad hunted for jobs, going out daily and prepared to take anything, even standing with groups of men at the gates of factories and dockyards, hoping for the offer of a few hours' casual labour.

Mam worried about him – each unsuccessful day resulted in him coming home cold, hungry and increasingly depressed. Despite her own fears, she tried to reassure him that this was just a temporary setback and things would improve.

He had managed to purchase some wood prior to the worst of the weather taking hold and, with help from his brothers, was extending the joint from fifteen to thirty feet. Mindful of the earlier sliced tarpaulin and theft, he gradually built side and back panels. The activity, along with planning for the summer season, seemed to offer him some solace and Mam chose not to keep reminding him of his promise – but she now worried that they were eating into the small amount of money they had.

They were just about getting by on Dad's earnings from the Kelvin Hall job. The lessee had been true to his word and hired some of the young travellers to build up and help to mind the dodgem.

Dad was in his element and life for him seemed normal again. He was in a familiar environment, working with his peers and bringing home a small wage. He announced proudly to Mam that even though he wasn't earning much, they would manage until spring when they started out again. He assured her the extra stall would guarantee double their takings at each fair.

She had no heart to tell him that she was scarcely managing to make ends meet now. Neither could she confess that the bowl of soup he was enjoying was thanks to the good auspices of his brother. When visiting, Harry – discovering the pot of bones boiling with no sign of any vegetables to add, left Mam a few coins saying it was 'for the bairn,' knowing Mam could now buy the ingredients for the soup. She managed to make that soup last another two days, albeit thinner with each serving.

She now knew the reality of being impoverished and the irrational feeling of shame and embarrassment that it brought. She was afraid for their future, despite Dad's optimism, and also angry with herself for being so faint-hearted.

She needed to take stock. Her baby was healthy; Dad loved them both and was doing his best to care for them; the Albion, albeit an unconventional home, was clean and warm; and she was accepted, even affectionately now, by Dad's family… apart from Rosie, who continued to keep her distance.

She thought back to earlier times – to losing her mother, her treatment at the hands of her stepmother, her happier life with her aunts and the heartbreak when leaving them. She remembered the trip to Liverpool and the war casualties being stretchered from the train and realised how lucky she was to still have Dad. She could so easily have been one of the many war widows.

This was to be a new chapter in her life and for the sake of her baby she had to be positive and try to look to the future with some optimism. All marriages came with responsibilities… and promises. He had promised her that travelling would be out of his system once they had done the summer run and she believed him, promising to help and support him.

Spring was only a few weeks away; they would move away from Vinegarhill and its stench to new grounds – to fresh air, and the feeling of a new start.

TWENTY

The summer of 1948 was eventful for many reasons. Nationalisation of essential services had begun, first with the coal industry and railways, then the gas and electricity providers. The Empire Windrush docked, its passengers – Jamaican immigrants – arriving to support the National Health Service; and that same year the NHS announced free universal health care. Bread rationing ended. Polo mints were created. The first episode of 'Mrs. Dale's Diary' was broadcast. And Prince Charles was born.

For Mam, the summer was tolerable only because of Dad's continued promise that they would settle down 'next year,' once they had recouped their losses. The additional joint Dad had built was a darts stall and he had explained the rudiments of the game to her.

'The punters have to score twenty-one or less with three darts. The darts have different coloured flights in sets of three, so if several punters are playing, you won't mix them up.' He pointed to the different score areas. 'Bull is fifty, the ring round the bull is twenty-five – so if a dart goes there you don't even need to count… the punter's lost already.'

He had every confidence in her ability to 'mind the joint' and she proved just as proficient in working up a 'pitch' as him. At times he even had to leave the can joint to help her, so many punters were playing at the darts.

She worked alongside him throughout the season, tackling every job without complaint, knowing that the only way out of the business was to earn enough money to support their exit.

The lack of sanitation was something she could never get used to, however.

Water was precious, having to be drawn from a variety of sources, and she became adept at carrying the two full cans, learning how to brace her elbows against her hips to give balance. She also was mindful to keep the spouts facing outwards, her first attempt having resulted in water splashing all over her.

Where there were no public toilets, the use of a bucket was essential – but abhorrent. Urine was emptied down any nearby drain, but faeces had to be tipped into newspaper and placed amongst ashes in the metal dustbin. During the summer months, especially if the weather was warm, the smell was awful, as were the flies, so it was prudent to place the bins in shade. Fortunately, the bin lorries always arrived at the end of each fair, the scaffies (bin men) hoisting the bins onto their shoulders and tipping the contents into the lorry.

She was also contending with her young husband's disinterest in personal hygiene. His pristine uniform and pride in his appearance when they had courted seemed to have vanished now that he was in civvy street. His ablutions consisted of a towel tucked into the neck of his shirt, and his hands, face and neck washed. The basin of water was treated as something distasteful and to be avoided if possible. His habit was to blow into the soapy water scooped up into his hands as he bent forward, making a noise that amused his young daughter but did not evidence an effective wash.

He did not own pyjamas and chose to sleep in the shirt he had worn all day (and often all week). Washdays were hard enough to organise when they travelled, but it became a constant battle for Mam to get him to change his clothes, and a major triumph when he did. Much as she disliked Vinegarhill, she longed for the use of the Whitehill wash-house again, and the constant supply of hot water.

Something else that rankled her was the swearing. It seemed that many of the travellers were incapable of completing a sentence without it being interspersed with swear words. She realised that this was just their everyday vocabulary and not designed to cause offence but she could not get used to it. Dad never swore in her presence, but she was sure he was just as capable of letting rip when not in her company. Even the children swore – predominantly the boys, some no more than toddlers – and this shocked her, especially when some of the adults found it funny and did not check the youngsters. It appeared to be an acknowledged part of their growth and development.

On one occasion, she saw one of the (many) nephews, who would only be about four years old, running around outside with a huge rip in his trousers, revealing an expanse of bare bottom. She found a needle and thread, hauled him into the Albion and effected a quick repair. Re-joining his playmates again, she heard him announce proudly to everyone, 'Ha… I had a hole in my arse and Aunty Winnie sewed it up!'

Earnings continued to be haphazard. There were some grounds where it was scarcely worth opening and others at least allowing enough money to pay their way, but never enough to allow losses to be 'recouped', as Dad called it.

At no time would any of the travellers admit to either profit or loss and Mam noticed with amusement that when someone asked 'how did you do?', Dad's answer would either be 'we made a living' if takings were good, or if not so good, just a shrug and grimace with no comment. She was never sure whether this was a business tactic to avoid competition, or just a tradition that required them never to detail takings.

TWENTY-ONE

'What's a hoor?' Dad looked at his young wife, not quite believing what she had just asked him. It had been a long day; the village they had opened in was notoriously tough. The local children were almost feral, rampaging through the ground during the day, causing all sorts of mischief despite being checked by the travellers. At night, as the pubs closed it was the drunks who caused the trouble. Everyone was glad to be moving on to the next town in a few days.

They were sitting in Granny's wagon with other family members, this almost a tradition at closing time, replaying the day with cups of tea, cigarettes passed round, and children sent out to local chip shops for suppers.

'What did you say?' he asked, trying to keep his voice down, and she repeated the question.

'I was just wanting to know what a hoor was.'

She thought no-one else was listening then realised that it was quiet, all eyes on Dad.

'Why on earth do you want to know that?' he tried to whisper, clearly not wishing his family to follow the conversation.

'Well,' she explained, 'a man was cheating at the joint and I refused to give him a prize. He swore at me and called me a hoor.'

Dad was mortified, not so much at his young wife being verbally abused, but at being expected to define the nature of the insult. Walter, already with teenager savvy, was helpless with laughter, while Dad's other siblings struggled to stifle theirs.

Rosie pretended not to be listening, helping Granny to put out cups and a plate of bread in readiness for the food arriving. Old Teddy sat in his usual corner, puffing furiously on his Woodbine, the scowl on his face indicating his disapproval of the conversation.

'Ehmm,' Dad cleared his throat. 'It's a Scottish name for women who don't have a very good reputation… fallen women.' He stopped, hoping this would suffice, annoyed now at his brothers who were in various stages of hysteria.

Mam, who was not entirely naïve, gathered that this was another word for whore… a prostitute. Seeing how much entertainment it was providing, she decided to tease Dad by pretending still not to understand, requiring him to attempt further explanations.

Walter was now rolling about on what little floor-space there was, while John and Tommy, realising she was pulling Dad's leg, joined her in the tease.

'So, how do you know so much about this subject?' asked Tommy.

John added, 'And have you needed to pick up many women that have fallen?'

Mam, still smarting from her first encounter with her sister-in-law, chipped in with, 'Is being called a hoor worse than an English fanny?'

She looked at Rosie, who continued pretending to be busy, noting that her cheeks were flushed – perhaps from the embarrassment of realising her earlier comment had been heard.

Mam smiled to herself. *Point scored,* she thought. Just then the boys arrived with the suppers, steam and vinegar fumes emitting from the hot, soggy newspaper parcels as the various orders were unwrapped. Dad, now rescued from any further interrogation, glared at his brothers, clearly annoyed at being the butt of everyone's humour.

Later that night Mam noticed a change in him. He scarcely spoke. Any attempt at conversation by her was met with curt monosyllabic responses. This behaviour puzzled her and she mentioned it to Granny the following day.

'Take no notice,' was the response. 'He always was a moody bugger, just like his old man. He didn't like being made a fool of by the boys last night.'

Mam felt so guilty. The last thing she wanted to do was hurt or embarrass him; she had just assumed that he would appreciate and share the joke with his brothers. She tried to discuss the event with him. This approach was counter-productive, seeming just to add further to his angst.

His silent treatment continued for another day then stopped… communication resuming as though nothing had happened. She thought no more of the matter, glad that they were talking again – albeit she did not understand his rather strange behaviour. Little did she realise that this was to be the portent for the future.

They were nearing the end of the season and takings were poor, the last two grounds not attracting punters mainly because of the wet weather. Rosie, the self- appointed family oracle, had issued dire warnings of 'tax man penalties' if they didn't keep accounts, so Mam had purchased a little notebook from Woolworths in which she was dutifully recording weekly income and expenditure. The evidence was damning and disheartening. As fast as they accumulated money they were having to pay out either for repairs to the Albion, diesel, or swag… always something.

'Well,' she sighed, pushing the little book across the table to Dad, 'if the tax man ever decides to audit this book, he'll be paying *us* some money!'

Dad gave just a cursory glance at the figures, not seeming to be too worried that they were consistently evidencing a loss. He looked at Mam, realising some response was expected.

'Never mind… we'll get this winter over and catch up. It'll take a bit longer, but I can pick up any wee jobs that are going and do some hours at the Kelvin Hall again. We'll be able to start out next summer in a much better position.'

Her heart sank. This was déjà vu and she started to feel trapped. She had not anticipated another winter in Glasgow… or the resumption of travelling the following summer. She looked at me, now a happy little three-year-old, and for a moment hated her husband.

What sort of a future was he planning… if he even had a plan? How on earth could he expect her to impose this lifestyle on their daughter… a life that so far had just been of hardship, worry and alienation from her own family. He seemed to assume that she would be happy with any decision he made, without actually including her in the process.

She remembered his covert activity with Rosie in purchasing the Albion and then the ramshackle joint, the rights to the grounds he'd arranged and the seasonal run he had planned ahead of telling her. It seemed that he was able to have these conversations with his family – specifically Rosie – but not with his wife.

Haunted by her aunt's comments that it was 'in his blood' and that 'once a traveller, always a traveller,' she began to fear that there was truth in the statements. However, bridges had been burnt and she was enough of a realist to know there was no going back… no parental home to run to. For her, the die was cast, but not for her daughter.

Checking that I was asleep, she tucked the soft woollen blanket round me, loving the sweet aroma mix of baby powder and soap, and smiled, noting that I was still contentedly sucking my thumb (a habit not broken until I was four).

She knew that Dad loved them both and would make sure that I grew up in a protected, caring environment and want for nothing. But she vowed that when I was old enough to understand, she would tell me of – and encourage me to want – a life beyond travelling.

She also made a promise to herself that one day, someday… they *would* have a house, be settled, and live a 'normal' life.

And so began Mam's odyssey.

TWENTY-TWO

There are some who say they can recall all their early childhood events, but I have no vivid memory of those early Glasgow winters apart from one incident when I was about three years old.

I remember it being very dark. I was half asleep. There was a knock on the door and men's voices. I was aware of Mam being worried, and a great commotion as the men carried in Dad; his head swathed in so much bandage it resembled a white turban.

I was frightened at both his appearance and the noise created by the men as they talked over each other in their attempts to explain to Mam what had happened while trying to reassure her, achieving neither.

Mam cuddled me, seeing my distress, and settled me back down to sleep. Apparently, while at the Kelvin Hall, Dad had been tackling maintenance work and had fallen from a height onto the metal plates of the dodgem. He landed badly, splitting his left ear almost in half and also cracking some ribs. Uncles John and Tommy had borrowed the lessee's car and drove Dad, his head wrapped in a blood-soaked towel, to hospital, where his ear was stitched back together.

They helped Mam to undress him and get him into bed, a difficult task as he was still medicated, dazed, and struggling with them. He kept insisting that he was alright, and they were to tell the lessee he would be back to work the next day.

As they left, John and Tommy looked at Mam and shook their heads.

'He's rambling, Winnie. There's no way he can go back to the Hall,' stated

John, adding 'but don't you worry luv, he'll be ok. In a few weeks he'll be good as new… apart from another trophy to add to his collection.'

This was John's reference to Dad's war wound. His left leg bore a large deep scar where the bullet had lodged. Mam scarcely slept that night, fearful of – and watching for – any sign of concussion or undiagnosed injury.

The following morning she answered the door to Rosie, who stood hesitantly at the foot of the small steps, unsure of her reception.

'I don't want to bother you… I just wanted to see how Dickie was.'

Mam realised that Rosie was genuinely concerned and invited her in. Dad, now dressed, was nursing a massive headache and wincing, his ribs complaining painfully as I tried to climb on his knee, and he was in no mood for company. Nevertheless, he recognised that this might be a 'watershed' moment between his wife and sister.

Rosie sat on the little locker seat next to the door.

'How're you doin'?' she asked.

'I'm ok,' he replied. There was an awkward silence.

This was the sum total of any talk between them on health-related matters. Their conversation turned to all things show-business… who was opening where, the price of swag, starting out dates and so on.

Watching the interaction between her husband and his sister, Mam began to realise that there was a lack of people skills. They did not seem comfortable discussing intimate matters such as health and chose the safe, familiar topic of travelling.

Rosie turned to Mam, who had now rescued Dad from my persistent clambering and was trying to keep me quiet.

'Would you like me to take Jean out to give you a wee break?' she asked.

Mam was taken aback and wondered whether she had misheard the question. Her sister-in-law, always seeming so stern and disapproving – someone she had considered an adversary – was actually offering to help. Dad jumped at the chance. This was an opportunity not to be missed.

'That's a good idea, Rosie. Winnie hasn't had much sleep because of me and the wee one could do with some fresh air.'

Mam looked at Dad and burst out laughing, perhaps from an exhausted hysteria, but more probably at the concept of 'fresh air' in Vinegarhill, the putrid smell from the gut-works prevalent everywhere again.

There was silence for a moment then he caught a whiff of the stink, not even disguised by his cigarette smoke, and held his painful ribs, trying not to laugh. Rosie gazed at them both, still waiting for some response to her offer of help, the humour of the moment lost on her, and Mam was afraid she might think that they were laughing at *her*. Her sister-in-law sat stiffly, hands rammed in pockets, looking so uncomfortable and reminding Mam of a frightened bird looking for an escape. For the first time, despite her earlier interference in their lives, she felt real compassion for the woman.

'That's really kind of you, Rosie – I'll get her coat.'

This was to be the start of regular walks with my aunt and a gradual but unspoken truce between her and Mam.

TWENTY-THREE

With no income now and little chance of Dad being fit for work any time soon, their few savings were vanishing rapidly again. What little they had was spent on me rather than themselves, but this resulted in their own neglect.

On one occasion Mam's brother Leslie visited. Now based in Glasgow, he had been given the Vinegarhill address by his father, probably with the instruction to check that 'all was well.'

He sat in the Albion opposite Mam, sipping tea from the only cup still to have a handle while she asked a multitude of questions about his family, her dad, her aunts, Fred. She was lost in the moment and hungry for information, her brother describing the life she had hoped she would always have.

She noticed Dad, who was standing behind Leslie, frantically trying to attract her attention without Leslie noticing, and pointing at something, his face contorting in all shapes with frustration as his signals were obviously not understood.

When Leslie left she asked Dad what the problem was. He pointed to her foot, and she realised with horror what he had been trying to tell her. She had a habit of wiggling her foot when sitting with her legs crossed. The newspaper padding over the large hole in the sole of her shoe had been clearly visible as she sat opposite her brother.

She was mortified, replaying the visit over and over, worrying what on earth Leslie must have thought and dreading to imagine what his feedback to her father might be.

'Stop worrying about it,' was Dad's response. 'You shouldn't care what other people think. We might not have much compared to others but look at what we *do* have. A happy, healthy kid with parents who love her, a clean warm home, loads of aunts, uncles and people who are there if we need them.'

As if on cue there was a knock at the door and a familiar voice asking, 'Can I come in?' It was the lessee, the owner of the Kelvin Hall dodgem. He stood in the doorway and cleared his throat. 'I'm not stopping,' he volunteered, apologetically. 'Just wanted to give you this.' He handed Dad an envelope. 'You forgot to pick up your wages when you were whisked off to hospital.' He paused here as though anticipating some reaction. 'So I thought I would drop them off when I was passing.'

He turned and made his way back down the steps, leaving an astonished couple who both knew Dad was not due any outstanding pay.

'Look at this,' Dad exclaimed as he looked in the envelope. 'There's enough here to keep us going 'til we start out.'

Once again Mam was reminded of the kindness of this community, but also that her dream of a settled life was still beyond her grasp.

And so it began, the nomadic cycle of summer fairs with unpredictable income and the inevitable winter struggles. The season started around March, generally finishing between September and October. Our first few winters were spent in Glasgow, this being the main base for the majority of Scottish travellers. Vinegarhill was the most commonly used 'yard', but several others existed, including sites in Springburn and Darnick Street.

Summers followed a specific schedule – each week timed to whichever Highland Games or gala day we had grounds reserved at. Often there would be a gap in the dates between events, which meant either a lay-over in Glasgow and no income, or a hurried stopgap event arranged by a lessee in some small hamlet just to keep the stuff open. These impromptu fairs seldom even covered expenses, and everyone hated them, but it was the preferred option to a week or two-week closure.

If Mam had any preference at all it was the Highland Games events. She felt that the clientele were a bit more civil than the 'rougher element' from the miners' galas. She was always mindful of the aggressive drunk who called her a 'hoor'.

Dad took a different view, based entirely on economics rather than social proprieties. The gala crowds spent more, especially when the pubs closed, whereas the Games people tended to drift away once the sports finished.

For me, life was wonderful, simply because this was the norm. I was fussed over by my uncles who saw me as the next Shirley Temple, since even at an early age I could hold a tune, albeit get the words jumbled.

Once, when travelling in a tram with Mam along Edinburgh's Princes Street during one of the rugby internationals, a group of Irish supporters seated around us must have felt homesick. One asked me if I could sing 'Hello Patsy Fegan' – an Irish folk song – and gave me half a crown (2/6d) for obliging. I was still only three and had been taught this song by the uncles. Relating the story when we got home, Dad joked that it was a 'nice little earner' and that we should go on the tram again.

The Stirlings were talented musically, being able to sing and play instruments, and all were self-taught, although Dad did receive some informal lessons. During his travels as a youngster he befriended a fellow enthusiast of similar age who passed on a few of the rudiments of mastering the piano accordion. The friend was Will Starr (later to become the acclaimed Scottish accordionist).

Uncles Tommy and Walter also favoured the accordion, while John was an accomplished drummer and could match the skills of any celebrity drummers of the time such as Gene Krupa, Buddy Rich etc.

The brothers had good voices, especially John, a born crooner with a silky-smooth voice remarkably similar to Nat King Cole's. They formed their own little band and became a feature of traveller dances, calling themselves 'The Stirling Boys'... the lack of an imaginative title belying their actual talent.

Dad never owned an accordion and always borrowed one when needed. He said this was not a problem since there was no room to store one in the Albion, and in any case, the damp would not be good for the bellows. He explained that some people pawned them during the winter, knowing that this offered dry storage until redeemed later. While Mam understood the logic to his explanation, she knew that he really would have loved his own instrument.

Drumming for Uncle John was a constant and he practised rhythms when standing in the joint, just by rattling coins on the shutters in time to whatever music the fairground panatropes were playing.

Dad was a whistler and his tunes, and the skill he had of adding wonderful trills and twists to the notes, could be heard daily (when not smoking).

Music was a regular feature of family life, and my memories of family singalongs and individual talents will be forever held dearly.

TWENTY-FOUR

By the summer of 1949 nothing in our circumstances had really changed, but life in the wider world refused to remain in limbo and many events took place.

National Service was introduced – men aged between eighteen and twenty-six were called up to serve eighteen months. This was a major inconvenience for travellers, having the potential to cause labour shortages again. However, there were sufficient numbers of men exempt from call-up to still keep things running, assisted by the womenfolk.

Traveller women could build up and pull down, and haggle over grounds and the price of swag, as well as do all the domestic chores, which were often more demanding. Many could also drive the lorries.

1949 was also the year that saw the end of clothes rationing. For Mam this had no real impact since her wardrobe was now sparse and replacements could not be easily afforded. Dad had one suit, one white shirt and two ties – a black one for funerals, and a blue for weddings. The saving grace for both was the dungarees for Dad and the pinnys for Mam, which – when kept clean – served to disguise any clothing shabbiness.

I, on the other hand, was dressed beautifully. Mam borrowed Aunt Rosie's Singer sewing machine and learned how to make little dresses using Butterick sewing patterns. Her first few early attempts were amateurish, mainly because she had problems trying to work the hand-cranked sewing machine. Rosie enjoyed being consulted and took pride in demonstrating how to thread the little silver shuttle, the best types of thread to use and how to adjust the tension for different types of materials.

Once she and the machine reached an understanding, Mam produced some very professional pieces for me. One in particular required her to pleat and smock the bib of the dress. She spent hours on this and even Rosie, who was not given to praise anyone, admitted that it was 'quite nice.'

Glasgow Fair Sunday was traditionally a day when traveller children dressed up and Mam made sure that I had my 'fairy frock' for the occasion. She also spent what little she had on a little pair of white buckskin shoes – completely impractical for the muddy ground – but it pleased her (and Dad) to see me dressed for the occasion.

She thought often of her aunts, both skilled needlewomen, and wished they could see her handiwork.

As well as clothing, sweet rationing stopped that year. Uncle John was delighted, having the greatest sweet tooth of all the brothers. Unfortunately, he gorged himself on so many of his favourite confections that he was unable to pass water and had to be taken to hospital. Sweet rationing resumed shortly afterwards, not because of Uncle John but due to sugar shortages again.

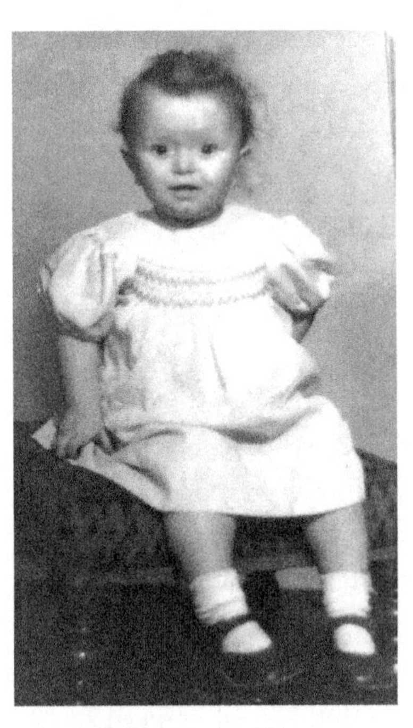

An eighteen-month-old me posing in one of Mam's creations

This was also the hottest summer recorded since 1921 and was when Mam suffered her first miscarriage. Since they were not registered with any doctor and it was a very early pregnancy, she did not seek any medical advice. She suspected that the excessive heat, long hours standing in the joint and the heavy lifts when helping dad to pull down were the cause. (Hinged double shutters from the front of the joints had to be loaded onto the roof of the Albion. These were extremely heavy, and Dad always enlisted various brothers to help, but often in their absence the task fell to Mam. This required her to somehow heave the shutters up to a level where Dad – standing on the roof – could reach them and haul them the rest of the way.)

Her sisters-in-law, apart from Rosie, offered reassurance and advice, reminding her of Granny's numerous miscarriages and the number of children she produced. She silently hoped they weren't expecting her to match Granny's record.

She noted that Rosie lacked any understanding of or empathy with illness. Anyone unwell, regardless of the condition, was described by her as 'having a wee chill'. Rosie dismissed Uncle Tommy's delirium as 'having one of his malarkeys' when he was actually suffering recurring bouts of malaria – the legacy of his war service.

By the time I was four, Mam had miscarried again and this time she decided to see a doctor, who advised her that she was perfectly healthy – just 'unlucky'. Dad tried to comfort her, saying that it didn't matter, that he 'loved the bones' of me, and that they were lucky to have one healthy child.

Nevertheless she was heartbroken, knowing that he longed for a son and feeling she had somehow let him down. His brother Edward was ensuring that the Stirling name would be perpetuated – Margaret, his wife, producing one boy after another while ironically Edward wanted a daughter.

Rosie was sitting on the wagon steps and talking to some women about the birth of another of Edward's boys, remarking that 'our poor Dickie was never going to have a son'. She hadn't realised that Dad was nearby and heard her.

'Listen, Rosie,' he snapped, 'we are proud of our daughter, and she will be more than a match for any boy... you'll see. And anyway,' he continued, now red-faced with anger and also embarrassment at such a personal confrontation with his sister, 'what right do you have to make comment on my family? Whether we have one child or ten, it's none of your business.'

He stomped off, leaving Rosie dumbfounded and embarrassed at being told off in front of the women, who were now leaving. Granny, who had watched the scenario from the wagon doorway, chuckled, this being the first time to her knowledge that Dad had stood up to his sister.

To add to Mam's worries, while we were opened at Hamilton there was a major smallpox epidemic. In March 1950, an Indian sailor, Mussa Ali, was admitted to a Glasgow infectious diseases ward with what was thought at first to be pneumonia and chickenpox. By the time it was identified as smallpox, nineteen people had been infected and six died. One of the fatalities was a twenty-nine-year-old doctor, Janet Fleming, who had been in the hospital ward when Mussa Ali was admitted.

Doctor Fleming had lived in Hamilton; therefore a mass immunisation campaign was launched in which three quarters of Hamilton's total population were vaccinated, this being part of a huge programme in East Lanarkshire, where thousands of possible contacts with the nineteen original victims were traced.

Various centres were utilised and stayed open into the early evenings to cope with the numbers queuing for the jab, and I have a vague recollection of my parents taking me to a large dark hall that was full of people. Mam comforted me as we stood waiting our turn, realising that I was afraid of the Bunsen burners and assuring me that they were just to 'clean' the needles.

Everyone was concerned about the after-effects of the vaccination and on the fairground for days afterwards, my anxious parents and relatives watched their children for any sign or symptom that might either be a reaction to the jag – or worse still, the disease itself.

Mam had experienced the worry of the earlier English flu epidemic and now the smallpox virus. She looked at me, a healthy five-year-old, and as though talking to herself, said, 'It won't always be like this. We will live in one place, not travelling all over the country, exposed to every germ. Things *have* to get better.'

TWENTY-FIVE

'I've got a good deal on a wheel-'em-in,' Dad blurted out as though the words scared him.

Mam had already figured that he was working up to telling her something. He sat on the little locker seat, fidgeting with a bootlace that didn't require attention and clearing his throat as he watched her ironing.

She didn't look up, his *fait accompli* tactics no longer a surprise, but he could see that she was annoyed. The flat iron was being thumped down more vigorously on the shirt creases, which obstinately refused to budge as the iron cooled.

He continued, unnerved by her silence, and feeling the need to explain and justify his purchase. 'You see… some of our grounds don't have space for both joints but there would be room for a wheel-'em-in. We could simply put the dart boards in the centre of it instead of the joint, and that way our takings won't drop.'

Having now travelled for three seasons she was familiar with the round stalls, known as 'wheel-'em-ins,' these being circular and designed to draw punters in from any direction. They tended to be either hooplas, where a ring was thrown over a prize, or roll pennies – or 'chutes,' as Rosie called them.

The chutes were Rosie's domain and she stood in the centre like a croupier, raking in or paying out the pennies depending on whether or not they landed on prize squares as the punters rolled them down the chutes and onto the oilcloth tables.

The roll-a-penny – or 'chute'

Mam often relieved Rosie for meal breaks and had quickly become adept at flicking, with one hand, cascades of coins across the table to any winners. While not actually enjoying working the chutes, she liked the security afforded by the wire cages around the tables, which stopped any cheating hands from sliding coins onto winning squares.

She could not picture the darts game being moved safely to a wheel-'em-in and did not relish the idea of trying to work this type of stall.

She put the now-cool iron back on the stove, wrapped a cloth round the handle of the hot replacement and tapped the base with her spittled finger, the brief sizzle indicating the iron's readiness to smooth the creases. She wished problems could be smoothed out so easily. She brushed her hair back from her face and chose not to look at Dad as she worked.

'And what sort of a deal did you do?' she asked, knowing that they were in no position financially to make any large purchases.

He hesitated momentarily, cleared his throat, and looked at the floor as though choosing his answer carefully. She knew him well enough by now to recognise that an excuse – or worse, a lie – was forthcoming, and waited, fearful of what he might have impulsively committed them to.

'Well...' He paused, still gazing at the floor. 'An old pal owed me money from way back and offered me the wheel-'em-in... instead of cash.'

Ironing now forgotten, Mam sat down and faced him, her eyebrows raised quizzically, her expression one of disbelief. Realising his story was not believed, Dad decided the best tactic was to tell the truth.

'Well… ok… I didn't want to tell you because you would think she was interfering, but I borrowed the money from Rosie.' He paused. 'And before you fly off the handle, I asked her for a loan, and it was my idea to buy the stall, not hers.'

'How much did you borrow?' she asked, trying to control her voice and keep calm.

He avoided a straight answer. 'Not much. The wheel-'em-in will soon pay for itself and anyway, Rosie said she's not in any hurry for the money.'

While her relationship with her sister-in-law had improved, she still felt there was an undercurrent of control by Rosie and decided to speak to her the next day.

'Rosie, that was really good of you to lend Dickie that money.'

She had chosen the moment carefully and would try to be diplomatic. They were in Granny's wagon, for once empty apart from me on the floor, playing with their old collie Bob. Rosie was on her knees, cleaning the chrome-work on the stove, and seemed surprised at this statement.

'Oh… he told you then.' This was more of a disinterested comment than a question.

'Yes, last night. But he really shouldn't be borrowing from you,' Mam replied.

Rosie shrugged, offering no response, and kept polishing the stove, so Mam continued, 'This wheel-'em-in thing he bought just seems like an unnecessary burden!'

She had Rosie's attention again; she viewed the comment as criticism of her brother.

'Winnie, he's thinking of your futures and planning ahead. He can reserve rights for extra ground space and the stall will be Jean's when she is old enough to mind it.'

Mam was horrified. She looked at me, still happily playing with the dog and too young to know what was being discussed. She realised that his family assumed Dad would always travel and his wife's aspirations were of no consequence. She had to set them straight.

'That wasn't the deal, Rosie, and no daughter of mine will be standing for hours in a joint, taking dog's abuse from drunks and living this hand-to-mouth existence. That was not the plan when I married your brother and it might take some time, but we *will* be settling down. Perhaps you were all unaware of it, but your brother *did* promise me this.'

Rosie could see that the young woman she had always considered a bit of a walkover had a mind of her own and was potentially a force to be reckoned with.

'But Winnie,' she rounded, 'show-business is such a full life.'

'No Rosie,' Mam countered as she ushered me out the door. 'It's a fool's life!'

Both women had reached an impasse. Rosie was desperately keen to keep her family together and for future generations of Stirlings to continue the tradition of travelling fairs; while Mam longed for a settled life, the one Dad had promised her, a bricks-and-mortar home with hot water and sanitation – a life that offered the security of employment and a steady wage, not a life constantly in transit and the unpredictability of fairground takings.

Mam's agenda remained unchanged, but she stopped talking about getting a house, realising that his family were not taking her seriously. At times this had been hurtful, one occasion being when my uncles had arranged for a wooden doll's house to be made for me. One of the men remarked, 'There you are, Winnie – you've got your house at long last.' No slight was intended but it did remind her that she should just keep her own counsel.

Similarly, she seldom mentioned it to Dad since the few times she had done, he changed the subject – or worse, refused to talk at all and reverted to sulking.

Despite this she was not unhappy, accepting his mood swings, which she realised were his attempts to avoid difficult subjects. She was convinced that they would eventually have a house somewhere. After all, she reasoned, the basic essential ingredients of their family life were already established.

They loved each other, Dad was a hard worker, they were living respectable albeit unorthodox lives. They had a healthy child who seemed bright – perhaps a little precocious, but keen to learn. All that was missing now was a settled lifestyle.

She saw education as the lynchpin to my future success and was determined that my learning would stretch beyond the three Rs. She read to me as a toddler, capturing my attention and imagination, then taught me to read.

By pre-school age I was reading everything, including the Sunday papers. This required her to stop buying the 'News of the World' when I asked her what intercourse meant!

TWENTY-SIX

It was now 1950. I was five and about to experience school life as a traveller's child. There was a legal requirement for school attendance and that a record be kept of the hours attended. At every town, village and hamlet, Mam checked where the school was and enrolled me, often for just a week, before we moved on to the next place.

My attendance record would be left with the relevant school, to be endorsed by them, showing start and finish dates, and to be collected by Mam when we left. These records filled rapidly, and over my school years evidenced more than fifty 'attendances.'

I have no memory of my first day – or even which school that might have been, there were just so many of them – but I *do* remember the terrible anxiety I felt each time I started a new school.

For most youngsters on their first day, the trauma of being left by their mothers and the fear of the unknown would generally vanish once they settled into and enjoyed the experience of their class and schoolfriends. For me, this trauma was a weekly, sometimes fortnightly, event during the summer months, and school friendships were impossible.

The night before each enrolment I would watch Mam as she carefully selected my clothes and Dad sharpening pencils he had hunted out for me. Both would see I was scared and try to reassure me, telling me that I would be all right after the first day. I would have a sleepless night, then hold Mam's hand as she walked me to whichever school I was to attend. Invariably anxious to the point of feeling sick, I would try to think of other things – my new leather Clark's sandals with the clean crepe soles, which were becoming dirty as we walked; my pristine white ankle socks, always to be removed when I got home; and the fun later of examining the patterns made by the sun as it shone through the sandals' leather openwork, 'tattooing' the tops of my bare feet. Anything rather than think of what might lie ahead in each new school. Sometimes we were accompanied by my cousins, who happened to be in the same town and also enrolling, which helped me to feel just a little bit more secure – but more often, it was just me.

Then the first day in class, curious eyes scanning me as teachers introduced me, and a week of lessons that I could seldom follow, apart from English.

Classrooms consisted of rows of wooden desks, the floor usually with a slight incline upwards, allowing teachers to see pupils at the back. Classes held as many as thirty pupils, which for me was extremely intimidating, and I spent an inordinate amount of time scanning the room, trying to identify which child was approachable and who might be the class bully.

Some schools were in poorer areas and half-washed children, tide marks visible and smelling of pee, were to be avoided at playtime – especially if they were scratching their heads. Other schools were sweeter smelling, helped by the bowls of hyacinths that seemed to appear annually on the teachers' desks.

Often, unnoticed by teachers, I would pretend I wasn't there and sit with elbows on the desk and hands cupped – binocular fashion – round my eyes, as though I was outside looking in. And oh, how I longed for this to be so!

At one school, the headmistress was clearly reluctant to admit me, telling Mam that it would be difficult to know at which class level I could be placed. She stated that the school had an extremely high standard and that this might place too much pressure on me as a transient pupil. Mam was beginning to bristle, feeling that the woman was pre-judging my academic ability.

'Let me assure you,' she asserted in the most business-like voice she could muster, 'this is a bright child, and her reading ability is excellent.' She remembered the scenario with the 'News of the World' but decided that it might not be the best example to offer.

The teacher looked at me, not sure what to ask next. 'Have you learned any poetry?'

I rose to the occasion, remembering a rhyme my uncles had taught me,

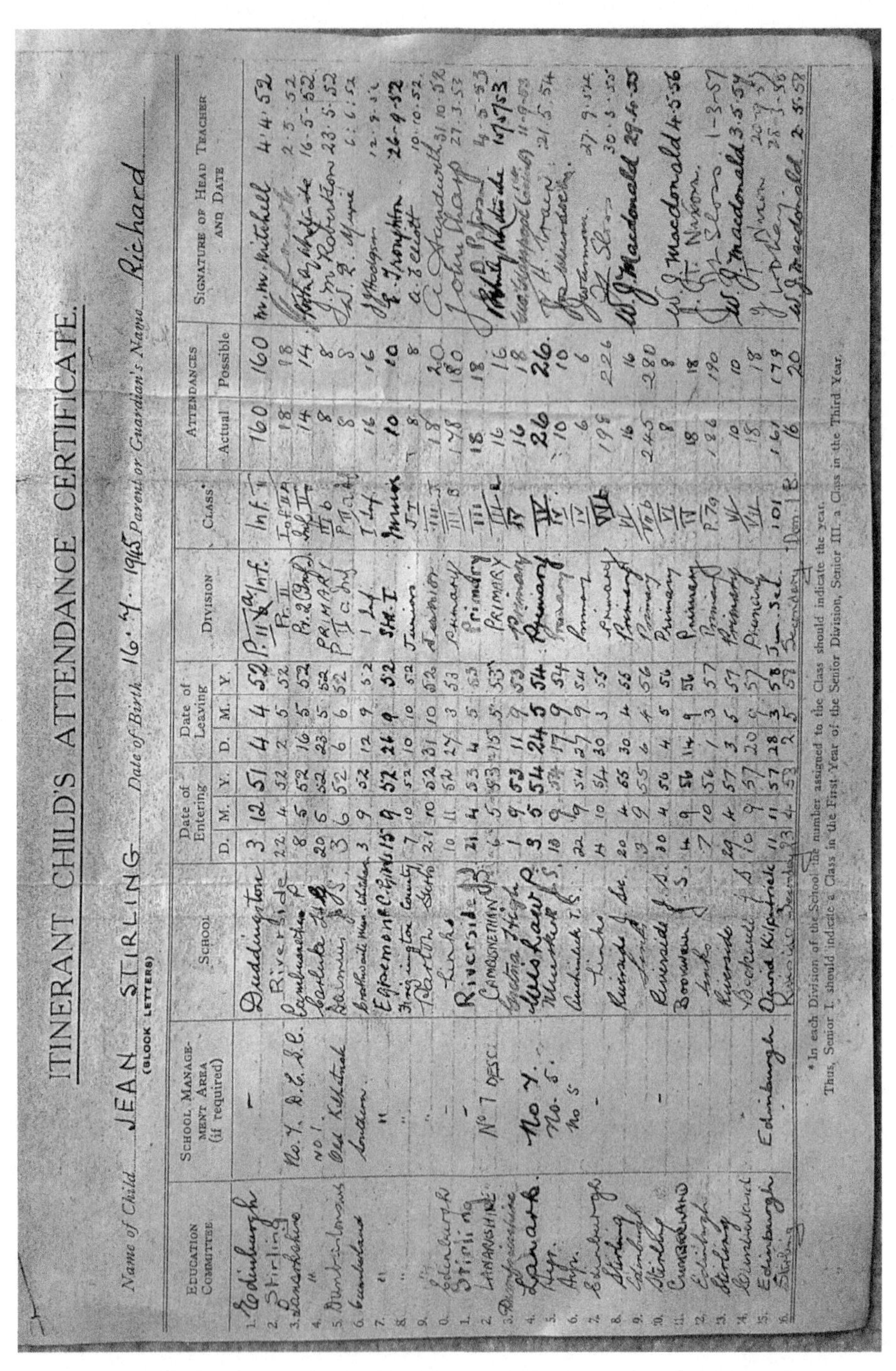

ITINERANT CHILD'S ATTENDANCE CERTIFICATE.

Name of Child JEAN STIRLING (BLOCK LETTERS) Date of Birth 16. 4. 1945 Parent or Guardian's Name Richard

	Education Committee	School Management Area (if required)	School	Date of Entering D.	M.	Y.	Date of Leaving D.	M.	Y.	Division	Class*	Attendances Actual	Possible	Signature of Head Teacher and Date

* In each Division of the School the number assigned to the Class should indicate the year. Thus, Senior I. should indicate a Class in the First Year of the Senior Division, Senior III. a Class in the Third Year.

One of many attendance certificates, which we called our 'leaving lines' (emphasis on leaving – rather than attending!) This was probably an indication of our desire to move on and to Mam's dismay, recited their comic version of the nursery rhyme 'Little Fly Upon the Wall:

Little fly upon the wall, ain't you got no shirt at all?
Ain't you got no shirt or shimmy? Blimey... ain't ye cold?

I sat back, pleased with my rendering, wondering why Mam was red-faced in her attempts to stifle laughter. The woman, still not convinced, decided to test me, and selected a 'Janet and John' book from the 'infants' first reader' section of her cabinet, asking me to read a small sentence. I looked at it disdainfully, then at Mam, then back at the book – my hesitation noted by the teacher.

'Oh, she is *way* beyond that level,' Mam hurriedly explained, and taking her cue, I rattled through each page without pause or difficulty – then, flushed with success, I offered to read from a Dickens book I'd spotted on her desk. The poor headmistress surrendered to this onslaught, and I was enrolled briefly in her school with no resulting damage to its high standard.

It was always a joy to leave these schools and I'm sure that the teachers were equally relieved. It must have been so difficult for them to know how to deal with us and they probably worried that we might be a disruptive influence in the class.

It was a 'tradition' with traveller children that we gave the teachers a 'going away' gift on our last day. This invariably was a piece of 'swag' – usually a coconut, sometimes a 'stookie' (plaster) ornament or glass salad bowl... and in later years, a goldfish. Our parents found this a costly business – swag looted and pillaged by their kids at the end of each school attendance.

TWENTY-SEVEN

At some point during these early years, it was decided that our winter base should be Edinburgh rather than Glasgow.

Aunt Rosie had tried unsuccessfully each winter to book a space at the Kelvin Hall Carnival in Glasgow. This would have been the pinnacle of her fairground ambition – the one fair where she felt they were guaranteed a 'bob or two.' Disappointed, she finally accepted that this was never going to happen and decided to try for a place in the smaller Edinburgh equivalent, the Waverley Market in Princes Street, and was successful.

The move to Edinburgh delighted Mam. We had opened a few times in grounds near the capital, which meant she had visited and shopped there (and had the profitable adventure with me singing to the Irishmen in a tram!).

That first winter we were based in Duddingston on what was really just a piece of waste ground. Access from the main road was via Mill Lane, so named because of the abandoned flour mill at the foot of the lane.

Mam arranged a place for me in the primary school, which was also in Mill Lane and just yards from where we were based. Not all of the travellers' children managed to get into that school; some of my cousins had to go to a larger and busier facility in Portobello.

It was a happy winter for many reasons, not least because we had some financial respite; our summer, especially the last fair at Egremont, had been a little more profitable. We were surrounded by family and friends, and it was like our own small, safe community.

The hub was Granny's wagon, a meeting place for everyone – a constant hive of activity with the kettle always on the boil. Grandchildren, myself included, wandered in and out just as we pleased, fascinated by the various conversations, and always tolerated.

It was always referred to as 'Granny's wagon,' probably because Old Teddy never really displayed any sign of affection, or even *talked* to any of us. We were there to be put up with, and occasionally cursed if too noisy. We just considered him to be a 'presence' – a watcher in the corner – and mostly ignored him.

Uncle Tommy had recently married Charlotte Paulo and their little wagon was parked behind us. Uncle John was courting Charlotte's cousin Marie, and there was great excitement for and anticipation of another wedding.

Dad's sister Lizzie and her family were also there, which meant I had two companions, my cousins Irene and Rosina. We enjoyed putting on 'concerts' for the family, which were just singalongs in one of the wagons, and we thought we were good – albeit encores were seldom requested.

'Where are we going, Mam?' I asked as we made our way in the dark, stumbling across rubble towards the old mill. I was aware of others heading in the same direction, carrying chairs and boxes, and Dad had the accordion.

'Shhhht,' she whispered. 'We're going to a party in the mill, but we aren't supposed to be there, so we have to be quiet.'

The 'party' was to celebrate either John and Marie's engagement or her twenty-first birthday, and I was not sure which, but it was of sufficient note to justify trespassing.

The building was dark but the men had torches and, having previously reconnoitred the property, guided everyone to a wooden ladder reaching up through a hatch to an upper level. Tilley lamps were lit and children and older folks were helped up the ladder, followed by chairs and boxes of food and drink. The room was dry and cold, one end cordoned off with boxes and rope, the men having found a huge hole in the floor and warning us children to keep away.

A wonderful night of music and dance took place, everyone forgetting about noise and potential discovery. It seemed that everyone could 'do a turn,' one man giving an hilarious impression of Jimmy 'Snozzle' Durante, another singing Al Jolson songs, going down on one knee to sing 'Mammy' better than the real Jolson.

Dad played the accordion, Uncle John improvised – drumming on a box

– and everyone danced, ancient remnants of flour dust rising from the cracks between the old wooden floorboards as feet stomped over them in time to the music. The cold of the room was no longer noticed as the night progressed, and neither did it occur to anyone that the noise might be reported to the police.

This was 1950, just five years after the war. People were glad to be alive and thankfully adopting a 'live and let live' philosophy, so our party was never reported.

TWENTY-EIGHT

That period between 1950 and 1951 was eventful for many reasons. Princess Anne was born in August 1950; tinned fruit, chocolate biscuits and soap rationing ended; NHS prescriptions cost one shilling.

The wireless was our main source of home entertainment and programmes were designed to cheer up post-war listeners. Mornings consisted of 'Worker's Playtime' broadcast from various factories, 'Housewives Choice,' 'Music While You Work' and the pilots of two radio soap operas, 'Mrs Dale's Diary' and 'The Archers'.

There were very few children's programmes but that did not bother me. I enjoyed the music and was engrossed in the two serials, 'The Archers' described as 'the everyday life of countryfolk' and 'Mrs Dale's Diary' about a doctor's wife who always had the opening line 'I'm rather worried about Jim.' Mam and I joked about this, always anticipating the line.

King George IV pre-recorded his Christmas speech, still not having recovered from the major surgery three months earlier and died in February 1951. Winston Churchill was re-elected prime minister after a seven-year absence and announced that Britain now had the atom bomb. Mam was horrified by this.

'My God,' she blurted out to Dad, not realising I was listening. 'Here we go again. Churchill has the reputation of a war monger and the last thing we need is his capacity to blow us all up.'

This scared me. I pictured the mushroom cloud associated with atomic explosions and remembered seeing photos of Hiroshima and Nagasaki in one of the newspapers. I was convinced it was only a matter of time before we were all incinerated and spent many sleepless nights worrying.

However, this was also the time when my parents were able to afford my bicycle at Christmas, a junior-sized blue and white beauty. Dad and Uncle Walter spent hours trying to teach me to ride it, running behind me and holding the saddle as I wobbled and invariably toppled over. One fall resulted in my knee being sliced open and requiring several stitches.

The day I eventually mastered it, Uncle Walter was my 'stabiliser,' letting go of the saddle and watching proudly as I flew solo. Dad was a bit miffed that he hadn't been the one to accomplish this, especially when his younger brother teased him about it, claiming to be the better teacher.

This happy winter was followed by the same, now-familiar round of summer fairs, some paying our way, others scarcely covering expenses. Mam longed for the return to Duddingston, only to be disappointed when Dad discovered it was closed and some development was planned. This would include the old mill, which was destined to be transformed into luxury flats. Mam knew it was irrational to feel as she did but was saddened by the news, remembering how happy she had felt there and how well I had settled into the little primary school.

Dad's parents still needed to be based in Edinburgh now that they had secured their place in the Waverley Market fair. They arranged to park for the winter on a showman's yard at Craigmillar, joined by Tommy and John – who was now married. (The Craigmillar yard in Niddrie Mains still exists as a showmen's site.)

Not wanting to return to Glasgow but with no space left at Craigmillar, Dad checked for other locations in Edinburgh and found Seafield. This was a yard owned by Calder of Leith, who were well-known tent manufacturers and hirers. The yard address was 68 Seafield Road, the facility only used for storage by Calders and having ground space to let out. The yard had on-site caretakers and Dad managed to negotiate our space with them. This was to become our permanent winter base, as was Craigmillar for Dad's family.

The ground was positioned between two railway lines – one on a raised embankment behind us, the other across the main road, and just beyond this... the sea. It seemed a cold bleak place to me. I missed the family all being together, the gatherings in Granny's wagon, the banter of my uncles and the company of my cousins.

Life seemed less secure without our extended family and although Dad knew everyone on the ground, they were strangers to me.

My illustration of Seafield... billboards at the top of the ground, and coal board trucks on the embankment

TWENTY-NINE

'I don't think we will be using those toilets. They smell and I think I saw a rat.' Mam had just returned from collecting water from the old brick toilet block, the first section having taps where everyone filled their cans. She continued, 'I've spoken to one of the women who has lived here for years. She told me that they are mostly used to slop out the buckets, although the men don't seem to mind using them. There is also a public wash-house in Portobello, so I'll strip the bed and get the sheets and blankets washed and dried.'

She seemed delighted at the prospect. Clean clothes and bedding were her constant trial. At every ground in the summer months she had to pester Dad to put up a clothes-line and borrow the boiler and wringer from Rosie. This was never high on his list of priorities and an interruption to his 'own' jobs of seeing to the joints or cosseting the Albion's engine.

On rainy days, trying to dry things – especially larger items such as blankets – was a nightmare for Mam so the prospect again of an abundance of hot water and dryers was so pleasurable. The fact that she would have to take a tram ride to Portobello carrying the heavy bath of washing did not dampen her enthusiasm for the task.

'There's a little shop along the road for anything we run out of, but most of the women seem to go to Leith for their messages. Oh, and by the way,' Mam was really getting into her stride now, 'I'll have to find our medical cards and register us with the local doctor.'

Dad was only half listening to her now, having decided that domestic arrangements were not really his domain. Mam had noticed that he seemed to be reluctant to make decisions or become involved in anything that took him out of his comfort zone or familiar territory. Anything involving talk on future planning was avoided by him, especially on the few occasions now that she mentioned settling down. His tactic was to be quiet and revert to a mood, which often lasted for days.

However, this discussion covered practical issues only for that winter, so now looking at me, she said, 'Oh, and I hear that there is a nice little school called Links Primary, which is almost opposite the doctor's surgery. I thought we could register with both places at the same time. You might even be able to start school on Monday.'

My heart sank. We had only been on Seafield a few days and I had hoped for some respite. She could see that I was not delighted at the news and continued, 'The school sits at the foot of Leith links, and we could easily walk there. Some of the other traveller children go there so you wouldn't be on your own.'

This was no great comfort to me, not having met any of these kids prior to arriving at Seafield; they would be just as much strangers to me as the 'flattie' schoolchildren.

And so, following another anxiety-fuelled night, I was registered at Leith Links primary as an 'itinerant scholar.' I remember every detail of getting there, but nothing of the actual enrolment or being installed in a classroom. Perhaps I was too traumatised for anything to properly register with me. I can recall the tram ride then holding Mam's hand so tightly it must have hurt, and the walk with her across the frost-covered Links, which seemed to stretch for miles, to the school. Already I had a feeling of being trapped with the realisation that I would have to come here all winter.

Day after day, Mam walked me to that school and was there to meet me without fail, regardless of the weather. She worried constantly about my safety, convinced that something awful would happen to me if she wasn't there. She soon had a little convoy as the children from the ground joined our march to and from the school. The walk took us past the railway signal box on Seafield Road and I loved hearing Mam's story of her childhood visits to her granda's signal box and her description of the levers and polished brassware he took such pride in.

Her escort duty was to continue all through my primary years and long after the others were flying solo.

Occasionally we took the tram instead of walking, the terminus at Seafield being the point where the tram reversed its route. This required the conductor to hook the trolley pole from one overhead power cable to the other. Some were able to perform the task effortlessly, but others had to suffer the embarrassment of several failed attempts being witnessed by the queue before admitting defeat and asking the tram driver to help.

The route took us along Claremont Park, the trees and footpaths lining the Links on our right, while on the left was a row of very grand Georgian houses. One of these was our doctor's surgery; another was a home for single mothers. Occasionally we would see young women on the tram, some with visible 'bumps,' others sitting with their little cases placed strategically on their knees. Often they were accompanied, but there were others who were alone, avoiding eye contact with passengers as they left the tram. I watched as they walked slowly up the drive to the big house and, while too young to understand what these girls would be experiencing, I felt sad for them.

THIRTY

The Seafield ground was to become our permanent winter base, and Links Primary my school for the period from October to March each year. Remarkably, classmates never questioned my absences, just accepting my return as they would some migratory bird. Hard though it was for me to catch up academically with my class each winter, it must have been an added burden for the teachers, and they were exceptionally patient, arranging extra 'remedial classes' to try to bring any lagging pupils up to speed.

The teachers all seemed elderly to me – possibly still a legacy of the war years, but more probably because everyone over thirty seemed old to a child.

My weakness was arithmetic, a mystery bordering on torture, as I struggled to understand numbers. While Mam had tutored me well with reading and writing, maths was not her forte. Dad, on the other hand, could work out square feet measurements and calculate any number of different equations effortlessly. Unfortunately he was no teacher, and try as he might. he was unable to explain to me in simple terms the intricacies of numbers.

It was all just a frustrating puzzle to me and my attempts to understand generally ended in tears, Mam trying to reassure me that it would eventually make sense and Dad at a loss to understand why it was such a problem. Both parents were relieved to learn that I would receive extra help with this via a remedial class.

The class was small, just four other children and myself. We sat round a little table as the teacher tried to encourage us to count, using tiny coin-shaped cardboard discs printed with numbers. Regrettably, all that I gained from those sessions was the memory of the floral-patterned Pond's powder box that held the counters, and the lingering scent as they were tipped onto the table.

In future enlightened times, this 'number blindness' would be acknowledged as a specific condition known as dyscalculia. Unfortunately, in the fifties the child was just classed as 'a bit thick,' and every session involving numbers was torture – and often humiliation – for me.

At one of the less sympathetic summer schools, the teacher was marking and handing back our jotters, having set a short arithmetic exercise. She walked up and down the rows reading out the scores as she returned work to each pupil, vocal in her praise of one or two children who had done well, and just handing back the books with no comment to others.

I cringed as she approached and stopped at my desk for what seemed an eternity to me, then opened the jotter and gazed at my efforts. I thought for a moment that a miracle had occurred, and I was about to be commended for my efforts. She looked at me.

'You don't *really* want to know *your* score, do you?' She made no attempt to lower her voice and I felt that she was enjoying the moment. Not sure whether she expected a reply and aware that the other children were gazing at me, I just shook my head, mortified at this very public and cruel exposure of my academic failings.

I hated that teacher, the school, the trial by numbers and the feeling of inadequacy and humiliation that woman inflicted on me. I was seven.

I had similar problems with the music class. While I loved participating in the singing part of the sessions, I was unable to understand or read music notation, which required symbol recognition and counting beats to the various notes. Fortunately I had a good ear for a tune, memorised melody and used the music sheets only to follow the words. The teacher was never aware of my 'blind spot.'

I would remain numerically challenged into adulthood, on one occasion having to phone a friend to ask how to work out percentages – this while I held a senior local government post and managed a huge staff budget!

THIRTY-ONE

I viewed Links Primary as my 'proper' school and all the others during the summer as just places to be contained. I looked at classmates in those schools with an element of pity, knowing they were stuck there while I would be moving on.

I adopted this same attitude when some of the towns or villages we opened at were a bit bleak and unwelcoming. By now, Edinburgh was home and the few winter months spent there were as near as Mam could get to a settled lifestyle.

At the end of each season, as we approached Edinburgh, I gazed out the lorry window looking for the first sight of a bus or tram heralding our arrival – the maroon and cream paintwork and the city coat of arms on the sides so familiar. It was even better if one of our 'own' buses (i.e. the route number 12, 25 or 49) was spotted. They were almost welcoming us back again. And then, as Dad drove us past the Links I would look across to the school, checking that it was still there, still a little anxious knowing that I soon would be enrolling again.

Seafield Road was the connecting road between Leith and Portobello, and we were parked at the outer wall of the ground, next to the road, with the sound of the trams waking us up every morning as they rattled past. From initially being an irritation, they soon became the familiar sound of 'home,' as were the foghorns at night from boats and from the lighthouse on Inchkeith Island as it flashed its warning across the Forth. There was an occasional sound of trains, and the coal board used a track that stood on the raised embankment above the ground as a siding for their NCB trucks.

During the winter of 1952/53, and primarily due to emissions of coal and wood smoke pollutants, London experienced thick poisonous smog that resulted in huge loss of life. The actual numbers are debated but range from 4,000 to 12,000. That December in Edinburgh, a combination of very cold weather and no wind also resulted in a thick smog, which fortunately only lasted four days and cleared when it became windy again.

Mam was afraid for my health and kept me off school, the little hostess stove being constantly fed with shovels full of coal and stoked by her in her attempts to keep us warm. Unfortunately, one night this resulted in our supply of fuel running out, with only dross, which was little more than dust, at the bottom of the coal bag. We both wished that Dad, who was working late at the docks, was home. The dark foggy night seemed frightening and the temperature in the Albion was now dropping at an alarming rate. I could see that she was worried.

'Right, pet… I'm just going to pop out for a minute.' I watched as she put on her coat and wrapped a blanket round me. 'Now keep that on until I get back. I won't be long but you must stay warm.'

I needed no second telling, gasping at the icy blast that hit me as she opened the door and disappeared into the darkness. I sat and waited, peering out the window, desperately hoping to see her coming back.

An hour had passed, the fire was out and now I was really scared. I wondered whether I should ask someone for help but there were no signs of reassuring life from anyone in the nearby wagons. Curtains were closed and lights were dim… everything contributing to my sense of helplessness and fear that something had happened to Mam.

I pulled my knees up to my chest and huddled under the blanket in an attempt to keep out the cold air. I could hear the foghorns outside; their noise, which previously had never bothered me, now sounded ominous and threatening, like a harbinger of doom. To my relief, and after what seemed like an eternity, the door opened and she was home, but her appearance shocked me. Covered in coal dust, her face was dirty and streaked with tears, which she had tried to wipe with blackened hands, her knees were scraped, bleeding, and one shoe was missing.

Without a word she hunted in a drawer, found a hammer and went outside again. By now my imagination was running wild. Had she encountered a fearful creature in the fog and was she arming for further battle?

A sound of hammering outside and she reappeared triumphantly with pieces of coal. As she tried to relight the fire, Dad arrived home and looked at her in horror.

'What on earth have you been up to?' he asked as she slumped down on the locker, clearly exhausted and yet trying to sound calm in her efforts to reassure me.

'We needed coal. I climbed over the wall to get some and couldn't get back.' She was shivering now, the aftershock of her ordeal combined with exposure resulting in her explanation being short and stilted. 'And you will have to go back in daylight and find my shoe.'

She described clambering over the brick wall at the foot of the embankment, not realising that the ground dropped away steeply on the other side, making it impossible for her to climb back. She managed to find a large lump of coal and heaved it over the wall but then had to stumble in the dark through rubbish and jagged undergrowth until she found a gap to get through. This was the whole length of the ground, near the billboards and she dreaded being seen by anyone as she limped back – for once thankful for the thick fog that was hiding her walk of shame.

And she did feel ashamed. Yes, she was driven by desperation, the instinct of a mother to keep her child safe and warm – yet she knew that this was theft. Even though the piece of coal was laying on the banking, it still was NCB property. She had never stolen anything in her life, yet perversely, was now pleased that thanks to her efforts they would have a fire again. Dad hadn't the heart to tell her that her 'booty' was mostly slate and wouldn't burn.

'Right, Cinders, I'll find your shoe in the morning.'

He laughed and she relaxed, smiling at the pantomime comparison as he left to borrow coal from a neighbour. Mam cuddled me and as we shivered and waited for his return I realised – for the first time in my seven-year existence – that our lives were actually quite perilous.

Those coal trucks were 'visited' fairly regularly that winter – and subsequent winters – by Dad and his accomplice, Johnny. This was only when normal supplies ran out and they took just enough between them to last until the coalman made his next delivery. Mam and I dreaded Sunday nights, these being the 'heist' nights, always at 8pm.

Johnny was ex-commando and heavily into tactical manoeuvres. His logic was that this was when everyone would be watching the London Palladium on television, especially when some of the big-name American stars were appearing. No-one would hear or see their trips 'up the banking,' as they called it.

There would be a discreet knock on the door accompanied by Johnny whispering, 'Are you right, Dickie?' Then they both disappeared into the darkness, Mam and I terrified that they would be caught, then breathing sighs of relief when hearing them return.

If the transport police or NCB were ever aware of this activity, they never acted to curtail it, and the 'up the banking' expeditions kept our fire – and a few other families' fires – alight for several winters.

Dad never considered this stealing, saying they only picked up coal that had fallen from the trucks. Mam had a suspicion that some of it had been given a little help to 'fall,' but said nothing.

THIRTY-TWO

As soon as we arrived on Seafield each winter, Dad hunted for work, taking any available job, and often working in terrible conditions.

Labouring on building sites meant suffering the vagaries of bad weather, and casual labourers such as Dad were laid off without pay. He tried to avoid this type of work if possible but sometimes there was no alternative. For a couple of winters he worked at the BOCM (British Oil and Cake Mill), which produced animal food. Then he got a job in the brewery that was opposite, and I remember the smell of the hops lingering on his clothing, and also the peculiar white canvas, rope-soled shoes he was required to wear when working. He explained that these were to avoid fires – boots with metal studs possibly causing sparks that might ignite the husks and debris on the floors.

One winter he worked in the British Rubber Mills and Mam was convinced that this could be the start of a real career. He was learning the mixtures for the different products and seemed genuinely interested in the job. He kept a little notebook in which he recorded the various formulas he needed to memorise, joking that it was homework. However, there was an unfortunate consequence to that job when he developed severe dermatitis, the result of exposure to some of the solutions he had been working with. He became allergic to rubber and could not wear rubber-soled boots or any synthetic clothing, and the condition plagued him for years, on one occasion causing him to be terribly ill with septicaemia.

There were winters when he worked at Leith docks, sometimes as a rigger and occasionally as a welder's assistant. He often would come home at night, the whites of his eyes scarlet and painful where a flash from the welder's torch had caught him. Mam would have to try and bathe them, and a little blue plastic eye bath seemed to be in regular use.

Sometimes he would present Mam with something a crewman had 'given' him from a boat. Once a bottle of Polish brandy that neither of them drank, but kept handy for any New Year callers, another time a box of shiny Canadian McIntosh Red apples. Fortunately, he was never stopped by the dock police, who did spot checks.

There was no doubt that Dad was a hard worker and that he was determined to provide for his family. His pay packet was always handed over, unopened, to Mam – his acknowledgement that she could budget and manage their finances better than him.

She somehow was able to shop and feed us economically, give Dad his cigarette money and still have something left for a treat, which was sometimes a trip to the Palace picture house in Leith.

I loved those visits to the cinema, not only enjoying the excitement of the film but also the anticipation of a bag of chips to be enjoyed while waiting for the tram home. Film programmes tended to run continuously, which meant that if the movie had started when you arrived, you simply sat through the remainder then watched the bit you had missed at the start. The final programme always ended with the national anthem, with the expectation that audiences would stand to attention until it finished. There was always a scramble to get out before it started, and Dad would be annoyed if we were stuck in a middle row with people slow to leave.

Everyone seemed to smoke – clouds of smoke visible and billowing in the beam of the film projector. We invariably left the picture house coughing, with eyes stinging and clothes smelling of the stuff.

One film that really captured my imagination and also resulted in a childhood crush on Doris Day was 'Calamity Jane.' As a fan of Westerns, I loved the image of the rip-roaring Calamity, who could take on the world and who feared no-one. I rode my bike around the ground, pretending it was a horse, and wished that I had the fringed buckskins she wore.

When asked by Mam and Dad what would I like for Christmas that winter, I had no hesitation in saying that I wanted a cowboy outfit. On Christmas morning I ripped open my parcel and could scarcely believe what was there. No

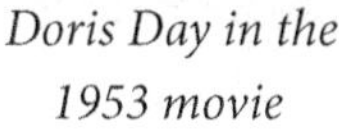

Doris Day in the 1953 movie

The Palace Cinema, Leith

fringed buckskin or 'proper gun-belt, holster and six shooter.' Instead, an outfit purchased from a fancy dress outlet, consisting of a short black canvas skirt and waistcoat with white cotton fringes. A white holster with red glass jewels was stitched to the skirt and held a small toy gun. The outfit was completed with a black 'cowboy hat,' trimmed with the same white fringes as the waistcoat and resembling a lampshade.

I looked nothing like my heroine and there was no way I could appear in public with this prissy outfit. I did not want to show my disappointment – my parents seemed so delighted with the costume – but I only wore it a couple of times just to please them.

Christmases were special times, Mam and Dad always trying to make sure I had at least one 'good' present and several little things. There was always an annual, a board game, sometimes a Reeves paint box, and every Christmas – the pack of corrugated strips of coloured plasticine. I loved this modelling clay and became quite proficient at making little figures, usually of cowboys (surprise, surprise} but also Roman gladiators.

The stuff was difficult to mould in the cold weather and I would stick lumps of it on a fork and heat it in front of the fire, sometimes raising blisters if I overheated the clay and molten bits dripped onto my fingers.

It was a while before it registered with me that my parents never seemed to receive Christmas presents. They explained that Santa (yes… I still believed) only delivered to children. In reality, they could only afford my gifts – nothing for themselves.

For Mam, winters on Seafield gave her a sense of stability and routine. My schooling was sorted for those few months, and Dad always managed to find work somewhere. Each winter she hoped that he would eventually agree that travelling was a precarious and non-profitable venture, yet without fail, come spring he would pack us up and set off once more round the circuit of fairgrounds.

Mam hated spring, not just because we were starting out again with Dad's usual promise of 'just one more year,' but because the scent of spring flowers took her back to her childhood memory of her mother's death and funeral. In her adult years and even with her own child, the grief and sense of loss still haunted her – the memory of the church bell tolling as the funeral procession approached… the men who doffed their caps respectfully as they passed… the young boys who mocked the men, pretending to raise imaginary caps and laughing. How could they be so cruel? She had wanted to run at them, kicking and punching, scream at them, 'Don't you know that's my *mam*?'

Always at the back of her mind was the fear that her heart condition diagnosed during her wartime medical would result in her own premature death. She worried that Dad might remarry just as her own father had, and that I might suffer the same unhappiness. She hated our being uprooted yearly and remained continually anxious for my future.

I held a different view, although I would never admit it to Mam. I looked forward to 'starting out,' excited at the prospect of reunions with cousins not seen since the previous summer. I loved the feeling of escape, and any interest I might have had in lessons at school was lost as spring approached.

On the Seafield ground, the first sign of preparations for starting out was when the men began working on their lorries and checking engines that had lain dormant during the winter. Although not necessarily a competition, it delighted some when *their* lorry started first time while other vehicles required considerable coaxing. Our old Albion caused Dad public humiliation each year, always obstinately refusing to come to life. Mam secretly hoped each time that it had died, and at long last we would no longer have to travel.

The men on the ground were always willing to help and a rope on the starting handle pulled to the command of 'one – two – hupp' eventually forced the reluctant vehicle to come out of hibernation. One spring a bird's nest had to be removed from the engine. Fortunately, there were no eggs or fledglings, but I felt great remorse that we had made a creature homeless!

THIRTY-THREE

Hamilton was the start of our season and was a huge fair held on the red ash grounds of what used to be Hamilton Palace. The ground sloped from the entrance down to tennis courts, a putting green, and swings.

We were pitched next to the swings, which really pleased me, and I played for hours on them, muscles aching from this unaccustomed exercise.

Hamilton was also where I re-joined my 'gang' – Uncle Edward's boys, my cousins. As usual, everyone congregated in Granny's wagon, and I loved these first meetings, especially catching up with the boys and marvelling at how an absence of six to seven months could change them so much.

Hamilton Palace grounds

'My gang' – (left to right) Erroll, Johnny, Harry, Ritchie, Eddie

Some had grown taller, others were less shy, and at least one was enduring laughter as his voice kept breaking.

The boys had been my constant companions every summer, always travelling to the same places as us. They tolerated my company, sharing their comics with me and allowing me to join them in various adventures. We built dens, swung from Tarzan ropes, made guider barrows, and raced bikes.

Sometimes there was an element of danger. One example was when I was only four and we were at a place we used to call 'Singers.' I had followed the boys to the top of a steep road that led down to the ground. They had an assortment of barrows and bikes, while I was on a tricycle, and they decided to race down the hill, assuming that I would just watch.

Nothing daunted. I followed them, the tricycle gaining speed as I careered downhill. Halfway there I realised that my brakes were not working and I panicked, praying that the gates to the ground – which were normally closed – would be open. The boys, who had all stopped now, watched in amazement as I hurtled past them, swerved through the gates, which thankfully were open, and tumbled off the trike as it bounced off along the ground.

Dad picked me up, trying to find out what had happened, but I was speechless, my heart thumping, and my legs grazed and wobbling like jelly.

Mam was horrified when she heard what I'd been up to, and I was banned from ever going out onto a road again with my trike. The boys, however, reckoned that I had been really brave and I had earned street some cred in their eyes.

It used to puzzle me why the gable end of the tenement block at the top of that hill had cupboards – and even stranger, I could see strands of wallpaper and fireplaces. I wasn't to know that 'Singers' was actually Clydebank, and the tenement was all that remained of the row of homes after the Clydebank blitz just three years before I was born.

Our fairground was part of the sports pitch owned by the Singer sewing machine factory. The huge Singer's clock was iconic and defined the area.

I played happily on waste ground opposite the fair with my cousins, unaware that we were running around a bomb site and of the tragic and recent history of that area.

The war years to us children seemed centuries ago, and the battles just scenes from the movies we re-enacted in play – with 'goodies and baddies,' commandos, sticks as pretend guns, and voices mimicking the rat-tat-tat of gunfire.

'Our' place on the fairground was next to the railings of a Catholic school and its church bells tolled out the Angelus with such regularity that we could almost hear it in our sleep. There was a tree on our side of the railings and Dad always tried to park the Albion with the windows facing it, knowing that Mam enjoyed the feeling of country and freshness when she looked out at it. She loved seeing that tree every year, almost thinking of it as *hers,* and was disappointed if there were summers when we could not park in our usual spot..

The downside of being next to the school was the chaos of playtimes, when dozens of over-excited children clambered onto the flat roof of the school shed to get a good view of us. Others, more adventurous, climbed up the railings and tried to reach over to the branches of 'Mam's tree' in their attempts to look in our windows. She breathed a sigh of relief when the school bell summoned them all back and our privacy was restored.

The wheel-'em-in opened for the first time at Singer's, but also justified Mam's concern over the safety element when – to her horror and as she had feared – a misfired dart hit a spectator, sticking into his forehead like an Indian arrow. As though it was an everyday occurrence, the man removed the missile, dabbed blood with his handkerchief and handed the dart back to Mam, assuring her that he was all right before walking away. Mam's only concern was for the man, yet Rosie's comment when hearing of the event was, 'I hope you didn't say you were *sorry* because that's admitting liability and he could sue you.' Fortunately, litigation in the forties and fifties was fairly uncommon, people seeming to just accept that life held risks – this again perhaps a post-war legacy. Nothing more was heard of the incident, but Mam was never happy thereafter to have the darts set up in the wheel-'em-in.

That same year, when we were opened at the Alva Highland Games, the boys were told to keep an eye on me. It was an exceptionally hot day, the ground was busy, and my cousins either forgot I was with them or simply got fed up with me. When they eventually wandered back minus me everyone was horrified. The adults were firing questions at them – where was I last seen? How long ago? Why did they leave me? The boys were becoming upset at the bombardment and not really appreciating the seriousness of the situation. Mam was inconsolable, sure that I had been abducted, or at the very least was dying from sunstroke somewhere.

Punters and 'earning a living' forgotten, Dad took charge, instructing the boys to retrace their steps and look for me while he and my uncles set off around the ground alerting every traveller to the fact that I was missing. All the travellers knew me, and they also joined in the hunt. Meantime, the Highland Games continued.

A piper was playing for the young dancers on the raised platform, who were competing for more medals to add to the glittering array already pinned to their velvet bodices; men were sweating in their efforts to toss a caber; and a tannoy loudspeaker announced that the hill race would soon begin. (The Alva hill-race was one of the main events of the Games, athletes having to race from Johnstone Park, reach specific checkpoints and then race – or more often tumble – back down again. This was a distance of 2.6km and a climb of 385m, and the highlight of the games.)

The man using the tannoy was whipping up the crowd's enthusiasm and also joking when some burly caber contestants failed to toss the caber, encouraging the audience to cheer a puny youth who had actually managed to achieve the task. The noise of the loudspeaker could be heard everywhere and this gave Mam an idea. She ran to one of the Games officials, explained that her child was missing and asked if it would be possible to broadcast a description over the tannoy. The announcer agreed without hesitation, his voice now changed to a serious tone as he broadcast that a child was lost, my description and an appeal to everyone to look for me.

Within minutes I was found. I had crawled under the wooden spectator seats that encircled the games and was sitting on the grass, watching the highland dancers and happily eating an ice cream kindly passed on by a woman who did not want it dripping on her clothing in the heat.

It was announced that I had been traced and spectators cheered as though I had won something. My relieved parents thanked the Games officials profusely and I was marched back home, my freedom curtailed and my cousins vowing never to look after me again. I had caused them too much trouble and cramped their style!

Alva would be the cause of many misadventures, including being knocked off my bike and into the paddling pool I was riding around when I was six by a 'machine man' (fairground casual labourer) who carelessly opened a lorry door without checking for any passers-by. There was no apology, just a series of curses as he left. Soaking wet, upset, and with bent handlebars, I returned home, trying to explain what had happened. Dad traced the machine man and reported him to his employer. Justice was done!

'Machine men' were employed by the owners of the large machines (waltzers, dodgems etc) and while a few travelled with the same owners every season for years, others were casual labour, often only helping at one or two fairs.

Some of these were runaways, either from the police or extreme domestic situations. Others were simply obsessed with what they perceived as a glamorous life on the fairgrounds.

Aunt Rosie did not hold machine men in any high regard. She regarded them all as ne'er-do-wells who gave travelling show-people a bad name. Unfortunately, newspapers of the time tended to contribute to her belief, recording various crimes or incidents as involving a 'showman' when it was invariably a 'machine man.' These reports infuriated Aunt Rosie and, while I don't think she ever did so, she always threatened to complain to whichever paper was at fault and to 'educate them' about the 'differences.'

THIRTY-FOUR

At some point in my early life, Bruce joined our family. Nowadays, in dog breed terms, he would be called a Labradoodle, but in the fifties he was just a mongrel. I don't know how we acquired him; he just seemed to have always been there.

Dogs wandered freely, often just tagging on to families, and it was almost unheard of for anyone to actually *buy* a dog. However, there was a legal requirement to buy a dog licence costing 7/6 (seven shillings and sixpence – 37p) and while the majority of people chose not to comply, Dad, always fearful of falling foul of the law, ensured that Bruce was 'legal'.

Bruce was long-legged, black and curly, with big brown soulful eyes and a tail that constantly wagged. He was also a ladies' man, disappearing regularly and enjoying the 'hunt' in each locality, but hating the actual journeys from town to town. He would run away and hide on 'going away day,' requiring Dad and various family members to search everywhere for him.

On one occasion, after several hours spent looking for him, Dad had to give up. The ground had to be vacated that day and all the other loads were leaving. Mam was heartbroken at the thought of abandoning our dog but understood that we had to go. Dad reassured her that he would borrow a car and return later to look for him.

A few miles along the road to our next ground, we were flagged down by another lorry. Pulling over, the driver, a traveller from the ground we had just left, rolled down his window and grinned.

'Hi Dickie… I've picked up Bruce. Just after you left he was running along the road after you. He must have done a couple of miles before I caught up with him.'

Dad looked in the cab and there was our dog, exhausted but still able to give an apologetic wag of the tail. After this experience, Mam tried to make sure that Bruce was tied up long before any journey. He still recognised all the signs of imminent departure and a weekly game of hide and seek became the norm between them both.

One summer, when we were at Bridge of Allan for the Strathallan Highland Games, one of the traveller women hurried across to Mam, who was in the middle of hanging out clothes.

'Here, Winnie – I've just seen that queer couple outside the shops with a dog. I'm sure it was *you*r dog. They had a can round it's neck and they were begging.'

The 'queer couple' referred to were vagrants, a man and woman – worse for drink – who had been hanging around the ground for hours even though nothing was open. The travellers had moved them on several times when they were found trying to break into stalls and at some point they must have left.

Mam was not particularly concerned by Bruce's absence. He had been missing for an hour or so, but this was just his normal behaviour. She suspected that the couple must have spotted Bruce and saw him as a crowd-puller when they were begging.

Now she was furious. The idea that someone could steal a family pet – *our* dog – unleashed a rage in her that might have led to violence had the twosome been there at that point. She dumped the washing basket down, rolled up her sleeves, smoothed down her pinny and – now red-faced – prepared for battle.

Dad was working nearby and on hearing the conversation, he decided he should try to be the voice of reason. 'It won't be Bruce. He'll come wandering back as usual, you'll see. The woman will be mistaken; there's lots of dogs like Bruce.'

Dad hated anything confrontational and clearly did not want to go chasing after two drunken people who might even be violent. Mam refused to be placated and, convinced that our dog had been abducted, stormed off the ground and along the street, determined to find him.

They sat on a garden wall, swearing and still drinking, while Bruce lay beside them with a rusty tin can tied round his neck. He spotted Mam and wagged his tail.

'HEY –THAT'S MY DOG!' Mam shouted as she approached, red-faced with anger.

Bridge of Allan, a former spa town situated just North of Stirling, was (and still is) quite a well-to-do place, and this event was unfolding outside the garden of a very posh villa in a beautiful tree-lined row of grand homes. The lady of the house was sitting in her front garden and now had the misfortune to be privy to the unfolding drama. Realising that the woman was watching, and that an explanation was required, Mam turned to her.

'These people have stolen my dog and they have been using him to beg for money.'

Bruce stood up on cue, the tin can rattling on the pavement as he ambled over to Mam as though he was confirming her as the bona fide owner. The woman was aghast, clutching her chest as though she had been assaulted. This was a situation she would rather not be associated with.

'Oh my goodness… That is terrible… Should I telephone for the police?' she asked, standing up and quickly backing away from them as she spoke.

At the mention of the police, the couple staggered away, cursing and spitting, leaving Mam to remove the string and can from Bruce's neck while thanking the lady for her support.

Walking triumphantly back through the gates and into the large field that had been the fair's site for years, she was met by Dad.

'Don't ever do that again,' he exclaimed as he grabbed the dog's collar, and for a moment Mam wasn't sure whether the comment was aimed at Bruce or her. 'Anything could have happened to you. Those people might have turned violent and really hurt you.'

Realising that he had been worried about her, she refrained from asking him why he hadn't just come with her instead of making excuses.

The two vagrants must have taken the threat of police arrest seriously and were not seen again on the ground, although one traveller said he had spotted them in Stirling with another dog in tow. This news upset Mam, who wondered whether someone else's child was missing their family pet.

We lost Bruce one Seafield winter when I was only eight. Always refusing to walk on a lead, he was accompanying Mam to the little corner shop and walking ahead of her. Black dogs and dark nights are a bad combination, and he was hit by a lorry when crossing the road. The lorry driver was as distraught as Mam when they both realised that the dog was dead. He covered Bruce with a sack and returned to the ground with Mam, who could not stop sobbing and was scarcely coherent. He explained to Dad what had happened, then took him back to where they had left Bruce.

The grief I experienced was beyond description and as much to do with witnessing Mam's distress as coping with my own. Bruce was a family member – always there for as long as I could remember, and I just assumed that he would always be there. Death was an alien concept, something beyond my comprehension, as was this gut-wrenching, agonising heartbreak.

Dad did his best to console us that night but there was nothing he could do or say to take the pain away. If he was upset he hid it well, and he seemed almost relieved when people from the ground kept calling in to see if we were alright.

I longed for winter to end, to be away from this place and the scene of the accident, which we had to pass every day en route to school.

There was a huge gap in our lives, a void never to be filled, and for the first time I realised that there were some things in life that my parents had no control over and could not protect me from.

The annual reunion with my cousins at Hamilton did nothing to raise my spirits. I sat on the motionless swing, arms wrapped around the metal chains, my legs dangling, in no mood for play. Then there was a familiar whistle and my dad shouted me over. Still in a black mood and wondering whether I was in trouble, I noticed that Dad was winking at Mam and both were acting mysteriously.

'Jean, go round to Granny's wagon, they've got something they want you to see.'

I rushed round to find my cousins examining the contents of a box under the steps. Looking inside, I could see there were two Alsatian puppies.

'That one is ours,' one of the boys stated firmly, pointing to the slimmer, darker-coloured pup, which seemed intent on snapping at everyone.

'You can keep the other one,' added Uncle Walter and he lifted the plump, uncomplaining little puppy out of the box and handed it to me. I was overwhelmed, not believing what was happening, and looking to Dad for confirmation. He grinned, obviously delighted that I had been given the dog and said, 'He's a wee boy so you will have to give him a proper name.'

Flash in his prime

Many years later and swaybacked!

I gazed at the little creature, which was now cuddling into me and looking sleepy. He was a golden colour with a streak of black across his back and a mark on his forehead resembling a lightning flash.

'I will call him Flash,' I announced proudly, and my cousins guffawed.

'That's a daft name,' declared one. 'We're calling ours Terry.' Then he yelped as Terry nipped his finger.

Back home, I could not take my eyes off the little dog. Bruce had been the 'family dog,' but this tiny animal was *mine*.

'Now you *do* realise that you will have to take care of him, especially just now when he is still just a baby?

I did not need Mam to remind me. I was besotted and wanted to spend every waking hour with him, worrying over each whimper and unusual sound he made, constantly checking that he hadn't died. He became my constant companion that summer and when we returned to Seafield for another winter, both Mam and I realised that while never forgetting Bruce, Flash had repaired us and brought happiness back to our family.

THIRTY-FIVE

That first summer with Flash had been wonderful for me. From the plump puppy of spring he had become a happy, leggy one-year-old, and my constant companion. He was gentle and good-natured as opposed to the brother Terry, which seemed to delight in snapping and snarling at everyone. It was hard to believe they were from the same litter, and I wondered whether my cousins had teased the dog and broken its temper. I was always careful to avoid it even when it was tied up and just so glad that I had been given Flash.

Unfortunately his first experience of winter on Seafield was to be a turning point for him. Mam and I had decided to take Flash out of the ground and give him his first visit to the beach. We were unaware that one of the travellers owned a Staffordshire bull terrier that was known to be savage. As we passed the owner's wagon, the dog suddenly appeared, took an immediate dislike to Flash and attacked him, throwing him to the ground and trying to grab his throat. The dog's owner rushed out and hauled the Staffy off, leaving us to take our traumatised dog home and examine him for any wounds. The owner later checked that all was well but offered no apology.

It was necessary to pass the Staffy's home every time we needed to leave the ground or go to the shed for water. Flash accompanied us and without fail, the Staffy would lie in wait, ambush him, and not let go – the noise of the fight invariably drawing a crowd.

Dogs roamed freely and skirmishes were not unusual, but this particular dog was a known battler. It had a reputation for locking its jaws around its victims' throats and not letting go. Its attacks on Flash became more prolonged

– buckets of water thrown over the dogs and even smoking newspaper thrust under the Staffy's nose were methods used by the men to make it release its grip. Somehow, Flash always managed to break free and escape, the Staffy content to have retained its status of alpha dog.

Just before we started out the following spring, we heard the noise of dogs fighting. Mam was in the middle of making dinner and I sat reading a comic.

'Oh no… not again! Where's Flash?'

I could hear the alarm and also exasperation in her voice. Tired from having to rescue our young dog and also angry with the Staffy's owner for his lack of control of his dog, she did not relish yet another encounter.

'Why does this always happen when your Dad's not here?' (Dad was at work and the dog fights usually took place during the day, requiring Mam to be the rescuer and remonstrator.)

We dashed out of the Albion and headed past the lorries and wagons towards the sound of battle, dreading what we might find this time. To our astonishment, Flash clearly had the upper hand.

The Staffy was on its back and Flash had it by the neck, snarling and savagely shaking it to and fro, refusing to let go, the Staffy now squealing in protest as hair and spittle from both dogs flew everywhere. The usual 'remedies' of cold water and smoking newspaper had not worked. One man was trying to prise them apart with a broom handle.

Not thinking of her own safety, Mam grabbed the muzzles of both dogs in an attempt to release them, only to be whacked over the knuckles by the man brandishing the broom handle. Then, of his own volition, Flash stopped fighting and let the Staffy go. The animal scurried, still yelping, back to its wagon and hid under the steps while Flash, bloodied but unbowed, walked home with us. Mam spent the next week nursing her badly bruised and swollen hand, complaining that she had fared worse than the Staffy.

Flash had now achieved 'top dog' status on the ground and his enemy avoided him at every opportunity. However, the experience that winter turned our gentle, good-natured dog into a fighter and he could not be trusted with other dogs, attacking any animal within range, regardless of size. He never seemed to resort to the savagery of the Staffy, content just to prove that he was the top dog and letting his victims go once he had made his point. Nevertheless he did cause casualties. On one occasion he lunged at a Pekinese, causing its eye to pop out of the socket. (This eye prolapse – we later discovered – was a peculiarity of the breed.)

Another skirmish resulted in the death of an elderly West Highland terrier, not from any wounds inflicted, but from the shock and subsequent heart attack. This particular incident really upset Mam.

'That family have every right to demand that we get rid of Flash.'

She sat opposite Dad, sipping tea, her hands clasping the cup, desperately upset by the knowledge that Flash was responsible for the little Westie's death. Her voice quavered as she continued.

'I went round to their wagon to see them. The old lady loved that dog. She's heartbroken and I just didn't know what to say. The wee animal was still there, lying on the floor… not a mark on it and just as though it was sleeping. I asked whether I could do anything, but they just shook their heads, told me not to worry and that it wasn't my fault. They are such a nice family and now we have caused them misery.'

Dad lit a cigarette and gazed out the window as though trying to grasp some words of comfort or reassurance from the December gloom outside.

'Look… it was a really old dog and would have died this year anyway. It did have a weak heart and the cold of this winter would have been enough to finish it off.'

His attempt to apply some logic to the situation did nothing to soothe Mam, the image of the little furry white corpse, Flash's victim, a memory she would never forget.

She glared at Flash as though he had transformed into a demonic creature. I sat on the floor with my arms around him, convinced that some authority would descend on us, and he would be snatched away from me at any moment.

The incident was never reported. I think the family realised that we had very little and that the dog was my sole companion. Flash was reprieved but continued to battle at the various grounds, attracting an audience whenever word got out that it was 'the Stirling's' dog.'

Mam felt that Dad was secretly proud of his dog's battle prowess, almost as though it gave him status amongst the men, and she realised this was another trait of her husband's character that she had been unaware of and disliked.

THIRTY-SIX

Our seasons followed the same pattern – the solitude of winters on Seafield, then the excitement of summer reunions with the various family members.

Mam missed the company of other women. There was no-one on Seafield really of a similar age to allow any friendships to form, and she had also become aware that Dad did not seem to need anyone other than his own family. He was uncomfortable when in the company of other people and assumed she was also happy with their cloistered existence.

This winter dearth of friends meant that for all her dislike of travelling, the summer months at least offered the companionship of her sisters-in-law, especially John's wife, Marie, and Tommy's wife, Charlotte. The women were cousins, their family being the Paulos, who were famous in the circus world.

As a young girl Charlotte was part of a knife throwing act, standing against a target board while her brother launched knives at her, each one pinning the board perilously close to her. She claimed to have been nicked a couple of times when her brother was having an off day and made sure thereafter never to annoy him before a show. When telling this story, Charlotte assured everyone that her brother was actually a skilled knife thrower, having been taught by the famous American 'Buffalo Bill.'

We thought this was just a colourful addition to her already exciting story until many years later we discovered that The Buffalo Bill Wild West Show *had* travelled to Glasgow twice. One site was in Whitehill, near the Gallowgate, and it was quite likely that the Vinegarhill travellers would have mixed with the Americans. (A statue of Buffalo Bill commemorating his visit is situated within a housing development, roughly on the site where his Wild West show opened.)

As avid Western fans, my cousins and I were fascinated by this, not only amazed that someone we knew had actually *met* 'real-life' cowboys and Indians, but also that they had been taught knife throwing by them!

William Cody, also known as Wild Bill Hickock

Aunt Charlotte was a born entrepreneur. During rationing she always seemed able to know where to get things… or at least to know someone who knew. She was addicted to sales, often spending money they could ill afford on items she described as 'investments.' This included her purchase of Italian Capodimonte ornaments – which to Aunt Rosie, with no eye for the aesthetic, 'looked like swag.'

Aunt Charlotte encouraged Uncle Tommy to secure extra ground footage when available and opened extra stalls. Again Rosie was quick to criticise, seeing the joints being opened with no-one to 'mind the stuff' apart from any local flattie children Charlotte employed. What Rosie failed to realise was that Charlotte was planning for the future. She was securing and preserving rights to grounds for a time when her own children were adults. She realised that pitches at

Buffalo Bill's statue, Glasgow

some point would become scarce and was ensuring that her family would benefit from her foresight in later years.

Uncle Tommy understood the rationale and tolerated his wife's passion for life even when her obsession for sales caused problems; on one occasion she spent their diesel money and almost stranded them on a ground without fuel for the lorry.

Mam loved Charlotte's uniqueness – especially some of the circus cant she used when not wanting to be overheard by flatties. 'Omies' were men, 'mozzies' were women and 'chavvies' were children. She also had the habit of affectionately addressing people as 'cock,' which amused us children endlessly.

Aunty Marie, unlike her cousin, preferred not to plan ahead but rather lived for the day. She was full of fun and loved socialising, especially if this involved dances – or a party. She had a sharp, often caustic wit and was skilled in her use of double entendre, often not requiring words, her facial expressions speaking multitudes when reacting to someone's innocent comment.

A young Aunty Charlotte (on horse) with siblings

Single tub washing machine

Together, the two cousins were almost a double act, Charlotte the willing foil to Marie's humour, and Mam enjoyed their good-natured banter.

Marie was the first in the family to own a washing machine and generously loaned it out to whoever needed it. Obviously the thing only worked when tapped into an available power supply, and any generator or nearby property allowing a 'tap on' during the summer was very welcome. The washer was a single tub and included a wringer, which folded into the tub when not in use. Mam borrowed the machine whenever possible and even though she hand-washed woollens and used a ribbed scrubbing board for any soiled clothing, she still considered the machine a boon.

Dad was not so impressed as the whole rigmarole seemed to demand more work for him in running a cable to the 'tap on', setting the machine up on flat terrain, and also the amount of water it required for the initial wash, then the rinse, then possibly a second wash.

Even Aunt Rosie borrowed the machine, albeit her first attempt at operation was a bit problematic, having unwittingly added too much soap powder. The resulting foam rose up and over the washer like a white volcanic eruption, much to the delight of the watching children. They scooped up the foam, which was gradually spreading across the ground, playing pretend snowball fights as Aunt Rosie frantically tried to chase them – fearing possible electrocution – as she summoned Marie's help. No harm was done and the experience did not deter Rosie's future use of the machine.

THIRTY-SEVEN

This was a time of fun and freedom. My childhood summers were happy, every week on a different ground and rejoining my cousins for new adventures.

Fairs that involved gala days and Highland Games usually also had large beer tents, which, when dismantled and removed, were hunting grounds for us. We hoped to find any coins dropped by drinkers but were always unsuccessful, realising that even under the influence, punters were careful with their money. Instead we collected the metal tops from different beer bottles and made 'badges', fastened onto our clothing and secured with the cork discs from the tops.

We also collected the soft foil from inside discarded cigarette packets and made pretend bullion by rubbing the silver foil over any copper coins we had. I loved the designs and artwork on the packets, especially the Capstan picture, which always seemed to have an antique look. Someone had actually made a decorative plate by gluing and varnishing cutouts of the design.

I tried to do the same, gathering many cartons and spending hours painstakingly clipping round the circle with the sailor's head, convinced that I would be creating a work of art. It did not work. The card refused to remain 'stuck' and my every attempt to shape the segments into anything resembling a plate failed. I was left with a bag full of smelly, partially glued remnants destined only for the bin.

While pleased that I enjoyed hobbies, especially crafting, Mam was not so keen on my smelling of beer and cigarettes, and those particular pastimes were gently discouraged.

Halcyon summer days though these were, it was still necessary for everyone, regardless of age, to pull their weight. Older children helped with the build up, pull down and minding of the joints, while the younger ones went for errands and, in the case of girls, assisted their mothers with cleaning and childminding.

A regular job for me was the milk run. In the smaller villages with few shops, milk was collected from any nearby farm. We carried our freshly washed and rinsed glass bottles to be filled with milk ladled straight from the churn and very often still warm. Just a bit wary of the cows, I generally accompanied my braver cousins to the farms, sometimes having to wait outside the dairy shed until the farmer had finished milking the animals.

The smell of cow dung was overpowering and our attempts to hold our breath proved impossible. Neither were we keen on the farmyard hens that insisted on clucking and scratching around us while we waited. There always seemed to be an abundance of cats peering warily out at us from behind old barn doors and we kept our distance, convinced they would pounce at any moment.

Our bottles had no caps and the walk back to the grounds invariably resulted in some liquid spilling over, but generally we arrived with most of the contents intact, albeit in a sticky finger-marked bottle that had to be decanted and washed again.

I am not sure what testing or hygiene processes existed at each farm but do know that the milk was the freshest and creamiest I have ever tasted.

Another task was water collection from a variety of sources that had been negotiated by the lessees, ranging from a stand-pipe in the middle of a field to an outside tap in a yard – or in some cases, for a small payment, a local householder.

Being sent for water was less of a chore if we had a barrow to carry the cans, and we borrowed Granny's whenever available (the two wheels on the cart being all that remained now of my Churchill pram).

At one ground it was arranged that water could be obtained from a house at specific times of the day when the tenant would be home. This consisted of a hose-pipe fastened to the sink tap and poking out through the kitchen window. Unfortunately there must have been a kink in the pipe and in my attempts to get the water to run through, I accidentally disconnected the hose.

I could hear water running at full force into the sink and in my attempts to push the hose back through the window, I knocked dishes that were stacked on the draining board onto the floor, with the obvious sound of breakages. The kitchen window was too high for me to survey the damage, but the angry curses of the woman inside the house was enough to confirm my need to disappear before she spotted me. My cousins, the boys, thought the story was hilarious but changed their minds when instructed to go back in my place and fill the still-empty cans.

On another occasion, water was sourced from a local farm. Accompanied by cousins Irene and Rosina, we located the tap in an old, rather dirty outhouse and started to collect the water. The tap was painfully slow to pour and the task was becoming boring. As we waited we noticed there was one window, cobweb-strewn and half covered with an old hessian sack. Fearing there might be huge spiders lurking, we poked the sack with a stick. Relieved that none were spotted, we looked out of the stained, dirty window and to our horror saw three large pigs heading down a hill towards the shed. Our water source was obviously in their enclosure; they must have heard us and assumed it was feeding time. Abandoning our mission, we dumped the half-filled cans into the barrow and ran, looking fearfully behind us as we escaped, convinced that we were about to be the pigs' next meal.

We headed back to the ground, the cans rattling and banging into each other as we took turns at pushing the barrow. We felt a little shame-faced and foolish now that we were safely away from the farm, wondering what explanation we should give our parents.

Our story grew with each re-telling. The pigs were now monstrous-sized tusked boars charging down the hill, intent on savaging us and leaving us just seconds to spare in making our escape. We felt that adding a little colour to our adventure would excuse the shortfall in water and also the dents we had inflicted on the cans as we flew the scene.

Water was such a precious commodity and it always amazed me when, during hot days, the teenage travellers could waste it. The young men chased the girls with buckets and basins full of water, ambushing them as they ran and throwing copious amounts of the stuff over them. The girls screamed as they were caught, blouses and tops soaked in the process.

Too young to realise that this was probably a type of 'wet t-shirt' game,

Escaping from the savage pigs!

and for the hormonal young males a type of preliminary courtship, I just considered the whole thing to be quite stupid and was glad that I was not tasked with refilling the cans.

THIRTY-EIGHT

We wandered in and out of Granny's wagon at will, never considering that this might be intrusive, and always referred to it as 'Granny's wagon' even though Granda (Old Teddy) was there. This was probably because he was a humourless carmudgeon who scarcely tolerated, let alone spoke to, any of us.

Granny had a problem coping with the names of her ever-increasing number of grandchildren and her strategy was to employ nicknames. These included 'Jean Dump the Midden Diver', 'Pansy Potter', 'Sally Slackcabbage', 'Weary Willie' and so on. We thought this was hilarious and always knew which one of us she was referring to. Aunt Rosie's tactic was different in that she just worked incrementally through each name until she reached the right one.

Granny's wagon was the family hub – the place where we could observe the adults, and hear Aunt Rosie talking about the latest deaths, births, marriages and distant relatives. According to Rosie, scarcely a traveller existed who was not related to us. She had a penchant for linking us to some well-known names in the fairground and circus industry, including the Rosaire family and Florence Shuffelbottom.

Shuffelbottom is a Lancashire name and the story goes that Florence's paternal grandparents owned a cotton mill and were wealthy. When her grandfather saw Buffalo Bill's circus, which was on tour, he was so impressed that he decided to open his own Wild West show, assisted by his wife Rosina, who was from a showground family. Since 'Rosina' was a family name – even of one of my cousins – I trusted Aunt Rosie's claim to the family lineage to be true.

Florence Shuffelbottom (c1950s)

William and Rosina Shuffelbottom (c1890s)

I loved to hear about Florence Shuffelbottom, who, among her many other performing skills, was an expert sharpshooter, famed for her use of a Winchester rifle and earning the name 'Britain's Annie Oakley'.

Seeing a picture of Florence in her Western regalia, I realised that this had been the inspiration for Mam's choice of my Christmas 'cowboy' outfit. The fringes, waistcoat, jewelled holsters etc had been replicated small-scale for me.

Apart from wishing I had the Winchester, I still had no desire to make any public appearances in my version of Western regalia and was quite pleased to have grown out of it. The rifle range – or 'pipe shooter', as she called it – was Granny's stall and when not in use, the rifles were stacked behind the door of her bedroom in the wagon.

These fascinated me (probably still the Calamity Jane influence) and I made every excuse – usually the need to use the toilet, which was the bucket in the bedroom – to see them. They were quite old, the wooden stocks polished and stained from years of handling. A ramrod and a pullthrough cloth on a string was used to occasionally clean the barrels; this probably the only maintainance they received.

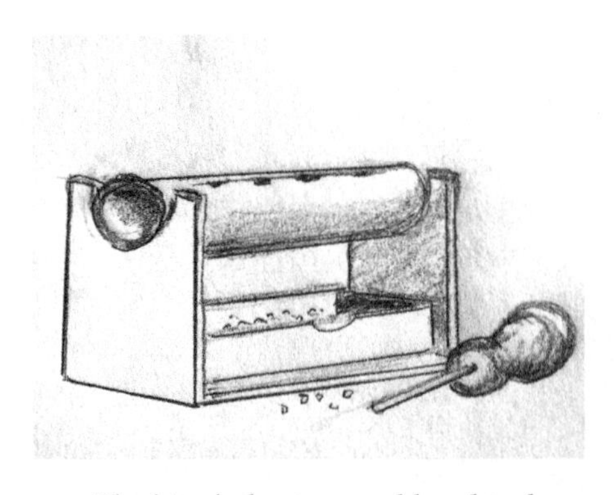

The 'rime', slug tray and hand tool

The small pellets (slugs), however, required attention. The soft lead could easily become damaged and misshapen, which would result in the rifle jamming. With only eight rifles, any of them out of action on a busy night would lose the stall money. The slugs had to be reshaped to fit the barrels and to do this, granny used something she called a 'rime'. This was a small metal tube suspended over a tin tray that caught the reshaped slugs as they were pushed through holes using a small wooden-handled tool similar to a screwdriver but with a rounded end. I was never sure whether 'rime' was the actual name of the apparatus or just something she made up, but I loved watching the process, always hoping she would let me have a shot.

She must have pushed thousands of these little slugs through the rime, often keeping some in her mouth as she worked. In later years she was to develop pernicious anaemia, her symptoms of weight loss and extreme fatigue not being diagnosed until almost life-threatening. Mam suspected that the prolonged exposure to lead was the cause, but Rosie dismissed the idea and Granny continued to use the rime despite being terribly ill.

The initial prescribed remedy horrified us children when we heard she must eat raw liver. (This was the acknowledged treatment of the time but fortunately replaced later with regular injections.) She never fully recovered

Granny and Old Teddy in their frailer years

and surrendered the 'minding' of the pipe shooter to Rosie, choosing just to sit at the side and take the money while Rosie dealt with the punters.

This was to become Aunt Rosie's domain. She could dodge underneath the rifle barrels while they were being fired with the agility of an athlete. She broke open the barrels and loaded slugs with a speed and deftness that even Ms Shuffelbottom would have admired.

She was fearless and ferocious with awkward punters, even grabbing the gun from one drunk and jabbing him in the chest with the rifle butt when he protested. She spent hours in the joint when it was closed, just rearranging and setting out the swag, prizes placed in rows on shelves, and in order of score value – the higher the target score, the 'better' the prize.

A stickler for the 'rules', she was furious with any traveller who dared to lift their shutters before the official opening time, which usually was around 5pm on Fridays and 1pm Saturdays. At tea time on Fridays she would be visibly on edge and clearly listening for any sound that might indicate a recalcitrant showman/woman trying to graft before anyone else. She often sent one or more of her nephews or nieces (including me) on a scouting mission to see who the offender was. While her brothers, Tommy and John, were now married, the youngest – Walter – was still at home and being bossed by Rosie. This was her world... she was in charge and she loved it!

Pre-war photos of my uncles (from left): Walter, John and Tommy

THIRTY-NINE

Each fairground was like a familiar village, all the families knowing each other and the wagons and stalls placed in exactly the same positions every year.

It was possible to identify which family was pulling onto a ground just by the colour of their vehicles. The paintwork on lorries and wagons was of great pride to travellers and almost their trademark. Most retained the same colour choice year after year. Those who could afford it employed professional signwriters to paint their family surname and often fancy scrollwork on the lorries. I can remember the fascination of watching one painter using small sheets of gold leaf to embelish his design and being assured by Dad that it was real gold. I scoured the ground afterwards, convinced that I would find valuable bullion.

Many of the traveller men were such enthusiasts they even customised their lorry engines; any part that could be painted or chromium-plated was treated, then the gleaming finished work, engine bonnet up, proudly put on display.

Wagons and living vans ranged in quality and design. Lessees tended to have particularly large, beautifully presented Mollycroft wagons, the windows often of faceted cut glass and dressed with the best of lace blinds, the side panels painted to a high standard and outlined in gold.

Granny's wagon, although a Mollycroft, was old and certainly not opulent. Always painted the same dark orange colour with cream bellyboxes, it still looked shabby when standing near some of the better wagons.

Displayed at exhibition

Beautifully painted and varnished

Nevertheless, it was Granny's home and a place where family reunions happened, uncles teased, arguments took place and were later resolved, and of course, the various cousins wandered in and out.

It never occurred to me that any of our homes might be considered sub-standard. Showpeople were non-judgemental, measuring their fellow travellers by their moral standing and honesty. Living vans – in all their shapes and forms – were acceptable and Mam had made our Albion comfortable, clean and homely. It was a place where I felt safe, loved and cherished.

The Hanley family favoured maroon and their loads can still be seen at various exhibitions, having been bought and restored by a fairground enthusiast. Our old Albion, however, trundled out every year with the same old bottle green colour and I don't think it ever crossed Dad's mind that he should paint it. His traditional spring humiliation –its refusal to start – meant that any new paint was begrudged!

FORTY

It was the fifties and a time of amazing freedoms and trust. Babies were quite commonly left outside in their prams while their mothers shopped. Dogs roamed freely, often wandering into the shops, the smell of food too good to resist. On one occasion Bruce followed Mam into the butcher's, sneaked behind the counter and stole a length of pork sausages. Mam had to reimburse the shopkeeper then explain later to Dad why the dinner plates were minus meat that day.

Children – especially showpeople's children – played ouside for as long as there was daylight, often only returning home for meals. Parents never worried, knowing that there was always an adult somewhere who knew them and would be watchful. Any youngster observed misbehaving would be scolded and the respective parent informed. This was an obvious deterrant and very few children of my generation dared to offend. No-one locked their doors and we wandered in and out at will.

To a certain extent everyone had dropped their guard. They had experienced all the fears and hardships of war, epidemics and death, yet had survived. Nothing could harm them now… we were all safe…

I was around five years old. It was early evening yet darkness was already closing in, the only light being from the various wagons nearby. It was mid-week and the fair was built up but not yet open. My parents had gone across to Granny's wagon, Mam promising not to be long and leaving me happily engrossed with my comics.

Around twenty minutes later, the door opened and a boy I vaguely recognised as a friend of my cousins came in.

'I've been sent to fetch you,' he announced. 'Your mammy and daddy have sent for chips. C'mon and I'll carry you over.'

This seemed odd to me. The ground was dry and I was quite capable of walking. He must have still only been in his early teens but was tall and muscular, and before I could protest, he lifted me from the Albion steps. The maneouvre was awkward and his hands and fingers seemed to be everywhere, especially under my dress.

He was breathing heavily and ignoring my wriggling attempts to get down as he carried me across the ground. Dumping me unceremoniously on the platform of Granny's wagon, he quickly disappeared between the booths and into the darkness, presumably to finish what his adolescent hormones had started.

Puzzled by the experience and thinking how stupid the boy was in his belief that I needed to be carried, I joined everyone in the wagon, sat on Mam's knee and shared her bag of chips. I made no mention of the encounter as it held no significance for me and I thought no more of the matter. I never saw the boy again, and only years later, when able to understand the concept of sexual abuse, did I realise when thinking back that I had actually been inappropriately touched by him.

Topics such as sexual abuse were never discussed by the Stirlings, and in any case it would have been pointless to mention my experience since I could not remember the boy, just the incident.

Apart from potential sexual predators, thiefs and epidemics, there were other hazards associated with the various places we opened. At Whitehaven the fair stood right on the edge of the harbour with nothing to stop any adventurous child toppling into the water. Similarly, the ground at Stirling was next to the River Forth and we were positioned just a few feet from its banks, the only barrier being a few bushes and weeds.

Fortunately (or unfortunately for the poor animals) the occasional carcass of a drowned sheep floating by was a disincentive to go near the river. At Egremont, Dad borrowed a car and took us to the beach at St Bees, where we spent a happy day paddling and exploring the rock pools. We were unaware that the atomic plant nearby (Windscale – later renamed Sellafield) had been guilty of radiation leaks, the most severe in 1957, when the worst nuclear accident in the UK's history took place following a fire at the plant.

The Windscale/Sellafield plant

Mam remembered the moon appearing to be shrouded in a peculiar blue-coloured mist. Soil was contaminated and all milk in the area had to be disposed of…much of this into the sea, consequently contaminating the water.

As a result of that radiation fallout, nearly 200 people developed cancer and at least half of those died. (This figure must have been based on casualties within the local area and probably did not include the travellers, yet later cancers and related fatalities within our group seemed to Mam proportionately too high to be a coincidence.) While she loved going back to Egremont since it heralded the end of the travelling season, there was always the spectre of that nuclear plant with its inherent dangers, and she could never fully relax until we were heading 'home'.

FORTY-ONE

By the time I was eight years old I was considered by Aunt Rosie to be a 'born traveller', an opinion based on my fascination with their 'wee machine' (children's toy ride). The ride was Uncle Walter's responsibility and he never seemed to mind my offers to help, although with hindsight, I must have been a nuisance.

I loved standing in the centre, helping to give the roundabout a push start and sometimes even being allowed to move the magnetto lever that engaged the motor and generated the speed. I was also a show-off, jumping on and off the moving machine and scolding any flattie kids who tried to do the same.

The platforms had various toys, on either side – a bus, Austin cars (now collector's items), toy jeeps etc. But of greater fascination to me was the panatrope, the collection of records and the little box of gold-coloured needles, a new replacement to be fixed into the player arm as each became blunt. I could tell from the quality of the sound when the needle had to be changed and was trusted to do this.

I knew every record of that time by heart – Bing Crosby, Rosemary Clooney, the Inkspots, and of course, Doris Day. The records were predominantly HMV and each had the circular paper emblem in the centre, of the little dog sitting gazing at the gramophone and listening to his master's voice. I always felt so sorry for that little dog. It looked so forlorn.

As the other traveller children, I was also beginning to help Mam and Dad in the stalls, being there for meal breaks etc. I was pretty hopeless in the dart joint, my inability to quickly count the scores on the dartboards a problem.

The requirement to retrieve the three darts and tell the punter whether or not they had won caused me endless anxieties, especially when doubles and trebles were part of their scores.

However, the can joint was easy – the punters either knocked the cans off the shelf – or didn't! No calculation required.

I periodically had to crawl under the shelf and retrieve any of the wooden balls that had fallen to the back of the stall. I hated that job. It was quite dark and cramped, and very often if we were open in a field I'd find that I had trodden on cowpats. The task was made more difficult by Flash who would join me, considering it a game, and constantly knocking me over as I tried to find the balls.

Mam hated to see me so involved in the business. This was not her plan and from a very early age I was aware of her desire to settle down. She talked of her life as a 'flattie' and how happy she had been with her aunts. While I enjoyed the stories I could not relate to them. She was describing something so far removed from my story that it felt alien to me.

I was happy in my eight-year-old childhood world, taking pride in helping Dad and being praised by Aunty Rosie as a budding showwoman. I loved the freedom, the feeling of not being tied down and the escape every spring to new adventures. I enjoyed the excitement of the local people when we arrived at each town or village to open, and the feeling that we were 'touring celebrities'... a sense that we were something special.

Poverty and hardships were not concepts I understood. Mine was a protected life with parents who loved me and made my happiness their absolute priority.

The Albion was the only home I'd known; the interior was filled with everything I associated with normal home life: my bedchair, an amazing contraption that doubled as an armchair during the day and folded out as my bed at night; the sweet smell of the freshly ironed candy-striped sheets, every crease and wrinkle smoothed out as she made the bed up for me; the little hostess stove, so carefully cleaned and polished by Mam, and the aromas of the meals she always managed to produce; the pretty curtains she made using Aunty Rosie's Singer machine and the patterned carpet, which, although a bit threadbare, still had to be hung over a clothes line outside and beaten with a cane carpet beater.

In the few years since Dad had first 'introduced' Mam to the Albion, she had made it comfortable and homely, and while not a match for the big Mollycroft wagons, she had ensured that it was my safe place – my home, containing all her loving touches.

I knew Mam's heart ached for her old life and a 'proper' home. I loved her and my sense of loyalty to her required me to agree that one day we would stop travelling, but secretly the prospect scared me.

Our 'settling down' conversations seldom now took place when Dad was present. Mam's early attempts to have him honour his promise of a house had failed and she realised that his pleas to wait another year were just delaying tactics. He no longer kept up any pretence of leaving 'the business' and whenever she tried to broach the subject he shut down… resorting to, or retreating into, a brooding silence that could last for days. She wished they could just have a full-blown row and clear the air but Dad refused to argue, his silent treatment a form of control that caused her endless frustration. And so, ten years on from Dad's promise, we were *still* travelling.

My parents had no friends, Dad not seeing the need – family being all that he required. For Mam this was tolerable, knowing that in the summer months she could enjoy the company and shared confidences of her sisters-in-law Marie and Charlotte. There was a bond between the three women and despite the end-of-year departures, it was easily and effortlessly reconnected every summer.

For my part, this 'catch up'was not quite so easy. My pals, primarily the boys, were growing up and developing new interests that did not include me. My two other cousins, Irene and Rosina Wilmot, did not travel to many of the same grounds as us, their family leaving our route part way through the summer to open in the 'black isles'. I was never sure where this was. It sounded so exotic and seemed miles away but was actually the Ross and Cromarty area of Scotland.

My friendships were reduced to specific fairs that coincided with any remaining cousins, plus a few traveller girls of a similar age, and the transient lifestyle did not allow for the development of school friends, either summer or winter.

Mam worried constantly that I might be lonely, especially during the winters, and made sure that I was always happily engaged in something, ensuring that there was always reading and art materials, teaching me to knit, and just talking to me.

Winters were miserable for her. There were no family members on the Seafield ground, the majority now based on various sites in Glasgow. In the absence of any other female companionship she increasingly looked to me as her confidante. I became the receptacle for every wistful longing for her old life, and also her fears for our future. Without realising it and quite unintentionally, she was creating an anxious, worried child. The stories of losing her mother, her own heart condition and her belief that she would also die young, terrified me. Whenever she was unwell I was convinced that it was something terminal.

These were not fears I could ever share with Dad; in fact, I could not recall any actual 'proper' conversations with him. His dialogue revolved around things that he felt most comfortable with – primarily showbusiness, or how much of a nuisance the Albion was becoming. He preferred to watch, listen and occasionally offer a brief comment.

Not that he was uncaring or unloving… just awkward with any dialogue of a grown-up nature. I often felt that *I* was more grown up than Dad and began to resent his lack of attention to Mam's misery.

FORTY-TWO

It was now 1955 and events continued to capture attention and offer distractions. We were spoiled for choice with films that year, which included 'The Colditz Story', 'The Dam Busters', 'Geordie' and countless Westerns; the papers carried stories of the heatwave and resulting drought; Winston Churchil resigned due to ill health; the polio vaccine was introduced in Britain; Alexander Fleming the bacteriologist died, as did Ruth Ellis – the last woman to be hanged in Britain; a state of emergency was declared in Cyprus as EOKA terrorists declared war on British rule; the Ark Royal aircraft carrier was launched.

The world was not standing still yet, for my family life continued to follow the same predictable yearly pattern of winters on Seafield and summers travelling from town to town, some fairs giving a small profit, others running at a loss, with never a chance to get ahead financially.

Dad was fighting a losing battle with the Albion, its engine seeming to require attention weekly. The idea that it might break down completely was too awful to consider. This was not just a form of transport, it was our home *and* our business. Everything we owned, little though that was, including the stalls and equipment, was packed into – and on top of – it. Somehow, usually aided by his brothers – especially Tommy, who was a proficient mechanic – Dad managed to keep us mobile.

'I don't think it will see another summer. To be fair, it was quite old when we bought it ten years ago so it doesn't owe us anything.'

Dad had just finished another repair to the engine and was trying to wash the oil from his hands. I watched, fascinated by the lines of black cracks appearing in the bar of soap as he tried to coax it into a lather, the water in the basin already like ink.

As Mam handed him a towel, she looked at me and I could almost read her thoughts. Without the Albion we could no longer travel and Dad would have to agree – at long last – to settle down.

He dried his hands, still not entirely clean and continued, 'We'll get the summer over, go back in for the winter and I'll look for something else.'

'What do you mean – *something else*?'

Normally soft-spoken, Mam's voice now had an edge I had not heard before. 'You *know* how we are fixed and what will be happening later this year.' She seemed to be talking in code, glancing quickly at me then back to Dad.

My stomach lurched, her reference to some 'later event' scaring me. She had been sick a few times in the last few weeks and I remembered her telling me of the awful bouts of sickness her mother suffered before she died. Was this to be what I most dreaded and was she going to die and leave me, just like her own mother?

I had been sitting on the floor playing with Flash and grabbed him round the neck, hugging him for comfort.

'It's nice outside. Why don't you take Flash to the beach?'

Mam obviously wanted to continue her talk with Dad in private and I was glad of the chance to escape. I did not want to hear awful words that would confirm my fears.

We were at Burntisland, the fair was pitched on the Links and the beach was just yards away, accessed through a tunnel that ran under the Fife railway line.

A miniature train skirted the boundary wall, passengers sitting astride the little carriages while the driver blew the whistle and drove them down the short track to the paddling pools and swings. Normally I would have enjoyed watching this, and also the activity of throwing sticks into the sea for Flash to retrieve, but worry overshadowed everything. Not even the view of Inchkeith island, 'our island' that could be seen from Seafield and somehow symbolised home – Edinburgh just being across the Forth – comforted me.

I remembered overhearing a conversation Mam was having that day with my aunts Charlotte and Marie.

Marie –'But *surely* Jean must have noticed *something*?'

Mam – 'No… she's too young.'

Charlotte – 'Well, you can't hide it forever and you'll have to tell her soon.'

Marie – 'Aye and you can't blame it on the new potatoes!'

The three women laughed. I failed to understand the last remark but clearly there was a secret not yet shared with me, only serving to add to my worries.

I delayed heading home for as long as possible, dreading being told of some awful event, anticipating a future without Mam, the possibility of some horrible stepmother and a life of constant drudgery.

Flash was now becoming bored and beginning to growl and bristle for a fight as he noticed some dogs approaching so I reluctantly walked back to the ground with Flash, rankling at not being allowed another battle, following me.

Mam, Marie and Charlotte were sitting in the shade on the Albion steps, the two aunts smoking and Mam sipping a glass of water. Dad was nowhere to be seen.

'Well… now's as good a time as any to tell her, Winnie.' Marie stood up, flicked her cigarette away and smoothed the front of her apron, nodding her head sideways at Charlotte to indicate they should leave.

Mam looked at me and sipped some more water. For someone who could talk on any subject, she was obviously having some difficulty choosing her words and the few seconds she took seemed an eternity to me. Was this *the* moment? The time I had always dreaded and of all my nightmares? Was she about to say she was dying?

'How would you like to have a wee brother or sister?' She gazed at me, unsure of my reaction, fearing that as an only child for almost ten years I might resent a sibling.

My face must have been a study. This was so unexpected and without realising it, I had been holding my breath and was almost at fainting point. The relief I felt was overwhelming. We were to have a birth rather than a death, and all I could blurt out was, 'Can we still keep Flash?'

Mam laughed and cuddled me. I could hear Dad whistling happily nearby, the sun still shone, a terrible weight had been lifted from my young shoulders and life felt so good again. Being an only child had never troubled me and the role of 'big sister' I viewed with some excitement, already picturing the new sibling able to walk, talk and play endless games.

Pregnancy offered no respite for travellers' wives and they still had to help with the business as well as run their homes. Women carried on as usual and being pampered through pregnancies was never their expectation. They did exactly as their mothers had done, working alongside their husbands until their babies were born.

Mindful of her previous miscarriages, Mam no longer helped to lift the heavy shutters or carry water cans, but she still had to mind the darts joint under the watchful eye of Dad. Her pinnys were now substituted for pretty cotton smocks, which were extremely practical, having pockets for the change and also concealing the ever-growing bump.

She breathed a sigh of relief when that summer ended safely, we were back on Seafield and she was booked into the Eastern General maternity hospital nearby.

Two weeks before her due date, Dad arranged for me to stay at Granny's. They were based on a ground at Falkirk and all I can remember of my stay was extreme home-sickness. I was with my extended family – grandparents, aunts, uncles and cousins – yet felt alone. I missed my parents and Flash, my home, the safety and reassurance of familiar routines. The Stirlings seemed unable to see me as a scared, anxious child who needed words of comfort. They were not unfeeling, just had different priorities – and show-business came first.

In a large family where childbirth was not a novelty – just a temporary blip and sometimes an inconvenience – I was only a temporary 'added extra' to be given bed and board until reclaimed by Dad.

'It's a boy!' Dad proudly announced to everyone when he came to collect me. 'You've got a wee brother now,' he said, looking at me for some reaction.

At that point I couldn't have cared less. All I wanted to do was get home and see Mam.

As of November 1955 we had become a family of four and within just a few weeks it seemed that the baby, to be called Richard (after Dad) and John (after Mam's dad), had always been with us. Any fears my parents may have had regarding mine or Flash's reaction to this newcomer were quickly allayed. We were both besotted with this tiny blonde-haired, blue-eyed addition to our family. Flash instantly took on a protective role, every sniffle or whimper requiring him to check the baby. Any visitor had to first get past Flash, who kept a close watchful guard, much as a bitch would with her puppies.

Mam attended the baby clinics regularly and was always anxious when they measured his head with a tape. The nurse explained that this was the procedure after a forceps birth and was just a precautionary check, but Mam worried constantly.

That winter, she was so caught up with baby care that she scarcely had time to notice Dad 'making other arrangements' for the Albion.

Dad had been away for almost a day with Tommy and John, saying they were just going to look at a lorry. They arrived back with a single-decker bus, Dad proudly announcing that they had been to Falkirk and 'got a good deal' from the Alexander bus company.

It probably *had* been a reasonable price; Alexander's were happy to sell to showmen, knowing the vehicles would not be used by any rival bus companies.

Mam was dismayed, realising that she had heard Dad's assurances of 'good deals' before – and in any case, no deal was a *good* deal if they couldn't afford it in the first place. She was tired. The baby had been restless all night and was still fractious.

'But we're just about living at subsistence level now,' she snapped, not meaning to sound quite as waspish or dampen enthusiasms.

'How did you manage to pay for it?' Almost before she had asked the question she knew the answer. 'Rosie loaned you the money, didn't she?'

Dad avoided eye contact and rammed his hands into his dungaree pockets, and for a moment she thought he was about to go into one of his silent moods again.

'It wasn't much and I'll pay her back next summer. A couple of good gaffs will do it.'

Assuming Mam's silence to be assent, he left her to join the group of men gathered round the bus, keen to join the debate on its price, reliability and potential lifespan.

Mam sat in the Albion, her despair almost palpable as she picked the baby up for its next feed. She was almost past caring now, knowing any argument was pointless. Her hope that the Albion's demise would force Dad's hand had been foiled by Rosie, who seemed determined at any cost to keep them mobile and stop Dad from settling down.

Yet somehow – especially with a baby boy now – she *had* to make it happen.

FORTY-THREE

During those winter months, assisted by his brothers, Dad spent every available hour converting the bus. His first task had been to disconnect the conductor's bell, my enjoyment at pushing the button quickly curtailed with his explanation that it would wake the baby.

Alexander's had removed the passenger seats prior to sale and Dad set about partitioning the interior into compartments. The front section immediately behind the cab was to house the dynamo, which powered the stall lights. This section had an access hatch in the floor that Dad explained would allow him to reach and drop the engine drive shaft when running the dynamo. Mam and I nodded our heads as though we fully understood the intricacies of the lighting system, both of us in awe of Dad's knowledge.

The next compartment was my parents' bedroom, just big enough to take their bed, dressing table and the baby's cot. Their room must only have been around six feet in length as there was no space between the head and foot partitions, the bed squeezed tightly against both 'walls'.

The interior of the bus was just over eight feet wide and there was very little space for storage. The dressing table drawers were solely for mine and the baby's clothes, while the few belongings my parents owned were kept in two suitcases and stored under the metal bed-frame.

Beyond the bedroom partition was the living area, and I was delighted to discover that I was to have a bed rather than the bedchair. This was an ingenious device built over the bus wheelbase that functioned as a couch during the day, the base – a series of wooden interlocking slats – pulling out to the size of a reasonable single bed. The space below housed all the bedding and even Mam had to admire the design and workmanship. All windows on the right-hand side of the bus had been covered over with hardboard panelling and a couple of cupboards were added, which held our pots, dishes and foodstuffs. Finally, the hostess stove was manhandled with great difficulty from the Albion and fixed in place, a hole having been cut in the roof of the bus to take the chimney pipe.

The vehicle was now habitable apart from the wooden paneling, which required some paint. Uncle John was a skilled painter, often called on by showmen to embelish their shutters etc with fancy scrolls and artwork. He suggested that rather than just slapping on a coat of paint (which was often Dad's technique), a woodgrain effect would be better.

Dad watched carefully as his brother demonstrated this on a small area of wood, first applying a special paint, then while still wet, running a hard-bristled brush down it, creating the illusion of knot holes and grains.

He left Dad to complete the job but hours later the 'grain' just looked like a mustard-coloured streaky accident. Dad was quite pleased with the work and Uncle John had no heart to tell him it was awful.

Mam was more philosophical, decreeing that a couple of coats of darker varnish would finish the job and somehow, once windows were cleaned and curtains fitted, and there was the aroma of food cooking on the stove, the place started to feel like home.

While the bus might have been more reliable mechanically, ironically the Albion had offered more storage space, and Dad had to fix brackets and holding boards on top of the roof in order to load the stall's shutters, poles, tilts etc. Smaller items were squeezed into the dynamo compartment behind the cab.

Dad's final task before the bus took its maiden voyage that spring was to paint the bodywork and remove the Alexander logos. There was no choice of colour, just an old tin of maroon Valspar paint he'd found in his parent's lorry, which he managed to eke out with the help of some thinner, and this time his artistic efforts were passable.

The old Albion, now emptied and stripped of any salvageable wood was no longer recogniseable as my home, yet I still felt sad, knowing it was destined for the scrapyard. It seemed akin to an old horse being taken to the the knacker's yard (but perhaps I was just in 'Calamity Jane mode' again!.)

The bus before any modification

(We had no photographs of the 'revamped' bus so this is my illustration)
'Modified' with maroon paint, roof storage and end door

Many years later on the Craigmillar yard, sadly waiting to be scrapped.

Starting out time saw the usual traditional flurry of the men starting, checking and fussing over their lorries. This time, however, to Dad's delight, with no requirement for the 'one- two -hupp' of the starting handle, the bus engine roared to life.

Regardless of all the work she and Dad had put into transforming the bus, Mam still considered it to be a stopgap arrangement. No matter how many times she had to tolerate Dad's moods or Rosie's interference, a settled life remained her target and she was determined, however long it might take, to make that happen.

FORTY-FOUR

Our 'start-out' followed the same yearly pattern, the first fair being at Hamilton and always coinciding with Easter.

My cousins and other traveller children were excitedly anticipating the various boxes of chocolate eggs they hoped to receive, but this was of little interest to me. I was totally engrossed with my baby brother, now four months old, and taking great delight in being entrusted with his care.

The hard-packed red ash surface and footpaths around the tennis courts and putting green were ideal for pushing the pram and I would occasionally be stopped by any traveller women who had not yet seen the new arrival.

Admiring the baby, some would pop a coin – which had to be silver 'for luck', under his pillow – usually a shilling but sometimes a half-crown. I would arrive home with our loot and try to describe to Mam, since I invariably did not know their names, which woman had paid us their 'lucky piece'.

Mam, always the worrier, warned me never to leave the ground, her concern for our safety only assuaged by the knowledge that Flash was with us and would ensure our protection without fail.

I could never wander too far from home in any case, since – with what I felt was monotonous regularity – the baby had to be breast-fed. One well-meaning woman, witnessing the process and assuming its inconvenience, advised Mam that she should feed him with oyster milk. It puzzled me how on earth oysters could be milked until Mam explained that the woman was mispronouncing a brand of powdered baby formula called Ostermilk! This became a joke between Mam and I that lasted for ages... milk from oysters indeed! Dad didn't see the humour.

Friday night opening always held an element of uncertainty. This was the start of the season for us, and as well as the worry of minding the joints and hoping punters would spend this year, the logistics of caring for a baby while we were opened were of concern. It was arranged that I helped Dad while Mam took the baby in for his feed, then once he was settled in his cot, it was my job to babysit. My parents would take turns roughly every half hour to leave the joint and come round to the bus to check we were alright.

This arrangement worked fairly well, partly because the joints weren't very busy. Every fair had 'crowd-pullers' (i.e. the large machines), which in our case were the yachts that were positioned at the foot of the ground and almost opposite our stalls.

Unfortunately that Friday the yachts had broken down, which meant fewer punters drifting our way. These machines were a rarity on fairgrounds by the fifties and I only ever remember seeing one at Hamilton. In earlier years they had been converted from steam to electric power and possibly the makeovers had caused problems.

Either way, the owner worked tirelessly to repair them and by Saturday they were working again and drawing the crowds, much to the nearby stallholders' relief.

Reassured now that the child-minding arrangements had worked, I was trusted to be left in charge that night while Mam and Dad stood 'out front' in the joints, trying to earn some money while the crowds were still there.

The fairground was brightly lit, which made the areas behind the stalls seem exceptionally dark. I'd read all my comics and had given up trying to listen to the wireless; the interference caused by the bus engine had reduced the signal to a crackle.

Richard was asleep, having been settled in his cot earlier by Mam along with her assurances that she would check on us later. I sat at the window, listening to the screams of punters on the yachts as the two boats swung back and forth. I could never understand why people happily paid good money to be scared witless.

I watched the tips of the boats just beyond the canvas tops of our joints as each one alternately appeared, then disappeared as they seesawed up and

A good example of the fairground yachts

down. In my ten-year-old imagination, I pictured them to be the soles of a giant's boots as he tried to climb over the tops of our stalls.

I was jolted back to reality by a sense of some movement at the back of our joint.

It was not uncommon for drunks to urinate and sometimes defacate behind the stalls, and occasionally couples took advantage of the darkness to indulge in some passion-fuelled groping. The behaviour always disgusted me, and I wondered how those people would like *us* to shit and copulate in their gardens or pee on their front doors.

I closed the curtains, realising that whoever was outside might see me at the window. Satisfied that Richard was still sleeping, I checked the time and was dismayed that it was still only 9pm – the fair would be open until midnight. I was bored. I poked the fire for the umpteenth time, adding more coal, then tried the wireless again, hoping for a play or some interesting programme. Nothing – just the same irritating crackle. I sat at the window again and pulled back the little curtains, hoping that Mam or Dad might appear… then my stomach lurched. There was still someone out there in the darkness and too near the window for comfort. I snatched at the curtains, almost pulling them off the wire as I tried to close them. I wondered how long the person might have been watching – the interior of our bus clearly illuminated in the darkness.

I moved away from the window, my heart pounding, then realised that the curtain on our door window was still open. Reaching up to close it, I glimpsed the face of the person, a man, who was now standing at the foot of our little wooden steps.

'Will you open the door just for a minute? I just want to ask you something.'

From my experience of being in the joints, especially after 10pm when the pubs closed, I was familiar with the sounds of noisy drunks, but this man did not seem drunk – quite the reverse. His voice was controlled and he sounded polite as he continued, 'I only want to find something out… if I can speak to you for a minute.'

Now he was quiet, possibly waiting for some response from me. Our bus was only about six feet from the back of our joint, yet with no way to alert my parents, it might just as well have been miles away.

Sitting on the floor, my back against the door, I strained to listen for any sound above the familiar noise of the fair that might indicate that he was still there.

I had to *do* something. I had total responsibility for the safety of my baby brother and the instinct to protect him took precedence over my fears. I gazed around the bus, reassuring myself that the man could not get through the windows, which were all sealed, the small ventilator slides too small for anyone to climb through. I turned to check that the snib was on the door, then realised that this was the flimsiest of fastenings, Dad's logic being that no-one would ever break into our place – after all, we had nothing worth stealing!

I decided that a barricade was needed and hauled our gate-leg table against the door. The little red formica-topped table was used for everything. It was an improvised ironing board, nappy-changing and baby bathing table as well as Mam's writing table. Now it would be part of my defence system, its flaps banging noisily against its frame as I dragged it across the floor. I listened again for any sound outside, conscious of my heart pounding and my breathing erratic from fear and exertion.

Deciding that more weight was needed, I placed Mam's two heavy flat irons on top of the table, reckoning that if necessary, they could be useful weapons.

Worried now that I might have wakened the baby, I checked that he was still sleeping then crouched down on the floor next to the cot and waited, watching the clock, listening for the man's voice, desperate for my vigil to end.

The door rattled and I almost cried with relief when I heard my mother's voice.

'Jean, love, what on earth are you doing? I can't get in. Are you alright in there?'

She could hear the table rattling as I dragged it away from the door.

'Oh Mam,' I gasped, scarcely able to catch my breath. 'There was a man outside and I was scared. He kept asking me to open the door, but I didn't... honest.' She could see that I was upset and her expression changed from concern for me, to worry and anger at what might have happened.

'Thank goodness you didn't. Did you see the man? What did he look like?'

I had to confess that I had only glimpsed his head, and even then it was hard to think of a description. I struggled to think of anything that might offer a resemblance.

'He had a hairstyle the same as that film star you like... you know, Robert Taylor.'

Mam understood what I meant. This particular American movie star had a pronounced 'widow's peak' hairline. She cuddled me then made sure the baby slept.

'Now don't you worry, pet. There's no-one outside now but I'll get your Dad and we'll check again. Snib the door shut and when we come back, this will be how you know it is us.' She illustrated this by giving a pattern of four knocks on the door. 'Don't open it to anyone else. You did really well...good lass.'

Despite her reassurances I realised how worried she must have been when she returned minutes later with Dad. This was 'gaff night' – the busiest time and the one chance to earn some money, yet they had left the joint to make sure we were alright.

'Your mammy told me what happened. It was probably just a drunk and there's nobody out there now. We'll be closed in a wee while but I've brought Flash in to keep you company.'

This was a real concession on Dad's part, Flash always being in the joint at opening times and a very real deterrent if ever there were problems with punters. Dad hated confrontations and only needed to point to Flash for any

Robert Taylor

Peter Manuel

potential protaganists to back off. Flash, who hated the sound of the engine running, was hauled reluctantly into the bus, where he sat quivering like a jelly for the remainder of that night.

Easter Sunday, sunshine and chocolate eggs meant my fears of the previous night were forgotten. Mam, however, had decided that we would never again be in that situation and for the rest of the summer, I was 'out front' with my parents and helping in the joints. Richard was always cosily tucked up in his pram inside the darts joint, under the watchful eye of Mam.

In 1958 newspapers carried the story and photograph of Peter Manuel, the Lanarkshire mass murderer, his victims including children and families spanning several years between 1956 and 1958.

I gazed at the photograph, horrified.

'You see Mam, the Robert Taylor hairstyle!'

Could he have been the 'prowler' at Hamilton that year or was it just a childhood fantasy? Certainly Manuel was active around Lanarksire at that time, but as Mam pointed out, many people had the widow's peak hairline, including women, and drunks were more commonplace at the fairs than mass murderers. I noticed, nevertheless, that Mam no longer enjoyed Robert Taylor films and I often wondered whether she had actually considered the Hamilton incident a 'near miss'.

FORTY-FIVE

'Aww… the pair wee sowl, dae ye keep him here awl night?'

The woman was so drunk she could scarcely stand, let alone throw a dart, and Mam had refused to serve her. Behind her stood two small children, one crying, tugging at her coat and asking to go home. The other child clutched a half-eaten toffee apple as though it was a treasured posession, his face smeared with its stickiness and unwiped snots. It was now around 10pm, the fair having been open since lunchtime, and a cold night, yet neither child had a coat or warm clothing and both were shivering.

The woman tried to lean across the shutter to look at Richard, who was sleeping in his pram, fed, warm and secure. Flash quickly intervened and the woman stepped back then tripped over her child, cursing the youngster for getting in her way. She staggered off, clearly not yet intending to leave the fair, the pathetic figures of the two children following her as they disappeared into the crowds.

Mam was furious. The idea that this awful woman was judging *her*, assuming the baby was kept out overnight in the joint like a dog in a kennel. How dare she? Especially when her *own* drunken parenting 'skills' clearly left much to be desired. Relating the event to Dad, he laughed – joking that it was quite a good idea and would save them a few sleepless nights when Richard refused to settle!

Fairgrounds during the day tended to be very family-orientated but some took on a different, sometimes menacing atmosphere at night, especially when the pubs closed. Generally, the drunks, usually men, were good-humoured and spent probably more than they could afford at the joints.

There was one occasion, however, when a punter decided to show off to his companions, and saw Mam as fair game. He was deliberately misfiring the darts, some landing amongst the few bits of glassware prizes she had carefully tried to display. He had also been running a 'tab', promising to pay after the next 'shot', yet no money was forthcoming.

After his fourth game and now owing Mam two shillings (it was 6d. per game) he refused to stump up and made to leave, saying the game was rubbish and so were the prizes.

He hadn't reckoned on Mam's tenacity. She was determined not to let him think he was getting away with it and her anger spurred her into action. She grabbed the man by his necktie, catching him off-balance and almost pulling him over the shutter as she brandished a set of darts, the points just inches from his nose.

'You will pay me what you owe or I'll stick these arrows somewhere you won't like!'

By now, Flash had appeared and was ready to sort the man out if needs be. Dad was unaware of the drama unfolding, his back turned and concentrating on the can joint, which was busy.

'Pay up or else!'

Realising that she meant business and also intimidated by Flash, who with hackles raised was edging towards him and growling, he produced a half crown (2/6d) which was 6d. more than he owed. His friends were now mocking him, enjoying the scene.

'And I hope you won't be expecting any change,' Mam snapped, taking the coin and letting go of his tie.

As the man and his cronies left, Dad – now less busy – realised he had missed something and was mortified to hear Mam describe her vigilante approach to cash collection. He expressed genuine concern, telling her never to resort to such means again as she could have been injured. Secretly though, he was so proud that she had stood her ground and would re-tell the story of her ability to deal with awkward punters many times. Mam, however, felt ashamed and degraded by her actions, realising her retaliation – despite provocation – might have had serious consequences.

There seldom was any real trouble at any of the grounds, but on the odd occasion it happened, assistance was always at hand. Somehow, word would get round the fair that there was a problem and potentially a row at one of the stalls, and within minutes there would be several showmen arriving, watching and prepared to intervene.

I witnessed this a couple of times, a crowd of punters giving a stallholder a hard time only to back off at the sight of the traveller 'posse' arriving. This self-policing facility was essential, since often 'rozzers' would only be seen at closing times, their presence just to ensure the fair finished at the contracted time.

Communal assistance was also offered if ever the lighting systems failed in any of the shows. Once or twice our joint was plunged into darkness when the dynamo decided to be temperamental. All the nearby showmen came round to help and when the problem could not be resolved quickly, a 'tap on' to someone else's lorry was arranged and within minutes, our lights were on again. This was not entirely altruistic since any stall without illumination was almost like a gap site in the row of joints and impacted on neighbouring showmen's ability to attract punters.

I always admired the knowledge, ingenuity and improvising skills of the travellers, including Dad. The men had engineering, electrical and joinery talents that could match the work of any journeyman, this knowledge seldom obtained from books but rather passed down from father to son.

Dad could tackle anything and was a hard worker, taking on tasks or projects with an almost obsessive diligence, often to the exclusion of anything else. He seemed to lack the ability to relax and just enjoy life… there was invariably something else 'to do'. He also had a habit of never throwing anything away, and picking things up – a screw, piece of wood, hinge etc, assuring us that it 'would come in handy'.

We ended up with a box full of bits and pieces, some of which, despite my view that it was all just junk, did come in handy when any repairs were required on our aging stalls, thus justifying Dad's salvaging talents.

There was no doubt that our joints were not crowd-pullers. They were already old and not particularly well maintained when Dad first bought them. Standing alongside some of the other beautifully painted and much newer stalls, ours were almost slumlike.

Our lack of 'kerb appeal' was exacerbated by the fact that almost every other joint was now either darts or cans, so competition was rife.

'How do you fancy drawing me a couple of big palm trees?' At first I thought Dad was joking until he explained his idea. 'Well, coconuts and palm trees go together, don't they? The can joint needs a bit of a tidy up. I was thinking we could have a palm tree at either side of the coconut display.' Now really carried

Can joint bedecked with 'triffids'

away with his vision of Tropicana, he continued, 'And maybe you could paint some hills or scenery on the big tin sheet at the back?'

I was flattered that he set so much store by my artistic ability, agreeing to do it, and the next day we set to. I traced the outline of what I thought resembled a palm tree onto a couple of sheets of hardboard, which Dad then patiently cut out using a fretsaw. I painted them and then tackled the 'scenic mountains', both tasks somewhat challenging my artistic muse, having only three tins of paint – blue, yellow and white.

The end product resembled two triffids about to invade the Alps, but Dad thought it was great and Mam praised my efforts. Uncle John, the artist of the family, joked that he didn't know palm trees grew in Switzerland. I was just so happy that he at least recognised the 'triffids' as palm trees!

FORTY-SIX

Each return to my winter school at Leith Links Primary served only to remind me that I was falling further and further behind academically. The dreaded 11+ exam was fast approaching and I knew that I stood no chance of passing, despite Mam's faith in me. We had already left Edinburgh when the exams were due to take place and I was so relieved to be missing them… but Mam had other plans.

When we were at Wishaw, I stood in a musty telephone box with her while she obtained the number for Links School, and once connected, asked to speak to the headmaster. I prayed that he would not be available but he answered immediately.

I listened, mortified, as she explained who we were and her concern that I would not be in Edinburgh for the exam. She asked – almost pleaded – that I be given some alternative date or location, or even exemption based on my 'ability'. I cringed, picturing the headmaster's reaction as he sat patiently listening to the comments of an over-ambitious mother, and I silently willed him to say no.

Exams and tests terrified me and I knew that I would never pass any of the required subjects. I have no recollection of ever receiving report cards, but had I done so they must surely have recorded my shortcomings – yet Mam's faith in me was unswerving. Her hope was that I would gain a place at Leith Academy, a Senior Secondary School with a 'gold star' academic reputation and many pupils becoming university graduates.

The poor headmaster realised that Mam was trying to secure an academic future for me as she pleaded my case and I suspect that he did not have the heart to tell her that I had no hope of meeting the grades. Instead, he offered his apologies and said that a delayed date was not possible, but that I would still be 'streamed' into the appropriate secondary school even without my 11+ qualification.

As we walked back to the ground, Mam, possibly assuming I was disappointed at not being allowed to earn my place, felt the need to reassure me.

'Never mind, pet. There's many a person made the grade without any of those exams. Look at Albert Einstein – he didn't read until he was seven and was even expelled from school. And Winston Churchill.' Mam looked at me, assuming that I was familiar with the histories of these men, and continued, 'He was rubbish at his school, always bottom of his class and struggled with exams, but he was a bit like you because he enjoyed the art classes and was good at English. So it doesn't matter which secondary school you go to… you'll get through with flying colours because, just like those men, you are already clever!'

While not appreciating the role-model examples of two old men – one fat, bald and cigar smoking, the other resembling a wild-haired eccentric professor – I appreciated her belief in my ability and just hoped that it was justified.

We all sat cross-legged on the Links Primary gym hall floor as the secondary school allocations were read out. The highest achievers were placed at Leith Academy, which had been Mam's dream school for me, then various other schools were gradually announced until just two or three children, including me, waited. Finally our names were announced with the statement that we were being placed at a school called David Kilpatricks, known as DK's for short.

In the playground later, everyone was excitedly comparing notes on who was going where, some delighted that their pals would be at the same school, others almost preening themselves in the satisfaction of achieving a premier league school.

'So where are *you* being sent?' a girl demanded as she spotted me sitting on the small wall that divided the two playgrounds.

I had never particularly cared for this girl and usually tried to avoid her. Not that she was a bully, just a bit of a prig and even worse now that she knew she would be a Leith Academy pupil. I could already picture her in the smart blue blazer, which would probably sport a prefect's badge at some point later. I did not really want to discuss my academic future with her but she stood in front of me waiting for an answer.

'David Kilpatricks Senior Secondary School,' I replied, trying to make it sound grand. She laughed and turned to a couple of her pals who had now joined her.

'Of course. You *know* what DK stands for?' She was obviously armed with some exclusive information that she now intended to enjoy sharing publicly.

I shook my head, ignorant of any local folklore and not enjoying this attention.

'DAFT KIDS SCHOOL,' she responded and ran off, probably destined for a future career in the diplomatic service, her fellow prigs in tow.

I felt humiliated and wondered how on earth I was going to tell Mam that I had apparently drawn the educational short straw.

FORTY-SEVEN

'It doesn't look *too* bad,' Mam assured me as we stood outside the school.

I was due to register on Monday and we had taken an exploratory trip to check its location, which buses to take, and how long it might take me to get there. Mam needed to be sure that I would be alright to travel alone. The requirement to make the journey by bus – and now with a baby – made it impossible for her to accompany me as she had done throughout my primary school years. I would be flying solo and she feared for my safety despite my assurances that I would be alright.

It was Saturday morning and a few boys were kicking a ball around in the large playground, their voices and the thud of the ball echoing around the building.

It was much larger than my primary school. We read the board outside, which stated it had been built in 1915 then been immediately requisitioned as a barracks. I half-expected to see ghosts of WW1 veterans at the windows. The place scared me; its appearance seemed more akin to an institution of penal servitude than one of learning.

We had been given a leaflet, describing among other things uniform requirements, which fortunately for us were not too prohibitive, the basic expectation being that at least one item of clothing should have the school colours.

Mam found a stockist nearby and bought me a scarf with the appropriate maroon and turquoise stripes, then, realising that I would have a considerable number of books to carry, suggested that we should shop for a new school bag.

David Kilpatrick Secondary School, North Junction Street, Leith

I knew that we really could not afford this.

'Aw Mam… only wee kids have schoolbags. Can I not just have one of those?' I pointed to a boy who had a khaki canvas bag with webbing strap slung nonchalantly over his shoulder. This looked so cool and grown-up to me. She was not impressed, remembering Dad's army equipment.

'That's an army gas mask holder. You surely don't want one of those?'

I pleaded my case, saying how much cheaper than a traditional school bag it would probably be, the amount of books it could carry etc. Despite her misgivings, we found an Army and Navy store and I was now equipped for secondary academia, the proud owner of the school scarf and a khaki gas mask bag.

The journey home felt strange and everything felt different somehow, as though some fearful thing was about to happen. We passed Leith Academy and I tried not to look at Mam in case she appeared disappointed. Then, at the foot of the Links – my primary school and it seemed unthinkable that I would never go back there.

It had been my one constant, albeit only a winter school, and a place that was familiar and safe. Now I would have to face yet another change and in an enviroment that was new and potentially threatening.

'You'll be alright, love.' Mam must have read my thoughts and squeezed my hand by way of reassurance, yet probably she felt just as anxious as me.

That first day at DK's was awful. To reach the girl's section it was necessary to walk up a lane past the boy's playground. We ran the gauntlet of their cat-calls as they clung to the metal railings, some shouting a mix of obscenities and also invitations to explore some 'social interactions' behind the toilets.

Hearing the backchat from some of the third-year girls, I gathered that some 'invitations' had already been previously accepted. This daily rat-run experience was either not noticed or ignored by teachers and I was never aware of any visible adult intervention. It just became a fact of school life that this would happen each day and I became so used to the routine and behaviour that I no longer noticed it.

If never particularly interested in schoolwork at primary level, I was even less so at secondary. The David Kilpatrick school operated a streaming system. Those who were deemed still to be educationally salvageable were 'C' (for commercial) category and were taught subjects that would prepare them for office work. The 'D' (for domestic) category offered none of this. We were the also-rans, being primed for domesticity, attending classes on baking scones (mine were always like biscuits), sewing drindle skirts (I was never sure what this was) and how to bath a baby. The 'baby' class was taken by the school nurse who demonstrated the procedure step by step, using a plastic doll, flannel and bath of soapy water.

Little did she know that I was already an expert, having helped to bathe my baby brother several times. I often wondered whether her time might have been better spent explaining how babies were made in the first place, especially when later spotting two pregnant third-year girls who probably had enjoyed the toilet block education just a little too enthusiastically.

Another class involved us being marched to a house that bordered the playground and being split into two groups, one allocated to weeding the garden, the other group to dusting and polishing all the furniture inside the house. This felt to me like cheap labour and a pointless activity, especially since I did not even live in a house.

It was a miserable time and I hated DK just as much as I had loved Links Primary. There was absolutely no comparison – the teachers at primary school had seemed genuinely interested in their charges and were skilled at encouraging pupils to do their best. DK, on the other hand, was like a prison – pupils as inmates and staff whose sole duty seemed to me to be the daily containment and control of us.

One teacher, who took the English class, was an absolute tyrant who terrified everyone and seemed to delight in giving miscreants the strap. (The leather belt, known as a 'tawse', was commonly used as a punishment and deterrent in

The dreaded tawse

Scottish schools, not being finally abolished until 1987.) Fortunately, English was a fairly safe subject for me and I managed to escape her potential wrath.

Teachers had their favourite belts, some with two thongs, others with three, and it was a common sight for the leather monstrosity to be displayed on the teacher's desk in full view of the class as a warning.

I *did* receive the humiliation and pain of the strap once, and through no fault of mine. Mam needed to catch the early turn at Portobello wash-house, leaving me in charge of Richard. Dad had already left for work and Mam was late back, causing me to miss my usual bus, resulting in a lengthy wait before the next one.

Arriving at the foot of Leith Walk, I jumped off the bus before it had even stopped, ignoring the conductor's rebuke as I raced along Great Junction Street. I felt sick with anxiety, my heart pounding, hoping as I ran that I might still reach the school before all the lines of pupils were marched inside. No such luck!

The playground was ominously empty apart from a few stragglers captured by the duty teacher and now coralled at the doorway. My legs turned to jelly as I realised that I had been spotted – the teacher, without speaking, pointing his finger in my direction and indicating that I should join the 'prisoners'.

He marched us to an empty classroom where, one by one, we were lined up to be punished. I was fourth in the line and waited, watching fearfully and hoping by some miracle that I might be spared as he wielded the belt.

There was a specific technique to receiving the belt, requiring the victim to hold both hands out, palms upward and one hand supporting the other. The belt was designed not to draw blood but rather to hurt, and one girl – who apparently was a habitual late-comer – received a 'double-hander', which meant first one hand was belted, then the supporting hand was placed uppermost to receive the same treatment.

The pain must have been awful yet she did not cry. In fact no-one cried, each one ahead of me submitting themselves to the punishment then rejoining our small line of victims. It seemed to be a sign of weakness to show the teacher that he had actually hurt them and I decided that I would have to follow suit.

The teacher was not interested in any excuses or even explanations of legitimate reasons for being late. I felt that it was pointless to plead my case and when it was my turn, held out my hands. The shock of the leather strap striking my outstretched palm, the pain, the burning sensation and the florid red mark on my hand stayed with me for most of that day. The humiliation, however ,was worse – having to go into my class late, all eyes on me and with the feeling that I had 'offender' stamped across my forehead.

I chose not to tell Mam that I'd been belted. I knew she would be upset and would blame herself for causing me to be late. Another reason for not telling my parents was my feeling of being ashamed. The strap had not only been painful but also felt degrading. The mark on my hand was nothing compared to my bruised psyche. Corporal punishment was unheard of in my family, and I had never been smacked or even spoken harshly to by my parents.

I could not fathom why anyone legally had the right to whip a child with a leather strap. Even criminals were entitled to fair hearings before punishments were decided. Being given the belt was tantamount to an assault and I found it difficult to think of any acceptable reason for an adult – especially a teacher – to believe such a barbaric punishment was justified.

The misery of that school was only tholed by the knowledge that I would leave each Spring.

FORTY-EIGHT

Winters on Seafield were different now. I delighted in having a baby brother and although the role of big sister brought child-minding responsibilities, I didn't care. I could share the excitement of Christmas surprises with him, telling him about this magical person Santa who would deliver wonderful presents; the annual Christmas party arranged by the Edinburgh travellers and held at the Inchview Ballroom in Portobello was an event I could now enjoy with him.

The presents wrapped by the committee members were gender-orientated and I always seemed to get either a little manicure set, or worse, a sewing kit. But now I had a little brother and *his* toys were wonderful, especially the silver six-shooter that could be loaded with gunpowder caps. (I just seemed permanently fixated with cowboys!)

It was so important to Mam that we had new clothes for the party and she took pride in the other women complimenting her on how well we were 'turned out'.

While money was always tight, somehow my parents always managed to ensure that our needs came first and that Christmas would always be a special time.

When Richard was three, however, I was forced to make 'the ultimate sacrifice'.

'Jean… we were just thinking that you have maybe outgrown your bike now?'

I was unsure whether Mam meant this to be a question or a statement of

Inchview Ballroom and all decked out for the Christmas party

fact. It was early December and my parents had been deep in conversation while I played on the floor with Flash. The bus was warm, we had just finished our tea and Richard was sleeping. Mam sat opposite Dad at the little gate-leg table and she seemed to be working out some calculations in the little Woolworths book she still kept faithfully for income and expenditure.

I tried to hide my mounting excitement, hoping her announcement might be a precursor to the promise of a new bike. My little two-wheeler was certainly just a bit on the small side now.

She looked at Dad and continued, 'How would you feel if we swapped it for one of the toys on your Uncle Walter's machine?'

I was dumbfounded. What could I possibly want with anything from the juvenile roundabout?

Mam realised that I was not really understanding what she had asked and checked that Richard was still sleeping before lowering her voice and continuing, 'You see pet, your dad and I want to give you both a nice Christmas but we need to try to economise.'

Her voice trailed off and she seemed to be struggling for her next sentence, looking to Dad for some support. I watched and waited as he took over the conversation.

'Your Uncle Walter said we could have one of the toy pedal cars from his machine for Richard, but that would leave a gap. He would take your wee bike as a replacement and fix it into the space left on the ride.'

My heart sank. My beloved bike – my make-believe Wild West horse, even motorbike when I stuck cardboard in the spokes to make a pretend engine noise – was being bartered by my parents.

They waited for my answer, clearly leaving the final decision to me. I was familiar with all the toys on the ride, having helped Uncle Walter during the summers. There were two Austin pedal cars, lovely things with proper blown-up tyres, a bonnet that opened, chrome hub caps and padded seats. Really a 'Rolls Royce' of pedal cars, albeit an Austin.

Any reluctance I may have had in surrendering my bike was negated by the thought of Richard getting one of *those* cars. I pictured him pedalling it along the broad Portobello promenade, or even the tree-lined footpath at Leith Links, with Flash and me trying to keep up. Already I was anticipating the fun we would have and to my parents' surprise, I readily agreed.

The 'swap' was arranged and I waited, excitement mounting, to see the replacement, then could scarcely conceal my disappointment when it arrived. Not the Austin – just an old tin car modelled to look like an army jeep. Khaki-coloured chipped paint, solid rubber wheels and a tin seat. I only vaguely remembered it being on the machine and doubted whether any child would have chosen to ride in it.

Uncle Walter's machine with one of the Austin cars

Dad could see from my expression that I did not consider this to be a satisfactory swap, and Mam – who had been watching, a conciliatory hand on my shoulder – seemed to share my view, requiring Dad to offer some reassurance.

'It looks a bit rough just now, but you can give me a hand to do it up and it'll be just like new. It will make a good present for Richard, and we will get you a bigger bike later on… honest.'

Mam realised that Dad was trying hard to make the best of a poor offering.

'By the time you and your dad have worked on it, the car will look so good your Uncle Walter will want it back.'

And so Dad and I spent the few weeks ahead of Christmas ensconced in the freezing front-end of our bus, away from Richard's toddler curiousity, as we repaired and painted the jeep. The end product, while not an absolute transformation, looked quite good. Now painted a glossy red with white wheels, seat and steering wheel, it awaited its Christmas debut.

Unfortunately, Richard was not impressed, being more interested in whatever might be in my parcels rather than the jeep, which stood forlornly outside.

'Why don't you take him out in it and let him pedal it around the ground?' Mam suggested, seeing our disappointment that the 'great reveal' Dad and I had looked forward to had not worked. For our sake, she needed Richard to at least appear to *like* his car, albeit he was too young to appreciate the pains we had taken.

He was lifted into the jeep and then we realised there was a problem. His little legs scarcely reached the pedals and he did not understand that he was supposed to propel and steer the thing himself.

The trial run ended in his frustrated tears and was abandoned. Over the next few days I tried to elicit some enthusiasm from him but to no avail. Since he was unable to pedal the car, I had to push and also steer the thing. The ground at Seafield was frozen and rutted, with no even surface to roll it gently along. My reluctant passenger protested at every bump, and I was not enjoying the sore back it caused as I bent over him to reach the steering wheel. For both of us, the vehicle had become a torturous instrument and I was so pleased when a few weeks later Mam suggested that the jeep be returned to Uncle Walter.

I had hoped that this would mean that I would get my bike back, but not so. In future summers, I tried not to seem bothered as I watched other children sit on *my* little bicycle while uncle Walter's machine whirled them round and round.

I did eventually get a second-hand adult-sized replacement bike and shared it with Dad, who needed transport to get to work. It never quite matched the fun and magic of the first… but perhaps I was just getting older.

FORTY-NINE

While winters were never easy, that particular Christmas seemed especially hard.

Dad had struggled to find a job, eventually picking up some labouring work on a building site. Unfortunately, every spell of bad weather resulted in him being laid off, which meant no pay. He tried to fill in his time by building a 'kitchen', which was really just a plywood shed that he somehow managed to nail together with wooden batons and then positioned on the platform. A door, a couple of windows and a few shelves completed his project. He assured Mam that he had obtained the materials by lawful means although she suspected they had come from the building site, bit by bit.

The end product was actually very handy, providing space to house the Calor gas tank, water cans, bucket and various pots and pans that took up space in the bus.

A little two-ring gas cooker was kept there with a whistling kettle to alert us when it was boiled, and this was also where any food with a particularly strong aroma (kippers etc) was cooked, thus avoiding lingering smells in our living area.

The kitchen also served as a bathroom, hot water from the kettle poured into a basin and ablutions hurriedly carried out in sub-zero temperatures. Richard, still too young for this exposure, enjoyed the luxury of baths in front of the hostess stove.

I, as a self-conscious thirteen-year-old, wanted some privacy and chose to use the 'kitchen'. This was fine until one evening, mid-way through my wash and in a state of undress, I heard someone coming up the steps.

Dad's 'kitchen'

I just managed to grab a towel and dash back into the bus before the door opened and Uncle Tommy walked in. Travellers never locked their doors and it was common practice for visitors just to arrive, with usually just a courtesy call of 'are ye in?' before opening the door.

I was mortified and also annoyed with Dad for omitting to put a snib on the kitchen door. He realised that it could just have easily been Mam who had been caught bathing and fitted a door catch the next day.

Mam and Dad were naïve when it came to any agency routes to financial help. The possibility of asking advice from the Social Security department was dismissed by Aunt Rosie, who stated that Dad had not put enough stamps on his books to qualify for payments. (It was a requirement that anyone self-employed purchased National Insurance stamps, and my folks had been unable to afford these with any regularity during the summer months.)

There may have been other forms of welfare assistance available but Dad believed Rosie's statement that they should steer clear of the 'Social' and accepted the offer of some hours helping her at the Waverley Market Winter Fair, which had just opened. (Every year thereafter, no matter how difficult things were financially, my parents did not seek help from any of the welfare services. I was never sure if this was a matter of pride, or just a continuing ignorance of what might have been available.)

As Christmas approached, Aunt Rosie suggested that Mam might also help out as the market had been busier than previous winters due to the circus, which had been drawing huge crowds.

Christmas day – a time Mam loved and which was almost sacrosanct to her, a time to cherish and spend with her children – was now filled with stress and anxiety. Dad stayed just long enough to watch presents being opened (Richard's disinterest in the jeep being noted with chagrin) before rushing off mid-morning to help Rosie.

Mam made our dinner – not the traditional Christmas fare, just home-made steak pie and vegetables. I didn't mind this as Mam was a wonderful cook and the pastry, gravy and tender chunks of steak were always mouth-wateringly good. Richard, just turned three, was still too young to bother and was happy to eat whatever was provided.

By mid-afternoon she had to go, yet I could see she hated leaving us and that she was terribly worried. Not only was she guilt-ridden at 'abandoning' us on Christmas day, but she feared for our safety.

Mam's anxiety was understandable. The ground at Seafield was a potential death trap. The electricity supply was from Calder's large shed and wires from this were strung across to a telegraph pole where everyone 'tapped on'. Lengths of cable criss-crossed overhead and sparks would flash from the connections on the telegraph pole in bad weather. Wagons, trailers and lorries were all parked closely together; Calor gas tanks, petrol and various other combustables were stored or stacked in or around our various homes; and every home had a coal fire.

The danger of conflagration was too awful to contemplate. Shifting vehicles out of the ground quickly would be impossible and emergency services would have major problems gaining access as there was only one way in and out. I doubt whether any health and safety officials ever inspected, or even if they were aware of our existence on the Calder's yard.

'Now I've left you some nice sandwiches for your tea, and the coalbox is full so there is no need for you to go outside. Be careful with that fire, the coal is full of slate so watch for the hot cinders jumping out.'

She was struggling into her long suede, rubber-soled boots as she ran through the litany of anxiety-ridden instructions. The front zip fastener on one of the boots snagged on the woolly socks she had borrowed from Dad.

Mam had poor circulation and was plagued with terrible chilblains, her toes and heels bluish red and painful, the socks being an attempt to keep her feet warm and also to pad out the boots, which were a size too large.

She continued, 'And try to get Richard into his pyjamas and to bed by eight o' clock at the latest. Now you will be alright, pet…won't you?' I was trying to work out whether this was a question or a reassurance as she continued, 'Now, don't open the door to anyone. Flash is here and he'll look after you both until your dad and I come home.'

Flash, hearing his name, dutifully wagged his tail then flopped over, stomach full and ready for another sleep. I watched as Mam pulled on a heavy grey overcoat that was almost ankle-length.

She had purchased the boots and coat from a jumble sale a few weeks previously. The combination made her look like a Russian Cossack but she was beyond caring about appearances and was glad of the warmth.

(Unfortunately I did not have her philosophical approach to hand-me-downs. A neighbour on Seafield had given Mam a woollen trenchcoat for me, her own daughter having outgrown it. The family were quite well-off and had obviously spent a lot of money on the coat, which was of excellent quality. However, I hated the garment instantly and refused to wear it, no matter how cold the weather was.

I felt ashamed that we were being seen as a needy family and was sure that I would be spotted wearing the 'charity' coat every time I left the ground. Realistically, the garment had been given for very practical reasons; it was too expensive to throw away and better to pass on to someone it would fit. But as a self-conscious and stubborn thirteen-year-old, I could not accept the perceived stigma and stubbornly chose to wear my own, albeit older, coat, despite Mam's entreaties.)

'Right, I'll have to go now, your dad will be wondering where I am. I'm really sorry to be leaving you but I promise you it won't always be like this.'

There was a catch in her voice as she spoke, then she hugged me and bent to kiss the top of Richard's head before leaving, turning once to give us another anxious look as she closed the door behind her.

It seemed that Christmas had suddenly ended when she left, and our tiny living area in the bus now felt empty without her.

FIFTY

The Waverley Market was busy, and in the darts stall that day, Mam was scarcely able to function. She resented the crowds of people, happy families enjoying the fun and excitement of the Christmas fair while her own children were home alone.

She imagined every possible scenario – Richard becoming ill and me not being able to cope, a Calor gas leak and us both suffocating, the fire going out and us dying from hypothermia. There was scarcely a horror left that she hadn't pictured.

Normally so efficient when dealing with the punters, she was giving wrong change and miscalculating scores; she was distracted to the point where, to Rosie's irritation, she was losing potential customers.

'I'm not coming back here tomorrow,' she whispered to Dad as they helped to close the joints. She was trying to choke back tears, her fatigue and distress now visible. 'I am not leaving those kids alone ever again. I don't know what we were thinking.'

Rosie seemed unaware of Mam's distress and was busy packing away the rifles. Dad checked that his sister was not listening then lit a cigarette and passed it to Mam, a non-smoker, in an attempt to calm her down.

'It's ok,' he reassured her, 'we'll manage. I'll tell Rosie that it will just be me helping and that you have to stay at home.'

Mam could see that he was uncomfortable about breaking the news to Rosie. Boxing Day at the Market was often busier than Christmas and losing a helper could be a problem. However, Mam reckoned that Rosie might be quite relieved to be rid of her since she had been dysfunctional for most of that day.

The bus home seemed to take an interminably long time. She gazed out at the crowds of people still milling the streets, the bright shop windows, Christmas lights, scenes of seasonal happiness. Yet her only thought was the potential catastrophe awaiting her at Seafield and her vision of ambulances and fire engines at the ground.

By the time they arrived home, Richard was asleep and I was having difficulty staying awake. Before she'd even taken her coat off, Mam was hugging me, asking if I had managed, if we had eaten, if Richard had been alright – a flurry of questions, scarcely giving me time to answer. Dad was still outside and talking to some men.

'We were fine, Mam,' I assured her, trying to sound grown-up and confident, but secretly relieved that they were home. Truth be told, the responsibility of being left in charge had worried me. I was convinced that every cough and snuffle emitted by my sleeping baby brother was the prelude to some fatal illness and I needed to check regularly that he was still alive.

Flash had added to my anxiety by periodically growling at some unseen sound, hackles raised, anticipating intruders. While pleased that he was constantly alert and knowing that he would protect us, the possibility of some fearful predator loitering outside terrified me, memories of the previous event at Hamilton still haunting me.

The following day, after Dad had gone back to the market, Mam – plagued by the guilt she still felt at leaving us – tried to recreate Christmas. Boxed games were opened and Snakes and Ladders, Tiddlywinks etc were attempted then abandoned when both Richard and Flash tried to eat the plastic counters. The remains of a selection box were finished, and a picture book was opened for Richard, who showed immediate disinterest then fell asleep on the floor next to Flash.

By early evening it was already dark outside and threatening to rain yet again. Mam and I sat in front of the hostess stove. The fire crackled and sparked, being stoked with a poker by her every so often to encourage the slate-impregnated coal to burn. A pot of her homemade vegetable soup simmered on the stove, a hot bowl to be ready for Dad's return and Flash gnawed happily on the ham bone that had flavoured the stock. Richard was now in bed fast asleep, and in the background our wireless was quietly playing some festive music.

I pressed Mam to re-tell the stories I loved to hear, of the Christmases she had spent with her aunts. She sighed as though the memory and the nostalgia was painful, yet realised that I was genuinely interested.

I listened as she described the feverish activity in the Pelaw household in preparation for Christmas. Her aunts planned and prepared the food with almost military precision weeks beforehand. Gifts really were an after-thought; the dinner was the primary focus. On the day, the dining room table was set with their best white napery, chinaware and serving dishes. Cutlery, having been polished to a mirror-like finish, gleamed alongside the shining water glasses at each of the place settings.

The delicious aroma of the turkey and trimmings wafted through from the kitchen, Hilda's cheeks were flushed from the heat of the range as she checked the progress of the various steaming pans, and Uncle Fred was being scolded by Edith as he tried to sample, ahead of dinner, some of the wonderful cakes and confectionery his sisters had baked.

Then, after the meal, everyone relaxed – the smoke from the one cigar Fred allowed himself at Christmas drifting across the room, while he tried tunelessly to join in with the carols playing on the wireless. It often snowed quite heavily and Mam would gaze out the window, fascinated as the Pelaw street was transformed into a beautiful white landscape. She would look at her aunts, who were usually now snoozing, calm after the day's events, and think to herself that she had never been happier and she wanted Christmases to always be like this.

Mam shared these memories with so much detail that I felt I was a guest at the table and could almost taste the food she described.

I looked out of our window, willing the darkening sky to snow, something to bring some semblance of Mam's Christmases back, but there was just rain, the black muddy ground and puddles illuminated by the few flickering lights from surrounding wagons.

I tried to picture the world she so longingly described, the home and family she still missed – people I had never met and could not relate to. This seemed a mythical place that, to my mind, could never be reached by us.

Reaching over and hugging me tightly, Mam seemed to know what

I was thinking. 'You'll see, pet. *One* day we'll have proper Christmases just like those… and *not* in this bus, but in our own *house*.' She spoke with such conviction it was hard not to believe her.

FIFTY-ONE

Despite Mam's hopes and aspirations, our lives continued to follow the same familiar pattern of winters on Seafield and 'start outs' again every spring.

The bus was proving to be a bit more reliable than the old Albion and my parents were now extremely skilled at packing up and loading the vehicle for each journey.

On one occasion, however, Dad forgot to remove the chimney extension, which became dislodged as he drove under a low bridge. The stove was still lit, a meal cooking in the oven as we travelled, and to Mam's alarm, the bus started filling with smoke.

She tried to alert Dad by banging on the wooden partition that separated the cab from our living compartment but to no avail and Dad drove on, oblivious to the drama unfolding behind him. Things were becoming quite serious now, the smoke causing us to cough and stinging our eyes. Somehow she had to attract his attention.

She opened the side door and hung out as far as she could, frantically waving a towel in the hope he would spot this in the driving mirror. We must only have been travelling about 20mph, but this maneouvre was still quite dangerous. Still no luck! We journeyed on, being slowly kippered while local people waved back to Mam as we drove past, thinking she was being friendly.

Realising she was unable to let Dad know his family were suffocating, she decided only one course of action was available and poured water over the fire, which then engulfed us in steam and soot as it was extinguished.

Arriving at our destination, Dad was shocked to hear of our drama and immediately reconnected the passenger bus bell, reminding me as he did so that it was not a plaything and only for emergencies.

The chimney pipe was reconnected, the fire re-lit, and the food that had been cooking in the oven as we travelled was still edible and eventually enjoyed.

Journeys from one ground to another were generally boring rather than dangerous. We hated travelling in convoy with the rest of the family since it was almost guaranteed that one of the lorries would break down, forcing all of us to park in the roadway, one behind the other, until the necessary repair was done. Fortunately, roads during the fifties were not terribly congested so our string of lorries and wagons did not cause too many problems for other vehicles.

The major offender was Granny's lorry, the old Scammell, which was on its last legs and clearly no longer up to pulling the heavy loads. Aunt Rosie always chose to ride in the Scammell's cab rather than in the wagon with her parents. With every breakdown, she would jump down from the cab and make her way back along the family convoy, seeing it as her duty to give an 'update'.

Seeming to have inside knowledge, she would advise us all that the lorry just had an 'airlock' and would soon be fixed. The first time Mam heard this she was impressed, marvelling at Rosie's mechanical know-how. However, later in the year and several breakdowns after this, Rosie continued to give the same 'diagnosis'. Mam realised that this was just a term that Rosie had heard somewhere and it sounded knowledgeable so she used it with monotonous regularity – so often, in fact, that it became a family joke. Every mechanical malady thereafter was referred to by us as an 'airlock'.

One thing I enjoyed about these prolonged stoppages was Mam's insistence that we still ate at the 'proper times', regardless of the location.

On one occasion we were parked alongside a forest and the scent of the pine trees combined with the wonderful aroma of bacon and fried tomatoes drifting out of the bus as she prepared a quick meal was a feast for the senses and a memory I still cherish.

Our established run of fairs followed the dates of whichever galas or Highland Games were scheduled. Occasionally there was a worrying gap between the weeks for these events. We had to go somewhere, and it was illegal just to park up on waste ground or roadsides for any length of time. This meant we either stopped over at Vinegarhill and faced a week without takings, or hoped that an alternative fair could be sourced quickly by a lessee. These stopgap fairs tended to just cover rent and diesel expenses but at least kept us going until our usual events were back on track. The offer of a pitch on one of the 'emergency' grounds was welcomed and the location was not to be shared with potential competition.

One lessee – the owner of a waltzer – was friendly with the Stirlings and always offered our families some pitches at any ground he'd identified. He knew that jointly, we had a good and varied selection of stalls and rides, and just enough to cover the ground space he'd negotiated.

Funfairs were very similar to theatre acts in that they needed to have a 'main attraction' (the big, thrill-seeker rides such as the waltzers, speedways etc), then a 'supporting cast' (stalls, kiddies' rides and so on). It was in everyone's interest to offer a variety of entertainments in order to attract punters. The lessee always warned us not to spread the word as there was no room for any extra – and potentially duplicate – shows.

One particular family were notorious for trying to latch on to these grounds. (This was the same family who regularly breached rules by opening their stalls before anyone else and not closing at the required times.) Their stalls were the same as ours – darts, a rifle range and even kiddies' rides. They were competition and to be avoided, but unfortunately they always seemed to know that a ground had been sourced somewhere and employed a specific tactic to find out where it might be.

This involved the husband, a 'weaselly' individual, sending his wife on a scouting mission. She would visit the various wagons, engaging the other traveller women (and sometimes children) in seemingly innocent chatter but actually –quite skillfully – wheedling the information out of the unsuspecting victims. Mission accomplished, she would update her husband, who then approached the relevant lessee and requested ground space.

Dad had warned Mam and I about this woman, and she soon stopped 'visiting' us when she realised we were giving nothing away. Mam always felt guilty about this and worried that the woman's family might suffer if they had no income that week. She wondered why Dad did not share this view and always seemed quite hostile to the woman's husband.

She was to discover later from Uncle Tommy that the man had been overheard by Dad to say 'we could do with another war'. This was a boasting reference to the money he had made, both on the fringe of some black market dealings, and also the fact that he had somehow avoided call-up and capitalised on some profitable wartime fairgrounds. The comment was made as all the men gathered round a bonfire, discussing how well – or otherwise – the fair had gone that week. On hearing the remark, Dad was furious and had to be restrained from jumping across the fire and punching the man, who quickly left the scene. Most of those who witnessed the event wished he had been allowed to go ahead and give the man a good thrashing, having – like Dad – seen war action and probably experienced some terrible things during that time.

The man always avoided Dad after this, leaving his wife to be his family 'spy'.

FIFTY-TWO

Our health care was a constant worry for Mam and anything that did not respond to the combination of cossetting and Vicks chest rubs meant either a trip to the doctor or, if *really* unwell, a home visit request.

During the winter months we were registered with the GP practice in Claremont Park, which was opposite Leith Links and in the same row of big Georgian houses as the unmarried mothers' home. Appointments were not required – patients just turned up at surgery times and sat waiting their turn. Often there was quite a queue, meaning the surgery would over-run its time, yet we were always seen.

Summer illnesses were not so easily accommodated. My parents would have to search for surgeries in whichever town we were at, Mam then having to explain to the various receptionists who we were, and why we weren't registered at that surgery – all this before they noted why she wanted to see a doctor, usually within earshot of curious others in the waiting room.

Dad, fortunately, never seemed to be ill. Mam reckoned he had been exposed to so many germs over the years that he had developed a natural immunity. We three, however, were not so fortunate, succumbing to almost every seasonal ailment. Often in the summer months it was food poisoning.

This was not really surprising, as efficient food handling and hygiene practices in many shops were not yet to the fore, and sell-by dates were unheard of. Wasps, bees etc could be seen crawling across food displays and I hated the coils of brown fly paper with the various insects sticking to them, dangling almost like gamekeeper trophies in shop windows. I was never able to eat a fruit slice, which Granny called 'fly cemeteries' after seeing these. (Fruit slices were square flat pastries filled with blackcurrants.)

Mam insisted that her nose was the best judge and if something smelled even slightly off, we weren't allowed to eat it. Despite her vigilance, we still occasionally suffered some bouts of sickness and diahorrea. The absence of any proper toilet provision might have daunted many, but Mam was our infection control nurse.

She disposed of any 'productions', boiled water and wiped bottoms, and ensured that all utensils (buckets and basins) were scoured and sanitised, as well as hands and fingernails, which were scrubbed until scrupulously clean. The smell of Dettol and Domestos lingered in our bus for days but was preferable to the alternative.

Richard was especially prone to throat infections with fevers so severe he was often delirious. Hot weather and some of the dusty fairgrounds we stood on seemed to trigger these bouts. On one ground, in her desperate attempts to keep him cool while waiting for a doctor, she tried to ventilate the bus by opening the rear emergency door.

Unfortunately this gave full view of the interior of our home to some of the local children, who seemed intent in causing mischief. They ran back and forward, gazing inside and pretending to climb in, with some being abusive to Mam as she tried to check them. Only the arrival of Dad, accompanied by Flash and the local doctor, shifted them. Mam was never sure whether the flattie children were scared off by the doctor or Flash, but was just so relieved that her tormentors had gone.

The lack of proper sanitation, the constant worry for her family's health, the hardships of the lifestyle and her fears for our future tormented her. Dad had promised to settle down once he 'got travelling out of his system' but it was clear to her, years after this promise was made and now with two children, that only some miracle or drastic intervention would make this happen.

FIFTY-THREE

It was now 1959 and the world around us was changing rapidly. 30% of households now owned cars and the first Mini was produced. Hovercraft was launched, the first 'Carry On' film was released, Cliff Richard recorded 'Living Doll', Ian Fleming published his book 'Goldfinger', and newspapers seemed to be constantly reporting stories of racial and political unrest. There were 'ban the bomb' marches, Notting Hill riots, and the Cod wars had started with an Icelandic gunboat firing on British trawlers.

We even had a television now, a monstrously huge thing that Dad had obtained from a second-hand shop. It never worked properly – the picture was either snowy or rolled from side to side, and sometimes – for variety – up and down! It also took up space in the bus, which we could ill afford. It was a continual nuisance to Dad when, having obtained a 'tap on' at whichever ground we were at, he had to fix the aerial on the roof, turning and twisting the thing until we called up to him that we had a picture.

Even with this additional, albeit unreliable, new entertainment, Mam's stories continued to be favourite and I loved hearing them. I was particularly impressed when she told me there was a heroine in her family tree.

Grace Darling was an English lighthouse keeper's daughter who in 1838, with her father, rowed out in stormy seas to rescue survivors from the shipwrecked Forfarshire. For this act of bravery she was presented with many awards and gifts, including a china tea set, which was passed down the generations and was now owned by Mam's aunts Hilda and Edith, along with some family Bibles signed by the Darlings.

I loved this story, convinced that I would inherit some heroic gene that would manifest itself in some future act of bravery.

We were unaware of any heroic deeds in Dad's family, although clearly some of the hardships his ancestors experienced as travellers must have demanded considerable resilience. One story was of a relative who somehow in his career became a clown in America, performing with the famous Ringling and Barnum circus. His act was with a dog and the twosome became quite famous. Then, for some reason, he must have fallen on hard times, and was found in the snow in Philadelphia, starving and clutching his little dog to his breast to keep warm. They did not survive and in February 1929, his death was announced in the New York Times with the sad statement that his body was not claimed. The story fascinated me and while sad for him, I was more upset for the faithful little dog!

Curiously, at some point in the history of the family, they changed their surname from Stelling to Stirling. We wondered whether some 1900s' skulduggery necessitated a new identity, or perhaps just a registrar misheard the name and the error was not noticed on the certificate by the parents.

Fred with his dog 'Dan'

Notice in 1929 New York Times

Fred Stelling, Clown.

Special to The New York Times.

PHILADELPHIA, Feb. 27.—Fred Stelling, who as a star clown of Ringling Brothers Circus for many years made millions laugh, died today in the Philadelphia General Hospital, with no one to claim his body.

Many travellers of that time were illiterate, evidence of this still noticed on the birth certificate of Dad's grandfather Henry, the mother signing her name with a cross. Literacy shortfalls continued in Henry's family, with Old Teddy being unable to read. Thankfully, Granny, Teddy's wife, ensured that *her* children learned the three Rs, resulting in my dad and his siblings being literate.

It is interesting also to see the occupation of Henry's father listed as 'Traveller and Exhibitor of living curiosities', this presumably being some sort of freak show. These were commonplace in Victorian times, the general public fascinated and sometimes frightened by them, yet still willing to pay to see the exhibits on show.

These included dwarfs, fat women, bearded ladies, Siamese twins etc. Some of the 'exhibits' became famous (e.g. Joseph Merrick, the Elephant Man).

I have no recollection of shows such as these when we travelled and can only assume they were no longer popular. The term 'showman' still existed nevertheless, travelling showmen/women keen to be distinguished from other groups who *called* themselves 'travellers' – these generally being hawkers, gypsies and sometimes societal dropouts.

Aunt Rosie defended the title proudly, angry that anyone might consider us to be gypsies, and she would have been delighted to see the 2022 census listing 'showmen/women' as a specific and unique cultural group.

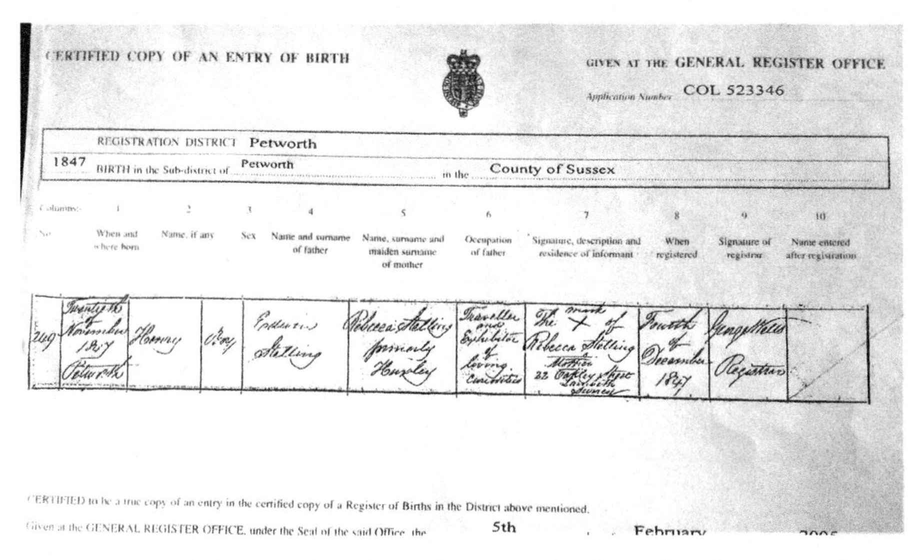

CERTIFIED COPY OF AN ENTRY OF BIRTH

GIVEN AT THE GENERAL REGISTER OFFICE

Application Number COL 523346

REGISTRATION DISTRICT Petworth

1847 BIRTH in the Sub-district of Petworth in the County of Sussex

Columns:-	1	2	3	4	5	6	7	8	9	10
No.	When and where born	Name, if any	Sex	Name and surname of father	Name, surname and maiden surname of mother	Occupation of father	Signature, description and residence of informant	When registered	Signature of registrar	Name entered after registration
249	Twentieth of November 1847 Petworth	Henry	Boy	[illegible] Stelling	Rebecca Stelling formerly Huxley	Traveller and Exhibitor of living Curiosities	The mark X of Rebecca Stelling Mother 22 [illegible] Street Lambeth Surrey	Fourth of December 1847	George Wells Registrar	

CERTIFIED to be a true copy of an entry in the certified copy of a Register of Births in the District above mentioned.

Given at the GENERAL REGISTER OFFICE, under the Seal of the said Office, the 5th . . February

Great Grandfather Henry's birth certificate 1847 (mother Rebecca's name marked with a cross)

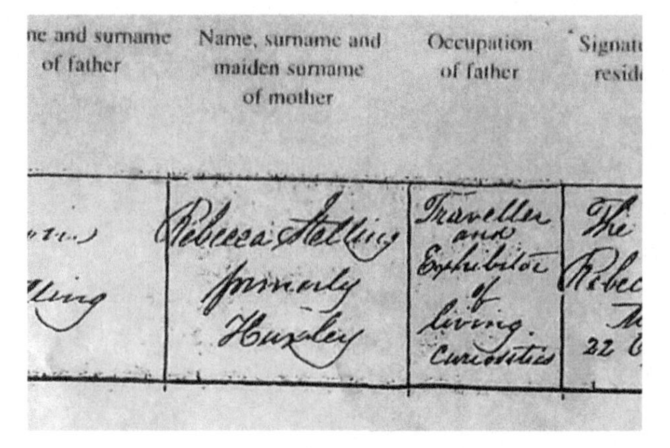

...me and surname of father	Name, surname and maiden surname of mother	Occupation of father	Signat... resid...
...ling	Rebecca Stelling formerly Huxley	Traveller and Exhibitor of living Curiosities	The... Rebec... 22 ...

'Traveller and Exhibitor of Living Curiosities'

Rose Foster (Miss Rosina, Miss Mermaida, Miss Tiny), born c.1890. Height 26 inches. Performed 1900s to 1920s: cutting paper shapes, and crocheting, with her feet

Daisy and Violet Hilton, Siamese twins, 1908 - 1969. Appeared in sideshows in England and America, and in the 1932 film Freaks. Photo 1933

'Freak Show' publicity

FIFTY-FOUR

My secondary school years gradually petered out and I eventually just stopped going.

Attendance to me seemed pointless and I successfully pleaded the case to my parents, claiming that I was not really learning anything and would be of more use at home.

Mam was convinced that an education board official would catch us and impose some sort of penalty for non-attendance. Realistically, we had travelled through so many school districts over the years that it was doubtful whether anyone noticed my seasonal absence. This meant that I was never 'officially' signed off and had no school leaving certificate or any qualifications. In truth I was not bothered, since I had hated senior school from day one and was delighted to be relieved of the burden.

Mam felt guilty, however, blaming our lifestyle for my educational shortcomings, but also reminding me of the 'brilliant people' who had been late developers, and saying that I would catch up eventually. I loved her faith in me but secretly felt it was misplaced.

It seemed to me that the world around me was moving too quickly and I was always out of step. Girls now pored over true romance magazines while I was still reading 'Bunty', and they back-combed their hair, only satisfied when beehive perfection was reached, and cemented with Bellair hair lacquer.

Fashion styles were strange and I could never understand why cardigans were reversed, buttons at the back. Someone said it was to show bosoms off to advantage, but I wondered why they couldn't just wear a jersey – and in any case, most had still to develop busts!

Boys were becoming a feature of their conversations and this was an adjustment I found hard to follow. Boys were pals and I never considered them as romantic possibilities.

My winter absences from these growth and development associations left me naïve and socially inept. My lack of friends worried Mam but never seemed to bother me. I was enjoying the company of my young brother, and with Flash, we were an inseperable threesome.

I also had responsibilities. As with all fairground children, I'd been helping in the stalls from an early age, and at twelve I was trusted to run my 'own' stall under the watchful eye of my parents. Mam hated the idea, afraid that I was being sucked further into the business and to a future she did not wish for me. Dad reasoned that an extra stall would surely bring in more money and since we still seemed to be living from hand to mouth financially, she reluctantly agreed. I didn't mind, seeing this almost as my 'rite of passage', and I was proud to have been trusted with the responsibility.

My stall was the wheel-'em-in (the round stall) and there was great debate about which game I should manage – darts ruled out as being too dangerous, setting aside the fact that I was 'numerically challenged'! And so it became the fish and globe stall, a prize of a goldfish in a water-filled plastic bag given to punters who successfully lobbed ping-pong balls into one of the rows of little glass fish globes.

A 'star' prize of a budgerigar was offered to anyone who managed to throw a ball into one special coloured bowl that was raised above the others. (This was before the Animal Welfare Act, which eventually banned live animals being given as fairground prizes.) Dad built a large circular aviary that was the centre-piece of the display and although only containing four birds, it was quite an attraction.

While feeling no affection for the goldfish and happily handing them to successful punters, I was relieved that no-one was managing to score the coloured bowl, and my heart was in my mouth every time someone tried. The budgies were my pets and all had names, including one I called Huey, named after a clumsy cartoon bird.

Huey was much larger than the others and I think probably had outgrown his brain, never managing to successfully work out how to edge along a perch without tripping over his feet, a maneouvre viewed with disdain by his companions.

Then, inevitably, someone managed to achieve the impossible. One bird must have caught the man's eye and he played game after game, probably spending more than the cost of buying a bird, but he was determined to win. I watched in horror as, almost in slow motion, the little white ball bounced up and into the coloured bowl.

I was so upset. These birds weren't just swag, they were my companions in the stall, and now I had to give one to this man. He waited patiently for me to hand over his bird while I tried to figure out how to *do* this. The cage was too heavy for me to lift across the table and also well beyond my reach. By now a small crowd had gathered, keen to see the winner receive his prize.

I was unable to call on my parents for help, their stall at this particular ground not positioned near mine. Just as I was about to ask the man to come back later to collect the bird, I spotted my cousin Ritchie nearby and called him over. I explained what was required and he assured me it was no problem, reminding me that I should find a cardboard box to put the bird in once captured.

I was so relieved now; my cousin was so confident and self-assured, taking command of the situation. Ritchie, now a tall, muscular youth, was well able to lift the cage un-aided. However, he decided just to lean over the rows of glass globes, reach into the cage and catch the chosen budgie.

Unfortunately, Dad's aviary design incorporated an exceptionally large wire door, and as it swung open the startled birds flew out. All, that is, with the exception of Huey, who sat firmly on his perch, either too stupid to escape or astute enough to know freedom would be hazardous.

Ritchie was mortified – especially when our 'audience' cheered as the three birds disappeared over the tops of the stalls and into the distance. The man shook his head in disbelief and refused my offer of Huey, the only remaining budgie, accepting instead a partial refund, a couple of goldfish, and my profuse apologies. Later that day, Dad and Ritchie removed the 'aviary'. (Huey was re-homed in a proper bird cage and never required to be in showbusiness again, spending his many remaining years as our pet before finally falling off his perch… a consequence of old age rather than clumsiness!)

Without the round cage as a centre display my stall looked uninviting, especially when pitched alongside others that were bedecked with an abundance of colourful swag. We decided to put it back and hung goldfish bags around it.

Ironically, the empty cage attracted more attention than when it contained birds. People were convinced that some exotic creature was inside, hidden from view and requiring closer inspection. Since this seemed to pull in a few more punters, and as in keeping with the tradition of good old-fashioned fairground 'trickery', we maintained the illusion!

FIFTY-FIVE

'How do you fancy painting some fish?'

I was helping Dad to build up the wheel-'em-in and he stopped for a moment, cigarette at the corner of his mouth, the smoke causing him to squint as he looked at the shutters. Seeing that I needed further explanation, he continued, 'I was just thinking, since this is a goldfish joint, we could maybe advertise by having some sort of fish on each of the panels.'

Clearly this was a vote of confidence for my thirteen-year-old 'artistic prowess' and I jumped at the chance, proud that, undeterred by my previous attempts at palm trees, he was trusting me to do the job. Mam, while agreeing that the idea was alright and not wishing to cast any aspersions on my ability, did not share the same enthusiasm.

'Do you not think you are asking too much of her? She's only a kid... and that's an awful lot of shutters.'

The shutters – or 'standing bottoms' – formed the circular base of the wheel-'em-in, and there were ten of them! Undaunted, and assuring her that I was up to the task, I quickly drafted out my ideas for two cartoon-style fish. My parents, always ready to praise my efforts, enthused over the 'designs'.

Dad, inventive as ever, showed me how to transfer each drawing onto the shutters using a paper stencil. This involved drawing the large image onto a brown paper sheet and then using a nail to poke holes round the outline of the fish.

The stencil was then placed over the shutter panel and a bag of coloured crushed chalk dabbed around the perforations. When the stencil was removed,

Our 'wheel-'em-in' resplendent with my cartoon fish

we had a reasonably accurate replica of my drawing, which we quickly inked in for painting before the powdered lines blew away.

My artistic endeavours took several weeks to complete, each shutter being worked on at various grounds and always well before opening times to ensure the paint had dried! Mam continually checked that I was not wearying of the task and while I assured her that I enjoyed doing it, by completion of the seventh shutter I secretly hated the job.

While the end product was still no match for the other brightly lacquered stalls, the large painted fish clearly advertised what we were about and attracted punters.

The wheel-'em-in was a hard stall to operate. Being circular, it was necessary to keep walking round and round to ensure no potential punters were missed.

Often when I had a pitch (several people playing) and when my back was turned, an opportunist would lean over the shutter, place a ball in one of the globes then claim they had won. Mam, ever vigilant, always alerted me, and taking her cue I then politely refused the various offenders a prize, telling them that they'd been spotted. Generally this was accepted without demur but on the odd occasion it wasn't, Mam or Dad left their stall, hurried across and told the various cheats, in no uncertain terms, to behave themselves.

I became quite skilled at identifying potential troublemakers, learning to keep a watchful eye as they played. They were often youths showing off to their girlfriends or companions, and sometimes drunks, who could scarcely lick their fingers let alone throw a ball. Occasionally there would be someone who was just downright nasty, seeing me as an inexperienced kid and a soft touch. I knew to ignore any derogatory remarks and this generally worked, the various offenders just walking away, disappointed that I was not rising to their bait.

Although terribly shy, I also discovered I had a talent for the 'spiel' and I seemed to adopt a different persona when 'out front' in the stalls. I shouted out with all the confidence of a fairground barker, encouraging passers-by to 'come and have a shot... three balls sixpence, seven for a shilling!'

I learned to read people, knowing which ones to call over and also the ones to avoid. Establishing eye contact as potential punters came near was important, making it just a bit easier to keep up the patter and draw them in. Even better if they had children – the combination of my spiel and the goldfish (and the large empty birdcage) never failed to catch their attention.

Often parents, frustrated at failing to win a game and now with a disappointed child, would ask if they could just *buy* a fish. I would then explain that this was not permitted as I wasn't 'licensed' to sell. However, if they spent another 'couple of bob' and tried again – then I would just give them a fish.

Two shillings bought fourteen balls and it was almost guaranteed that one would plop into a globe eventually so this was a bit of a 'hustle' on my part but I felt no shame. Those who still did not manage to win went away with a fish and a happy child, while my takings were boosted by two shillings.

The prices for games in fairgrounds were fixed and no showman was allowed to charge more than anyone else. During the fifties and sixties, sixpence was the cost per game on stalls, while the large rides charged a little bit more but always at the agreed rate. Showmen would have to sell forty games at sixpence per game just to earn one pound, and by the end of a busy Saturday, having been open for nearly twelve hours, and often experiencing anti-social behaviour from punters, every coin was hard-earned.

Despite my numeracy problem, I was at least able to count takings at the end of a night, delighted often to find that 'my' stall had earned more money than my parents' when we compared notes.

On one memorable Saturday, my takings from the fish and globe stall came to £22.00. This was a considerable achievement, since the average weekly wage for women in the sixties was £7.00, and at first Dad thought I'd miscounted, resulting in a quick re-check. In Granny's wagon that night with the usual crowded gatherings of uncles, aunts and cousins, Dad could not resist boasting about how much I'd taken.

'Aye, I told you so,' remarked Aunt Rosie, 'you're a born wee showwoman.'

This comment was not missed by Mam and although pleased that I was enjoying the praise, it only served to reinforce her resolve that this would not be my future.

She smiled, engaging in the happy banter, enjoying the fun and backchat of her in-laws, yet even with an integration of over ten years, she had not changed her agenda. Somehow – no matter how long it might take – her family would stop travelling.

FIFTY-SIX

Swag (prizes) were an obvious incentive to attract punters, and the bigger, brighter and more attractive these were, the more chance there was of drawing in the crowds.

The traditional fairground mainstay prize of coconuts continued, but in addition there was assorted glassware, chalk (stookie) ornaments, soft toys and boxes of sweets.

It was the highlight of Aunt Rosie's day when the swagmen's van arrived on any of our grounds. Often this would be 'wee Barney', as she called him, and at other times his competitors – 'wee Evelyn' and her brother.

I don't know whether Aunt Rosie ever knew their surnames but this seemed to be of little interest to her... and they certainly were small people!

She favoured wee Barney's swag as it was fairly cheap and she could buy lots of 'entry level' prizes for her rifle range. I considered the stuff to be junk – (plastic skeletons, egg cups, ash trays, combs, pencils etc) but it filled the bottom shelf of her display – better prizes to be won further up the shelves as the punters scored more points.

'Wee Evelyn' and her brother stocked better quality swag and also tried to keep up with any popular trends, these often being toy spin-offs from children's TV characters such as the little pink pigs, the Pinky and Perky puppets.

The swagmen were always sure of reasonably good trade and it was obviously essential that the travellers purchased the latest and most topical swag. Aunt Rosie kept an eye on what her competitors bought, keen not to be outdone and often, to Granny's dismay, buying those same items even though she had no need to stock up. She considered this to be a justifiable expense while Granny, who still held the purse strings, saw it as a waste of money. Old Teddy held no view, the purchase of swag being 'women's business' and not his concern.

Mam was fully aware that neither of our stalls had much to offer by way of swag, but she had to prioritise financially, and avoided the temptation to follow Rosie out to wee Barney's or Evelyn's vans. Money was still tight and not to be spent on unecessary tat just to keep up with the competition.

And so our display of coconuts was supplemented by little boxes of Bassetts or Dunhill sweets and fluffy toys called monkeys. The only resemblance to any monkey was the rubber head, the body being just multi-coloured cotton wool, glued and stapled to a toilet-roll-sized cardboard tube. Elastic string poked out of a fez on the monkey's head, presumably to allow some bounce if dangling from a car mirror or baby's pram. The things were badly made and possibly a choking hazard if given to a child, but they seemed popular, were colourful and also cheap to buy as swag.

Dad's can joint offered nothing breakable. Missiles being hurled at tin cans was not conducive to the safety of any glassware. These were reserved for Mam's stall and placed on a tier of three shelves with backing mirrors. When the few prizes of vases, salad bowls, sugar/cream sets etc were set out, the reflection gave the illusion of considerably more on offer.

The only additions to this central display were the round plaques that no-one ever seemed to want. These were painted chalk (stookie) wall ornaments dinner-plate size, with a design of something resembling a water-wheel. Mam, like me, thought they were awful but they at least filled up display gaps and amazingly, survived many seasons of packing/unpacking and damp weather.

'Setting out' the joints was something Dad liked to do, especially when a fresh order of coconuts arrived. We soon discovered he was keeping these for *his* stall, leaving Mam with all the old ones. This resulted in punters coming back to her and complaining that the nuts were rotten. It certainly was beyond dispute, the offending items broken open to reveal mouldy blue – rather than milky white – flesh.

Dad then enjoyed 'coming to the rescue', producing a fresh coconut from his display, and with an almost theatrical flourish, shaking it to prove the thing was fresh and full of milk. Punters were happy with the replacement but Mam always felt aggrieved, not happy that anyone thought she was offloading stale goods.

I decided that some subterfuge was required and regularly sneaked into the joints before we opened, switching the displays so that there was an even mix of old and new nuts on both stalls. Dad must have eventually realised what I was doing when punters started returning to him with complaints. He never admitted to any pre-selection of the stock, but knew we were on to him and distributed the things fairly thereafter.

My parent's darts and can joints never offered anything particularly appealing; in fact, it was a wonder to me that anyone actually came over to play.

Mam was ashamed to offer the dog-eared darts to punters. The plastic flights were misshapen and very few were original sets, being of different weights and the metal points blunt from years of use. The dart boards were also showing their age, the metal wires that separated each bed being loose, resulting in many a challenge from punters who insisted their dart was in the correct bed.

She dreaded the men from mining villages playing, since most were expert dartsmen, many becoming professional players (Jocky Wilson from Kirkaldy was world professional champion in 1982). Often these men, having paid for a game, would produce from their jacket pockets their own favoured darts, the feathered flights and pristine points contained in little leather wallets. To Mam's dismay, these players won game after game, almost clearing the stall of prizes. This required Dad to paint a notice stating that only three prizes per winner were allowed. When the skilled men continued to win, Dad painted another notice stating that players were not allowed to use their own darts. Mam joked that there would soon be more 'notices' than swag on display.

If anyone dared to question these 'rules', Mam – always quick to think on her feet – told them that players using their own darts would have an unfair advantage over novices and it was to make sure the game was fair for everyone. Her explanation was usually accepted, the men grudgingly throwing our mismatched darts at the pock-marked boards, yet as a testament to their talents, somehow still managing to win – but limited now to three prizes.

My 'swag' was primarily the goldfish, with just a few supplementary boxes of sweets and some coconuts. The fish were ordered from an aquarium in Glasgow and delivered to us in a thick polythene bag filled with air and water. I always liked seeing what had arrived, since the term 'goldfish' was a misnomer. They varied in colour from all gold to piebald, silver, albino and even black.

I was never so keen on the black ones; they looked predatory, like little sharks. The process of putting individual fish into the little prize bags required me to catch them by hand. I found that this was quicker and easier than using the small net Mam bought for the task. My cousins, during our various adventures, had shown me how to guddle fish so handling the little creatures was not a problem for me.

Much as I loved animals, I could only think of the fish as swag… a fairground prize and source of income. Nevertheless, we cared for them as best we could, ensuring they had clean water and fish food.

FIFTY-SEVEN

'Mam… Dad… Something awful has happened… come and see this!' I cried.

We were at Burntisland and due to open in four hours. It was the Glasgow Fair July holidays and this was one of the few places where we might earn some money.

The thunderstorms of the previous few days had cleared, the sun shone and the grassy Links was drying up nicely. Day-trippers were already arriving by the coach-load and a good 'gaff' seemed possible.

I had gone to check on the fish only to discover a catastrophe. Mam, Dad and my young brother joined me and we all gazed in horror at all the little golden bodies floating in the bath. Dad was the first to speak.

'I don't undertand it, I put clean water in the bath last night and they seemed ok.' He swirled the water with his hand, the motion moving the fish around, and I wondered whether he was attempting some form of resuscitation.

Mam was struggling to find some logical explanation and turned to Dad. 'Where did you get the water?'

Dad's face paled and for a moment he was quiet, gazing down at the lttle corpses.

'I think it must be my fault. I had to drain all the water off the tilts after the thunderstorm last night. They were sagging under the weight of the water but it seemed a shame to waste it – it was so clean – so I poured it into the bath.'

He lit a cigarette, clearly upset at apparently becoming a mass murderer, while I tried to understand how on earth clean water could kill fish. We stood solemnly around the bath as though attending some aquatic wake.

'You see,' he continued, 'I forgot that fish need oxygen, and rainwater after lightning and thunderstorms doesn't have any. The wee things suffocated.'

Whether or not there was any scientific basis to Dad's explanation, we could think of no other reason. Whatever the cause, they were all dead – nearly one hundred fish.

I was horrified, not only at the lives of these little creatures being extinguished, but also, realistically, they were my swag, and without them I could not open my stall. My parents were desperately trying to think of a solution. We had neither the money nor the time to re-order from the Glasgow aquarium. The fish and globe stall with no fish to offer as prizes was an economic disaster.

The stall had been a means to extra income, often meeting shortfalls in the can and darts joint's takings, and we depended on it week by week.

At this point Dad's sister Becky and her husband Jim arrived. Although settled on Vinegarhill, Becky still considered herself a traveller, regularly visiting fairgrounds and family, chauffeured by long-suffering Uncle Jim.

As one of the few family members to have a car, Dad immediately enlisted Jim's help, explaining the situation and the need to drive to Edinburgh. Our budgies had been purchased from a pet shop in Edinburgh (Dofos) and he remembered they stocked fish. He was accompanied by my young brother, who was enjoying the adventure, and they returned a couple of hours later but with only twelve goldfish.

Mam and I gazed at the little bag as Dad tried to explain the shortfall. 'I had to pay full price for them and only had enough cash for a dozen. Jim couldn't help because Becky has his wallet.'

Mam could see that Uncle Jim looked slightly embarrassed by this announcement, and was quick to thank him for coming to our rescue, assuring him that we would manage somehow.

I didn't share her optimism. We would soon be opening and I realised that twelve fish could never adequately make a display or be enough to keep the stall open all day, but then I had an idea. A trick of the eye had paid off previously with the empty bird cage attracting punters, so why not replicate this by hanging up bags of water?

We tried this, spacing every 'live' goldfish bag to six empty water bags. Unfortunately it was still possible to see these contained no fish and we looked at the display wondering what to do next. I remembered seeing a man pretending to take a goldfish from a bowl and eat it. It was actually a sliver of carrot but sufficiently realistic to horrify his audience.

'How about putting a fish-sized slice of carrot in each bag?' I suggested. I tried a prototype, carefully paring a thin piece of carrot and dropping it into the water. It was hopeless – the orange-coloured shaving floating in the water certainly *looked* like a fish... but a *dead one*! Then Mam had an idea.

'Tell you what, why don't we try colouring the water? That way, no-one can see if anything is in the bags.'

'But Mam... what if a punter chooses a coloured bag as a prize?' I asked.

'Then you explain that these are just decorative bags and if there are no fish left, offer them a coconut or box of sweets.'

Half an hour later, and with several drops of watercolour paint added to the empty bags, the twelve fish and tinted water supplements were on display, ready for the punters.

By the end of that night, somehow I had managed to eke out my meagre offering, the last fish being won just before we closed. Discussing the day's events, I mentioned that punters – especially children – kept requesting the coloured bags when they'd won a fish. This seemed to be a selling point and I asked if we could do this again when we had our next delivery of goldfish – add a small amount of colour to each fish bag.

Dad, still guilty about losing our previous stock, pointed out that fish would not survive in water contaminated with paint. Mam, keen to support my idea, offered a solution.

'Well... why not use food colourant?'

Dad and I looked at each other, not sure what she meant but open to any suggestion that might give our swag the edge and attract punters.

Mam continued, 'You can buy little bottles of food colourant. I remember Aunt Hilda had a couple of these in her cupboard. People use them for baking and they obviously are not toxic. I'm sure that one tiny droplet added to the water won't harm the fish.'

We were amazed at Mam's ingenuity and when next we opened, my fish were displayed in a glorious array of coloured water bags. Interestingly, punters seemed to choose their prize based on the colour of the water, rather than which fish they preferred.

I was so proud of Mam's ability to find solutions and convinced that no problem existed that could not be solved by her. Dad, confident by this time that Mam was now fully engaged in the 'business', enjoyed her participation. He was convinced, after her years of experiencing the travelling life, that she had adapted to the lifestyle and she was accepted by everyone in his world as a bona fide show-woman. She worked alongside him, kept a spotless, warm and loving home, and seldom mentioned settling down. He had won her over to his way of life and assumed she was happy, and life – for him – felt good. They even had a son now who would carry on the family business when he grew up.

Mam's agenda, however– albeit that it was taking time – remained unchanged. She found that any talk with Dad about settling down was pointless. He refused to discuss the matter and retreated into yet another mood if the subject was ever raised.

Undeterred by this behaviour, which cleary was his avoidance tactic, she knew that somehow she would make him see sense and give his family the settled life he had promised when they first married.

FIFTY-EIGHT

'Do you think it's maybe time we looked for something better to live in?'

Mam's heart leapt at this unexpected statement from Dad. She had noticed that he had been quiet all week – not in one of his usual 'huffs', but seeming thoughtful, as though planning something.

We had just finished lunch. Mam was sipping a cup of tea and dad was gazing around the bus that had been our home since Richard was born.

'I mean, Richard's getting older and really needs a proper bed now,' he continued, as though needing to justify his statement. Richard had progressed from his baby cot to my parents' bed and now, aged three, he was sleeping in the bedchair, previously mine from the old Albion. Dad drew heavily on his cigarette, his eyes squinting as the exhaled smoke caught him unawares. 'And you've got that wee Post Office account now so it would probably be enough for a deposit.'

He paused, looking at Mam for some reaction and then to me, seeing that I was suddenly interested. Mam had been managing to save a little money each week during the summer, our income having improved slightly with my extra takings from the wheel-'em-in. She could hardly believe what she was hearing. Was it going to actually happen at long last? Her dream of a house… a proper home with a bathroom, water on tap and not having to be carried… A settled life might almost be within reach now.

'Rosie was telling me of a place in Caldercruix.'

Mam was only half-listening, scarcely able to contain her mounting excitement, already thinking ahead, picturing their new home, Dad's voice just background noise. She was puzzled at his choice of Caldercruix. They had opened there a couple of times, but it would not have been at the top of her places to settle. It was a small mining town in North Lanarkshire, twenty miles from Glasgow and thirty-two from Edinburgh.

However, she reasoned to herself, a house *anywhere* was preferable to living in a bus, and perhaps properties were cheaper there. Then, jolted from her reverie, she heard him say, 'There's a woman who can arrange cheap deposits and hire-purchase. Lots of the travellers use her. We can go and have a look if you like?'

Now she was puzzled. Why would 'lots of travellers' be looking at houses? Just as she was trying to make some sort of sense of of this, he delivered the sucker punch.

'I hear there's a cracker on the site. It's twenty-six feet long and ten feet wide and has lots of room… even a separate bedroom with twin beds.' Clearly excited and not giving her any chance to comment, he turned to me. 'How do you fancy living in a nice new trailer instead of this old bus? It would have lots of room… even your own bedroom. You would have to share it with your wee brother but that's ok, isn't it?'

I didn't know how to respond. I looked at Mam, her disappointment almost palpable, but she said nothing. I was her ally, always on her side, supporting her dream of a house, and I felt that any show of enthusiasm by me would seem a betrayal. Yet I pictured us arriving at our various summer grounds, our old bus now towing a brand new trailer. This was something that seemed achievable and conformed to my familiar world and lifestyle, whereas in all honesty, I couldn't really imagine life in a house. Mam intervened.

'Now hang on a minute! You can't just spring something like this on us.' She was sounding angry now. 'This is you all over. You jump into things without talking it through with me. I bet Rosie and the rest of your family know all about it though? Did you tell them I had been saving money? You *know* what that was for… it would go towards a bricks and mortar home… *not* another tin box on wheels.'

Never good at arguing, her voice faltered and tears of vexation were near, made worse by Dad's lack of any response. Seeing things were not going to plan, he simply walked out, the bus door slamming behind him as he left.

Realising that I had witnessed everything, she tried to reassure me. 'Now don't you worry, pet. Your Dad and I will talk about this later on and sort things out, I promise. Now away you go, out with Richard... take Flash for a walk. I'll finish the ironing while you're away.'

While a laborious job, I knew that she vented occasional frustrations on the task, thumping the heavy flat iron down on the clothes, creases being shown no mercy as she smoothed them out. It was a form of therapy that she obviously needed today, and I was glad to be leaving her to it.

For several weeks after this I was aware that things were still not resolved. Mam seemed constantly worried and upset, while Dad remained in another prolonged 'huff', not speaking to any of us. To describe his moods as mercurial would be an understatement, yet none had lasted as long as this and we all suffered. Even Flash lurked in corners, tail between legs, whenever Dad appeared. I became a communication 'go between', instructed to 'go tell your mother' or 'see what your father wants' etc. I was continually walking on eggshells, and each day was a misery.

Then it all changed and my parents were talking again. Whatever promises he had made, somehow Dad had talked Mam into viewing the trailer at Caldercruix.

Three weeks later, the twenty-six feet Donnington Castle caravan was delivered to us at Seafield along with a hire purchase contract tying us for four years to the Bowmaker Finance Company.

Dad spent the remainder of that winter stripping out the interior of the bus, pleased that all the equipment for the stalls could now be loaded inside rather than on the roof. He also arranged to have a towbar welded to the back of the bus. The only item salvaged from what had once been our home was the little gate-leg table that when folded fitted nicely into a small recess in the trailer.

Mam missed the hostess stove, cursing the trailer's Calor gas oven, which always seemed to run out of heat just when the Yorkshire puddings were about to rise.

We were soon to find out that our move from the bus was not offering many of the improvements we had anticipated. Our new home had obviously not been designed for winter residents! The only form of heating was a small fire in the lounge area, which burned anthracite. This certainly was effective but only in one room, there being no radiators or piped heating anywhere else.

The twin bedroom at the other end of the trailer was so cold during the winter that our blankets stuck to ice caused by condensation freezing on the wall panels. Richard and I went to bed each night wrapped in woolly jumpers and bedsocks, with coats piled on top of the blankets for extra weight and warmth.

This was a major disappointment and also of great concern to Mam, who constantly worried about the possible impact on our health. The old bus, albeit too hot during the summer, had always provided winter warmth; the additional interior panelling along with the robustness of the vehicle's bodywork gave very effective insulation, retaining the heat provided by the hostess stove. It seemed we were now living in a refrigerator.

The trailer was not fitted with any plumbing or bathroom facilities, so our toileting arrangements were just as primitive as they had always been, and water stil had to be carried. Then travelling from ground to ground when we started out became an uncomfortable experience. It was against the law to remain in a two-wheeled caravan when being towed on the highway, requiring many showmen to convert their homes by transferring them onto four-wheeled chassis, their caravans now resembling modern wagons. Dad was not able to do this and realised that we would somehow all still have to travel in the bus, which now housed all the stalls and equipment.

There was still some space behind the cab, containing the dynamo, and also the hatch in the floor that gave access to the engine drive shaft. He built a small bed across the dynamo and this functioned as a seat for Mam, Richard and I, while the remaining area of floor space was taken up by Flash, who howled and shed hair for nearly every journey.

No longer would it be possible to enjoy the aroma of bacon cooking when we had roadside stops… or the facility to have the Sunday roast cooking in the hostess oven as we travelled. It felt that there were considerably more losses than gains.

Also, athough he did not admit it, I suspected that Dad initially did not feel confident towing the trailer, especially during the first year. Trying to maneouvre the thing round tight bends and narrow lanes was difficult, usually requiring one of the uncles to leave their own lorries and guide us through.

A sliding glass panel behind Dad's cab meant that we could talk to him as he drove, but this became quite stressful for both Mam and I, Dad expecting us to constantly watch out for signposts and give him directions, even on routes he was familiar with. Often it would result in frayed tempers if we happened to miss a signpost, and yet more huffs at the end of the journey.

I couldn't help thinking our lives had been so much simpler and more enjoyable in the self-contained environment of our old converted bus.

FIFTY-NINE

Hire purchase (i.e. the means of buying things on credit and repaying monthly) was not something my parents had ever previously considered. Despite financial constraints, they were never in debt to anyone and if they needed anything, it had to wait until they had enough money to pay for it. The purchase of the trailer was to be their first experience of what Mam considered to be debt.

Now she had to factor into her budget the monthly payment for the trailer, Dad still leaving the responsibility of correspondence and finance management to her. Not having a bank account, she bought postal orders for the required amount and sent these off to Bowmaker whenever their monthly invoice was received.

For a while, she somehow managed this, but then there started to be occasions when a payment was delayed. This was usually due to poor gaffs, no savings to fall back on, and hard financial choices between diesel, swag, ground rents and, of course, feeding her family. Payments to the finance house did not take precedence when faced with all those other, more urgent priorities.

She became familiar very quickly with Bowmaker's procedures, and when necessary, used this to defer payment until there was enough money. First there would be the monthly invoice stating when payment was required, then, if not received, a 'reminder', followed by a second reminder a few weeks later. If payment was still overdue, the heart-stopping brown envelope printed with bold red lettering that stated 'Warning! Final Notice!' would arrive. She always tried to avoid the final notice stage, managing somehow to accommodate the second reminder.

The threat of repossession was a constant worry and 'red letter day' had a totally different connotation for us. But to all outward appearances, our lives were improving, and at each ground, travellers came over to admire the trailer.

'Well Winnie, you've got your nice new home at long last.'

Aunt Rosie sat in the lounge area, enjoying the latest shiny addition to the family fleet and the attention it was attracting.

'Look, Rosie… it can have gold-plated hub caps for all I care and it *still* wont be home.' Mam wished instantly that she hadn't spoken so harshly, but the financial burden and constant worry was taking its toll.

Rosie must have realised that all was not well and made no comment, but felt just a little irritated. She had assumed by this time that her sister-in-law had abandoned any idea of settling down. Surely the purchase of the trailer had confirmed that?

Although she had become fond of Mam over the years, she still found it difficult to have any conversations of a personal nature and certainly could not ask her if everything was alright. She decided it was best just to wait. Her brother would probably tell her if there were any problems.

Towards the end of the year and back at Seafield, things were becoming really difficult. Mam had been unwell for some time but I tried not to worry, having read somewhere that women of a certain age went through 'the change'. I was relieved that she no longer sent me to the chemist for Dr. White's sanitary towels, a job I hated, always too embarrassed to ask for these if the chemist was male. I reckoned that 'the change', plus the fact that dad was having difficulty finding work and the finance company chasing us again, was the cause of all her upsets.

'I can't see any other way. I know you don't like the idea but you are just going to have to ask her.' Mam talked quietly to Dad, but with an urgency to her voice that alarmed me. They sat at the little gate-leg table, one flap extended to accommodate the red-letter correspondence from Bowmaker, Mam shuffling and rearranging the papers as though the activity would somehow magic them away.

My parents were so caught up in the emotion of their discusion that they probably had not realised that I could hear them. Richard was on the floor, engrossed in the task of trying to put the wheels, which he'd removed in the first place, back on a toy car, while Flash dozed close to the fire; I could smell his fur beginning to singe. I pretended to be reading read a book, but instead was watching and listening, realising that something serious was happening.

'She's your sister. She won't mind, and I can't think of any way out of this.'

Mam pointed to the letters again as she spoke. Dad shook his head and drew heavily on his cigarette, looking as though he would rather not be having this conversation, and sighed.

'I never thought I would have to ask her for a sub again.'

'Well… she's done it for some of the others, after all… and we *will* pay her back once you start work. You always have.'

It dawned on me now,that they were considering asking Aunt Rosie for a loan, and I could see that Dad was not keen on the idea. It was fairly well known that Rosie had helped out other family members financially. She always seemed to have money, living frugally, never seeming to spend anything on herself or even enjoy an occasional treat, resulting in her probably being the only member of Dad's family with savings.

Mam dropped her voice and I strained now to hear what she was saying.

'You can tell her about *me* if that helps.'

This puzzled me. Why on earth would Aunt Rosie be interested in Mam going through 'the change'? At this point, she looked up and realised that I'd been listening to everything. She smiled and turned to Dad, raising her eyebrows – the gesture being an unspoken question, which he understood, and he nodded his head in assent.

'While you are there, love, we have something to tell you.'

My heart lurched and I was suddenly afraid. Was it not the 'change'? Was it something serious? Perhaps even terminal? Was I going to lose Mam? I didn't want to hear… I needed to escape, to run away from the terrible news I was anticipating.

She continued, 'I'm expecting a baby. You are going to have another little brother… or sister.'

Within those few seconds I experienced a whole gambit of emotions: overwhelming relief that she wasn't about to die, then worry – thinking that it must surely be rather risky for a woman in her forties to have a baby – and then I felt angry,

'Awww… MAM! Everybody will think it's *MINE*!'

I was remembering the young girls, probably my age, going up the drive to the unmarried mothers' home at Claremont Park, clutching their little suitcases. I also could recall the often less than sympathetic glances from passengers as they watched the girls, bumps scarcely hidden, get off the bus. People were very judgemental and I could already see that they might jump to the wrong conclusion, when seeing me – a fifteen-year-old – pushing a pram containing a new baby!

My exclamation of horror and indignation, however, seemed to ease the previous tension and my parents burst out laughing, relieved to have told me and enjoying the moment, Bowmaker's letters temporarily forgotten.

SIXTY

Dad eventually plucked up the courage to visit Rosie, arriving home later with enough money to cover the instalment demand. The experience might have been humiliating for him, but his sister had been quite approachable and did not seem surprised… in fact, she appeared to almost be expecting the request.

Somehow they managed to repay her, but they were required to ask once more when Dad was temporarily laid off work, and as before, this was repaid.

The winter carnival at the Waverley Market had opened again and Aunt Rosie suggested that I might help out as well as Dad.

Mam was not keen on the idea, her own earlier experience of the market being miserable, but she eventually relented, agreeing that the extra money would be handy.

Each opening night thereafter, I became Aunt Rosie's assistant in the 'shooter', taking money, loading slugs into the rifles, ducking out of the way as punters took aim, and regularly getting in my aunt's way.

The only highlight was the fish and chips we had in the Princes Street Woolworth's cafeteria. We had to battle against gale-force winds to climb the Waverley steps, a notorious wind tunnel, but the meal was worth it.

With hindsight, I probably was as much use as Mam had been previously, and Aunt Rosie's 'employment' of me was her discreet way of giving us some extra cash.

Somehow we managed to survive financially that winter, but anticipated spring with some trepidation. This was not only 'starting out' time, but also when the baby was due. Mam was booked into the Eastern General Hospital for the birth, the hospital only being about a mile from the Seafield ground. There was no way she could risk leaving Seafield so close to her due date, so the decision was that she should stay behind in the trailer.

Dad would start out just with the bus, and I was to travel out each weekend with Richard to help him in the joints. Mam assured us that she could safely be left on her own. The first ground was Hamilton, followed by two weeks at Stirling, Richard and I shared Aunt Rosie's bed, top to tail with her and another young cousin who was visiting, while dad bunked down on the small bed he'd built earlier in the front of the bus.

Those weekends were awful. Lack of sleep, the inevitable bites from the 'nocturnal visitors'... the constant worry of leaving Mam on her own was hard enough. Trying to mind the darts joint...which I'd never been very good at... and also caring for my young brother was even harder, and we were desperate to get home to our own beds and the welcome from Mam.

'Where *is* she, Dad? What's happened?

We had arrived back at Seafield around lunchtime and as we opened the trailer door a scene of chaos met us. Wet towels were scattered on the floor and the wall-bed was still down, the blankets dangling over the side, pulled back from the sheets, which were soaking wet. I was shocked. No-one had ever explained to me the stages of childbirth. I had been farmed off to Granny's when Richard was due, eventually being presented with the end product, and being only ten, I had not really been interested in the 'preliminaries'.

Now, in my ignorance... I just thought she must have been terribly incontinent.

Dad found a hastily scribbled note from her: *'SORRY... I COULDN'T WAIT!'*

He saw how anxious I was, and Richard, tired and fractious from the journey, was becoming upset.

'It's ok, kids, looks as though your Mammy had to go to hospital without us.'

At this point, a woman from the wagon next door realised we were home and came in.

'It all happened early this morning,' she explained. 'I spotted Winnie at the window, pacing up and down, and realised things must be starting. We didn't have any transport and of course there's no phone, so we had to walk to the hospital. Winnie needed to stop at nearly every lamp post. I was frightened she would have it in the street!'

I felt so grateful to the woman. In our absence she had taken responsibility to care for Mam, holding her arm and reassuring her every time they had to stop. The effort and time it took to make that laborious walk to the Eastern must have felt like climbing Everest.

Dad thanked her and without even a wash or change of clothes, charged off to the hospital, calling to us as he left, 'You'll both be ok 'til I get back… I won't be long.'

Such optimism! Mam almost had a tradition of long labours and this was to be no exception. Not knowing what else to do, I bundled up all the wet bedding and towels, put up the wall bed and tidied up, then after a quick snack, Richard accompanied me to the nearest launderette, which was in Portobello. We sat watching the clothes go round in the machine, neither of us speaking – tired, bewildered and just a bit scared by what had happened.

Dad had been back and forward to the hospital, coming home only to wash, have a snack and check we were alright. The hours dragged on with nothing happening and I worried that we might never see Mam again. Someone had left a magazine behind in the launderette and I'd unfortunately read an article about women dying during childbirth.

'You've got a wee brother!'

He bounced into the trailer, so pleased to be giving us the news, and the woman who had assisted Mam seemed equally pleased, delighting in spreading the word round the ground that 'Dickie had a second son', and how she'd helped. My parents now had a fifteen-year-old, a five-year-old and a newborn. Clearly their family planning had gone awry!

My initial concern that I might be perceived as a teenage mother was soon forgotten. I was enjoying the role of big sister and the additional responsibility. It took Richard a little while to adjust to being the middle child rather than the youngest, but he soon warmed to the idea of another boy in the family, especially when Dad reminded him that Santa would need a bigger bag at Christmas.

The choice of a name for the baby had not been an issue. Mam decided to avoid the tradition of repeating family names, Richard and I both being called after relatives.

She liked the name David, and Dad, who wasn't fussy about family protocols, agreed. The next step was to arrange David's christening. I had been baptised when they lived in Newcastle, and Richard's ceremony had taken place in Edinburgh.

We were midway through the summer and now in a West Lothian village for two weeks. Mam, after checking the area and finding a nice little church, invited the minister to come and discuss the possibility of christening the baby there.

Richard and Dad sat outside the trailer with Flash, who had to be restrained, having taken a dislike to the clergyman. Flash was as protective of the new baby as he had been of Richard. I stayed in the trailer, curious to know what would be discussed, and watched the minister as he perched on the edge of the couch, nervously shuffling his papers while trying to balance a cup of tea on his knee.

'You *do* know that baptism is not just some form of magic spell, Mrs Stirling?'

This was absolutely the worst question the man could have asked and I could see that it had offended Mam. She gave a theatrical cough and cleared her throat.

'As a matter of fact, I have been confirmed in the Church of England by the Bishop of Durham… I have also, in my youth, taught at Sunday school. Both our children have been christened, and while our current lifestyle precludes church membership, we nevertheless do consider ourselves Christians.' Cheeks flushed now, both with the heat of her statement and also the feeling of injustice that she was being pre-judged by a man who should know better, she waited for his reaction.

The minister's demeanor changed immediately. It was as though Mam had presented him with some sort of ecumenical passport. A date was arranged for the christening without demur.

The fair was over, it was 'pulling down' day and also the Sunday we had to go to the church. Dad needed to leave what he was doing, wash and change out of his dungarees and into his (only) suit, but did this without complaint.

It rained en route but fortunately it was only a short walk from the ground for our small procession, Dad walking with Mam, who proudly carried the baby, me holding tightly to Richard's hand.

Aunt Rosie and Uncle John had agreed to be godparents and as we approached the church, trying to dry ourselves before entering, Uncle John joked that we had all been baptised now and might as well go home.

Inside, we were amazed to find that the church was full, almost every pew taken by people in their Sunday best, turning to smile at us. We froze at the door.

Dad, looking so embarrassed, whispered to Mam, 'Did you get the date wrong for this?'

The minister must have feared we were about to flee and ushered us in, explaining, 'I hope you don't mind but I mentioned to the congregation that there was to be a christening after this morning's service and I invited anyone who wished to to stay on and witness the event.'

Every single member had stayed and David had a full house. Dad, still trying to cope with his nerves as they walked past everyone, lowered his voice and commented to Uncle John, 'It's a pity this lot didn't turn up last night and punt. It would have saved the gaff.'

This was a reference to the long Saturday opening with very poor takings. Uncle John laughed, and Mam, overhearing the comment, scowled at them both, her expression reminiscent of a teacher reprimanding naughty schoolboys.

I did not feel comfortable in church environments. My experience of them was limited to the few family weddings I'd been taken to and also Richard's baptism. My discomfiture was now exacerbated by the sense of many eyes burning into my back as I stood watching my parents at the font.

Fortunately the ceremony did not take long and finished with the congregation singing Rutter's hymn – 'The Lord Bless and Keep You'. This was unexpected and Mam's expression was of delight, followed by some emotional tears when, almost on cue, a shaft of sunlight burst through a window, just as the verse 'and make His face to shine upon you' was reached.

We walked back to the ground, now enjoying the sunshine, Dad ahead of us along with John and Rosie, carrying David, who was now fast asleep. The baptism already forgotten, their conversation was now about the remaining joints to be pulled down, the long drive to the next gaff and concern that the ground would be like a swamp after the rain.

Mam was still thinking about the ceremony, comparing it with Richard's christening five years earlier. She had often talked about this and I vaguely remembered it being a bitterly cold January day, the old Kirkgate church in Leith empty apart from Mam, Dad, me and the baby, plus Aunt Rosie (who must have functioned as everyone's godmother). Mam cherished the memory, remembering how good Richard had been, not crying when anointed and remaining in fine fettle for the whole event.

David, on the other hand, had protested loudly when sprinkled with the baptismal water, this greatly amusing the congregation and adding to Dad's discomfiture.

'You know,' she said, 'despite what the minister said when he visited, I reckon the service today was truly magical.'

I had to agree.

SIXTY-ONE

Now aged fifteen, it was my turn to find winter employment somewhere. Other traveller girls took work in the breweries, or at the biscuit and chocolate factories in Leith. Those firms welcomed the seasonal staff, knowing from past experience that they were hard workers. I did not fancy working in a brewery; the smell of alcohol turned my stomach. However, the task of packing chocolates seemed quite appealing, especially if samples were available. Mam had other ideas. We sat at the small gate-leg table, scanning the 'situations vacant' columns of the Edinburgh Evening News.

'Now look, love, you should really be checking for something that will give you opportunities and the possibility of a career. *There's* one that seems promising.' She pointed to a small ad for an office junior in a solicitor's office. 'That could be a really good start for you. There is a telephone number. Why not nip down to the phone box, give them a call and see if you can get an interview?'

'But Mam!' I protested, 'I don't have any qualifications.' Memories of my education at DK's secondary school equipping me to sew a drindle skirt, burn scones and bath a baby. None of which, I thought, being particularly conducive to an office career.

'Don't be silly. You will pick things up quickly, you always do.'

Apprehensive, yet trusting her faith in me, I applied for the job and was granted an interview. As she had done during my school days, Mam accompanied me on a preliminary run, days before the interview, to make sure I knew which bus to take, how long the journey took, where exactly the office was and if it looked 'respectable'. That done, I was taken for some new clothes

– something 'officey', as Mam called it (which really was not so different from what I'd worn to school). I was ready!

The office was in one of a row of quite impressive buildings in the town centre. I was shown into a room that smelled musty, as though the large grimy window had not permitted any fresh air to enter for years. The walls were lined almost from floor to ceiling with books and there seemed to be a general lack of tidiness in the room. My initial thought was that this firm needed a cleaner rather than a clerkess.

The interviewer, a woman, sat behind a large desk, head down, seeming totally absorbed in some paperwork and not looking up as I entered.

I stood for what seemed an interminable time, wondering what the correct etiquette was. Should **I** speak first? Sit down on the wooden chair facing her? Did she even know I was there? Nerves were impacting on any little bit of confidence I might have possessed. I could feel my legs wobbling and my instinct was to run.

Then she looked up briefly, gave a rather weak smile, pointed to the chair – indicating that I should sit – and then commenced the interview.

I found myself trying to assess the woman, almost as I did when in the wheel-'em-in and evaluating potential punters. She was probably in her forties, poker-thin, her hair pulled back so tightly in a bun that I imagined if loosened, her face would collapse.

Her fingernails were long and varnished red and two fingers were nicotine-stained. Her teeth carried remnants of some hastily applied lipstick, and her voice was waspish. There was nothing about the woman to either put me at ease or warm to, and I decided that I didn't like her.

However, the interview seemed to be going well until she started to describe various mandatory courses I would have to attend, most of these being in the summer. I panicked, feeling trapped, my future being captured and controlled by this awful person.

'Oh, I'm really sorry,' I blurted out, 'but I can only work until the spring.'

Time seemed to stop, even though a large wooden clock on her desk still ticked like a metronome. I was beginning to wonder whether she had heard me, then she snapped, 'AND *WHY* IS *THAT*?'

Her eyes had narrowed almost to slits and her voice was so harsh it startled me. I tried to offer some sort of acceptable explanation

'Well... you see...' My voice faltered. I had no wish to share details of my unique family life with this woman, who in my panicked imagination was beginning to resemble Cruella DeVil, the wicked character in Dodie Smith's book, '101 Dalmatians'. I continued, 'My father's job means we have to leave Edinburgh.'

I hoped this explanation would be enough to satisfy her, but to my alarm she stood up and tossed her pen onto the desk, clearly annoyed with me.

'Did you *ACTUALLY* intend on *TAKING* this job... with *ALL* its benefits... then just *LEAVE... after SIX MONTHS*?'

By now she was red-faced with flecks of spittle at the corners of her mouth as she spoke, every second and third word loudly spat out like verbal bullets, hitting their target as I flinched. I pictured her in a courtroom, nicotine forefinger stabbing at the accused, and I felt myself shrinking back in the chair, the hard wooden frame pressing into my spine.

She terrified me and I wondered whether she was about to charge me with some sort of illegal activity.

She stood up, tore the notes she'd been taking and walked round her desk to the door, indicating that I should leave. My bottom lip quivered and, feeling so humiliated, I stumbled out, wishing the ground would swallow me up as she added, 'And I would suggest that you should be more *HONEST* in any future applications.'

She slammed the door behind me, adding emphasis to her annoyance, leaving me with a bitter experience of my very first interview and thinking how much easier it might have been just to follow the other girls and take seasonal work in the chocolate factory.

On the bus home I kept replaying the scenario in my head. Over the initial fear, now I was angry. The unfairness of it! How dare she claim I'd been dishonest when I had actually been upfront about leaving? I decided that in future, I would never declare this, and if being 'dishonest' – or rather, just a little economical with the truth – secured a job, then so be it!

Home felt like sanctuary. Mam was cooking dinner and wiped her hands on her pinny as she gave me a welcoming hug while Dad pretended to be reading a comic with Richard.

'How did you get on, love?'

Still smarting from the experience and realising that they had been waiting anxiously for my return, I decided not to describe the event and simply shrugged as I removed my coat and patted Flash.

'No luck.' I tried to sound nonchalant, hoping my quivering lip would not betray my humiliation and disappointment. 'They wanted somebody with qualifications.'

'Never mind, pet. There will be other jobs and probably better ones. Just keep looking. You'll find something. Qualifications aren't everything, you know.'

Mam was right. My second interview a few weeks later was successful and I was employed as stockroom assistant with a small firm of wholesale jewellers. The 'interview' basically consisted of 'when can you start?'. I soon discovered that this firm was experiencing financial difficulties and by the spring, they were quite happy to let me go – my £3.10/weekly wage possibly one less burden for them.

SIXTY-TWO

My third winter job was as a telephonist/receptionist with a firm of seedsmen and nurserymen in Portobello. Mam was so proud, convinced that my career was assured, despite my reminding her that I would be leaving again in the spring.

I had become quite adept at avoiding any awkward questions during interviews, the two previous employers having accepted my reason for leaving (family relocating), which wasn't exactly 'lying'... just bending the truth a little. Each employer assumed this to be a one-off rather than a yearly occurrence and sent me off with best wishes and excellent references.

I felt just a little guilty accepting this third job, knowing I would only be with them for six months. They seemed a nice crowd and were already including me in their plans for a staff outing to a Christmas pantomime. I had my own little office and was not required to do anything beyond manning the switchboard, which – in fairness – was quite busy.

Since the phones were my responsibility, one of my tasks at the end of each week was to cleanse all the handsets. This required me to go round the building, find the various telephones and sanitise them with Zoflora, which was a perfumed disinfectant.

After a few weeks, the GPO engineer had to be called in as some of the phones were developing faults. It transpired that I had been over-zealous with the Zoflora, pouring the undiluted liquid *into* the handsets instead of just wiping them with the disinfectant cloth.

I was so embarrassed and also afraid that I might be fired for damaging the phones. Instead, everyone seemed to think it was funny, especially when the manager quipped that no-one would catch flu that winter.

It was during one of these sanitising rounds that I came face to face with two of the traveller boys from Seafield. They were working in the seed packing storeroom and made no comment as I passed, but had obviously seen me. I tried to pretend that I hadn't noticed them and hurriedly wiped the phone, praying they wouldn't speak to me.

I felt so guilty ignoring them and reckoned they must have thought me a stuck-up bitch. Each disinfecting week thereafter, I dreaded meeting them, convinced that they would 'blow my cover'. Not that I was ashamed to be associated with travelling, but rather I was afraid of getting the sack if it was discovered I had no intention of staying beyond Easter when taking the job.

However, after a few weeks of these awkward and non-communicative encounters, it dawned on me that they were also avoiding me, and probably for the same reason. Seasonal work, especially for the men that winter, had been scarce and the majority of jobs advertised for permanent staff. Taking on anyone and training them, only to have them leave a few months later, would have been a disincentive to any employer. I reasoned that the two boys, who were the same age as me, had resorted to a similar tactic to mine by being a bit economical with the truth when applying for work.

We managed to keep a respectful distance and pretended not to know each other for the whole of that winter, but were so relieved when spring arrived.

I was sorry to leave that job and regretted having to hand in my notice, especially when staff were being so solicitous as I explained (yet again) that my family were relocating and I had to move with them.

I suspected that the two boys had given a similar explanation for their resignations and wondered whether anyone thought it strange we were all leaving at the same time. But it was 1962 and people were desperately afraid of the Cuban missile crisis. Our departure was the least of anyone's concerns.

SIXTY-THREE

For a while we seemed to be managing. Dad was handling the trailer confidently although he still required us to be his navigators. I had become expert in helping him to couple up the bus to the tow-bar, and I made a great show of lowering the trailer jacks and levelling it off when on uneven grounds.

An assortment of 'packing', which was just offcuts of wooden blocks, needed to be available not just for balancing the jacks, but also to place under the stall baseboards to level them. I hated handling the bits of packing since they invariably were wet, muddy and covered with an assortment of slugs from the various grounds we'd been on.

I was a show-off, keen to prove that I could not only earn money in the wheel-'em-in, but also help Dad build it up, pull it down and pack it away with all the skill of my male counterparts. I knew every pole, arch, shutter (now seemingly called 'standing bottoms') and how they all linked via hinges and 'cottars', which were long Allen-key shaped metal rods Dad had probably made to fit the large hinges. Why he called them cottars puzzled me, since this was actually an old Scottish/Irish term for a farm worker living rent-free in a cottage in return for labour. I fancied the hinge must be the 'home' to the cottar (i.e.labourer)!

Mam did not enjoy seeing me tasked as Dad's right-hand man but the logistics of caring for her two young sons, as well as everything demanded of her as a showman's wife, required her to accept this as a temporary necessity.

She was managing to maintain contact with her father, who still lived in Gateshead but now alone – Janet, the stepmother, having died in 1961. Mam

Hilda and Fred outside the newly purchased shop

kept him up to date with photographs of her children along with assurances that we were all fine and that she would try to visit at some point.

Sadly, there was still no word from her aunts, but her dad informed her that they were now living in Barnard Castle, Co. Durham, having bought a shop that sold chinawear.

Their brother Fred, by this time retired, lived in Cotherstone, which was only four miles away, and kept an eye on them.

Leslie, her brother, kept in touch and she followed his career with great pride. Now a senior manager in the transport industry, and as the official spokesperson, he was regularly being interviewed by the press whenever there was an issue with the organisation. He enjoyed holidays abroad and we received postcards from some quite exotic places. I heard Mam comment on this once to Aunt Rosie as she showed her one of the cards.

'You know, Rosie, our kids have never known what it is to have a holiday.'

'Oh Winnie,' Rosie snapped back. 'This life is one big holiday – haven't you realised that after all this time?'

I waited for some acerbic response from Mam but she said nothing and changed the subject. When I asked her about this later, she explained that Rosie could see no life beyond showbusiness; she was a zealot and any apparent criticism or adverse comment about the lifestyle was to be avoided. Showbusiness was the sum total of her world and she would always defend it with a passion.

I realised that despite Rosie's interference in her early married life, Mam had, over the years, grown to understand and respect her. She had learnt to bite her tongue and not criticise the life that Rosie loved, knowing this would both hurt and offend her.

'That's not to say that I want this to be *our* fate,' Mam added, concerned that I might think she had been won over. She looked at the most recent postcard from Leslie.

'I *know* I keep saying it, but I promise you, some day *we* will be the ones living in a nice house, going on holidays and sending postcards, you'll see.'

I loved Mam's optimism and it seemed her prophecy might actually be possible, the summer weather having been kind and our season showing a little profit, allowing us to return to Seafield that winter with a small amount of savings. Dad obtained work at Leith docks again, I found another office job fairly quickly, Mam enrolled Richard – now five – at Leith Links, my old primary school, and David, the baby of the family, was thriving. We anticipated a comfortable, trouble-free Christmas, but fortunes changed yet again.

Work at the docks stopped. No boats were coming in – or expected for some time – and all the men on temporary contracts were paid off. Dad was now unemployed and despite trying every possible avenue was not able to find work elsewhere.

Their few savings quickly disappeared, the only income now being my small wage and the family allowance paid by the state. (The Family Allowance Act of 1945 was a child benefit payment of five shillings per week for each child other than the first.)

No matter how hard Mam tried to eke this out, we found ourselves on the Bowmaker red-letter list once more and were haunted by the fear of our home being repossessed.

The Waverley Market winter carnival opened and Dad helped Rosie again, but this small additional income only ensured that we at least had food. Having already borrowed twice previously from Rosie, Mam would not let Dad approach her a third time, saying we would manage… somehow. I felt I had to do something and had an idea.

When premium bonds were introduced in 1956 it was possible to buy single £1 bonds. Whenever she could manage Mam bought me a bond, and I now had five.

Without telling my parents, I visited Aunt Rosie and asked her if she would give me £5 and take the bonds as surety. I gave the excuse that I needed some extra cash to buy Christmas presents for my brothers and I promised to repay her and reclaim the bonds later.

She agreed. I handed her the bonds and rushed home clutching the £5 note, feeling so adult and smug, convinced that I had saved the day by solving our family problem without actually 'borrowing' in the true sense of the word.

Dad was out job-hunting and Richard was preoccupied with the baby so I had Mam to myself and eagerly awaited her praise.

'Here you are, Mam. You can add this to the pot.' I proudly brandished the £5. 'And if I also help at the Waverley Market we should have enough for the payment.'

She was strangely quiet and it seemed an eternity before she spoke.

'Don't you worry, love. We can manage this month. I've sent the postal order off to Bowmaker's.'

I was puzzled. We had no cash earlier so how was she able to work miracles today? She appeared to be upset; her eyes were red and she fished in her pinny pocket for some non-existent hankie. I checked that Richard was still outwith earshot.

'What's wrong, Mam?

She looked at me, seeming anxious and almost shamefaced and I really began to worry.

'Now promise not to tell your dad… I had no other option… I had to do it.'

I nodded, terribly concerned now that I was about to become privy to some awful confession. I'd read about women being so desperate for money, they'd resorted to 'the oldest profession'. Surely not this! I dismissed the idea quickly, the thought too awful to bear.

'I've sold my engagement ring.'

I was lost for words. While relieved that she had sold her ring rather than her body, I was heartbroken for her, knowing how hard this must have been. She only possessed three pieces of jewellery – her wedding band, the gold locket and her engagement ring. She could never part with the locket, and always wore her wedding ring. The only option left was the diamond ring.

She tried to explain, telling me, 'Your dad won't notice that the ring is missing. I only ever wore it to special events and just kept it in its box.' She pointed to the now-empty little ring box. 'I sold it to a jeweller's in the High Street. He didn't give me much but it was enough to cover this month's instalment. Now *please* don't tell your dad, you know what he's like, he won't understand – he'll be hurt and probably ashamed, and we'll suffer his mood for weeks.

'Oh… and while I was in the High Street I went into the housing department to try for a council house, but we're seemingly not eligible because we don't live permanently in Edinburgh. Now promise me, keep all this to yourself.'

I nodded, lost for words and heartsick that things had reached this stage.

I pictured Mam hesitating outside the jeweller's, looking at the trays of second-hand rings and wondering what fate had befallen all the previous owners.

I imagined her handing her little ring to the manager, who, having given it a cursory examination, offered a price. I wondered whether she had tried to haggle, or was she just too upset to even try?

I pictured her in the council office hoping to be placed on a waiting list for a house and her disappointment when told that as itinerants, we did not meet the criteria.

I felt the bile rise in my throat, first with the emotion of it all, then anger that circumstances had driven her to this. I needed to blame someone and Dad, in my mind, was responsible for the predicament we were in. His determination that we should continue to follow his lifestyle was the root cause of all our problems.

I experienced at that moment a resentment bordering on hatred towards him.

Dad never seemed to notice that the ring had gone, or even asked Mam how she'd afforded that month's payment, just assuming that it was good budgeting.

We somehow eventually managed to pay off the loan but always on a financial seesaw, Bowmaker always being paid –sometimes *on* time, but often late. Although I hated the reminders and red-letter warnings, I felt also that whoever was handling our account must have been a sympathetic soul, our erratic payments being tolerated when we probably should have been foreclosed.

SIXTY-FOUR

Time passed at an almost frightening speed. The boys were growing rapidly. Richard, now of primary school age, was experiencing the traumas of the various summer schools and then settling into the rhythm of winters at my old primary, Leith Links.

David, now a toddler, was a lively and constant chatterbox, whereas Richard was shy and introverted. While he enjoyed the freedom of travelling life, he hated *being* a traveller, and at a very early age he made it quite clear that the lifestyle was not for him.

Mam felt some guilt about this, fearing that her stories of settled life as a flattie had influenced him. Whatever the cause, Richard had decided he would not be following in his father's footsteps. He disliked helping in the joints, opting to look after his young brother, both of them exploring round the grounds when we were open and only returning for meals – or when bored.

We never usually worried when they wandered off, knowing Flash –ever vigilant – was with them, and also reassured by the fact that every traveller knew the boys and would quickly intervene should they get into trouble. There was one occasion, however, which caused us great concern.

We were at Bridge of Allan for the Highland Games, the fairground pitched in a huge field next to the games arena. This was a large fair and one of the few events where we might earn some money.

The field was notorious for its instability, the ground turning into a muddy, saturated mess whenever it rained. Saturday, 'gaff day', was fast approaching. It had rained all week and the ground was like a quagmire.

David, Richard and cousin Stephen, on the chairoplane steps at Bridge of Allan, mud-caked wellingtons evidence of another wet week. (Behind them in the distance, the famous Wallace's Monument can just be seen.)

The lessee arranged truckloads of ash and cinders to be delivered and spread, and everyone hoped this might provide a dry walkway, but it was wasted effort. The surface of the footfall areas was still swamp-like, the ash on top of the mud just wobbling like sprinkles on jelly, and it continued to rain. Dad desperately tried to make improvised duck-boards, placing bits of wood and hardboard in front of our joints, but despaired as these slowly surrendered to the mud.

On the Saturday, the crowds that traditionally came to the shows when the Games finished were hurrying home, obviously reluctant to wade through the soggy mire, with only a few wellington-clad stalwarts venturing onto the ground.

By late afternoon the sun condescended to appear and while the ground was still a muddy, steaming mess, people started to drift back. Potential punters were bypassing our joints, choosing to side-step Dad's slippery duckboards, and our takings were poor, but the bigger worry for us was that Richard had disappeared.

He had last been seen at lunchtime when we opened, and had wandered off

– leaving David and Flash in the joints with Mam and Dad. By teatime, Mam was beside herself with worry, convinced that something awful had happened to him. I questioned any of the young cousins Richard usually hung out with, but no-one had seen him. Despite Dad's attempts to appear unconcerned, both Mam and I knew he was just as worried as us. He was chain-smoking, pacing up and down the joint, scarcely speaking to us, and even missing the occasional punters who wished to play.

'Where have you been?' Dad demanded as Richard climbed over the shutters and into the joint. Just as he was about to receive a combined interrogation and telling off, a crowd of about a dozen men arrived and spotted Richard.

'Ah, there ye are, laddie. We wondered where you'd got to. So you work here as well?' The man, resplendent in his kilt, a rosette pinned to the lapel of his tweed jacket denoting some sort of committee membership, realised some explanation was required and turned to Dad. 'He's been a great help to us today. We've been running the Round Tablers' charity balloon race all day and he helped us to blow them up and tie all the labels on the strings. That smile of his was a great crowd-puller and our table did quite well.'

Dad was dumbfounded. His son was not keen to help in the joints yet had happily worked all afternoon on a charity stall, and for no payment apart from a bottle of orange juice.

Mam and Dad waiting for punters, David telling Dad such a story!

The Round Tablers, probably having enjoyed a few visits to the beer tent, were full of bonhomme and started to spend money at our joints, laughing and joking with Richard as they played. They were attracting the attention of other people, keen to see what was causing all the noise, and soon we had crowds playing at our can and darts joints again.

By the end of that night, while not a fortune, we had managed to make a small profit thanks to

Richard, his Round Tablers, and the wellington-clad die-hards who returned that day to support the fair.

Richard promised never to disappear again and managed to avoid the scolding he really deserved, his absence forgiven in deference to him – albeit inadvertently – bringing us the much-needed punters.

SIXTY-FIVE

'Friggin' hell... what do this lot want?'

Dad always made it his rule never to swear in front of us but he sounded alarmed and we realised something must be wrong. As he slowed the bus down, Mam looked out the window and was quick to spot the cause of his concern.

'Oh Lord… we're being flagged down by a police car.'

Heart in mouth, I followed her gaze, hoping she was mistaken, but there it was – a large traffic patrol car, its flashing blue light adding to the drama as we stopped and it pulled in front of us. We watched as Dad jumped down from the cab to talk to the two policemen. Richard and David were now jostling with each other for a better view of the patrol car while Flash clawed at the bifold door, trying to get out.

'Do you think we maybe have a puncture, Mam?' I asked, trying to picture any scenario that might force us to stop. Mam scolded the two boys and pulled the dog, who was now howling, away from the door.

'I think it might be a bit more serous than a puncture, love,' she replied, her voice trembling as she spoke.

We both looked out again and saw Dad, now visibly wide-eyed and upset, walking to the back of our trailer with the two officers. They seemed to be gone for ages and we sat in the small compartment behind the cab worrying, aware that this was not a normal occurrence. Our journeys over the years took us around all of the Lothians, central and western Scotland – even across the border into Cumberland – and at no time had we ever been stopped.

We now were stuck at the side of a busy road, vehicles slowing as they passed, the spectacle of the patrol car, our bus and trailer, plus the two policemen, attracting great interest.

The two officers eventually reappeared, one winding a tape measure back into its holder as he talked to Dad, while the other sat in the patrol car, notebook in one hand, radio mike in the other, obviously making some sort of report.

'Are ye alright, Dickie?'

A traveller en route to the same ground as us realised we were in trouble and was about to stop and help. Dad quickly waved him on, warning him that he was blocking the road and assuring him that everything was ok.

Mam and I realised Dad would be mortified, not just by being stopped by the police but that the traveller would share the news and now everyone on the next ground would know. There would be great speculation. Had we been caught without tax or insurance? Were we speeding? Had we been in accident? etc, etc. (The answer was much simpler but the cause would have a far-reaching consequence for us.)

We watched as the patrol car drove off and waited for Dad to return. Instead of climbing back into the cab, he pushed open the bifold door and joined us in the little compartment. Hands shaking as he lit a cigarette, he paused, then looked at Mam.

'Well… we're in a right mess now.'

We all sat quietly, fearful of what we were about to hear, the swish of the traffic and the road noise no longer noticed as we waited for him to speak.

'It's the trailer,' he continued, drawing heavily on the cigarette then offering it to Mam, almost as a precursor remedy for shock. 'It's too long to be towed on two wheels.'

I almost laughed. This seemed ludicrous to me. I thought that surely a trailer equipped with a towbar was designed to *be* towed? There had to be a mistake.

Dad continued, 'Those rozzers told me we were spotted by their inspector when we drove through Linlithgow. He'd been sitting in the Black Bull pub having his lunch when we passed his window. He got right on the radio and ordered the patrol crew to stop us. That's why they had the tape measure. They told me that any trailer longer than twenty-two feet has to be either on four wheels or escorted by the police as an 'abnormal load'. Our trailer exceeds the legal limit by four feet.'

Mam was trying hard to work through the implications of this.

'Well... so we can't stay here, and we aren't allowed to travel. We don't have a magic wand to change two wheels into four and I wouldn't think the police would be happy to grant us an escort on every journey. Did those two policemen suggest *anything*?'

Dad grinned ruefully and we hoped there might be a solution.

'They actully weren't too bad, as rozzers go. They didn't book me and let us off with a warning, providing we get the trailer off the road. I told them we're heading for Edinburgh and I promised to park up once there. They said they would wireless ahead to make sure we wouldn't be stopped again en route.'

This was no solution! We were supposed to be heading for the next fair in West Lothian but were now expected to travel to Edinburgh, which really was just our winter base. Not only were we possibly going to lose our pitch at the fair if we failed to turn up, but our enforced detour to Edinburgh was possibly going to be tracked and monitored by the police to ensure we complied with their warning.

There was a risk that the Seafield ground would not be available during the summer, but Mam suggested that we should try there first, even if only to park overnight until we considered our predicament and any possible options.

The journey to Edinburgh only took about twenty minutes but felt like an eternity. We sat on the little bunk behind Dad's cab, eyes fixed on the road ahead, afraid that we would be stopped again.

No-one spoke; even the dog was quiet. I could see Dad's white-knuckled hands clenched to the steering wheel as he drove. We were all shocked at this turn of events and our future now seemed desperately uncertain.

Even if we were allowed to park at Seafield, it still did not solve the problem of how to get to, and open at, the next fair.

Our previous years of travelling, first with the Albion then the bus, combined home *and* business. We were self-contained, our home, life and livelihood – *everything* – under one roof.

Now, the trailer, which ironically was supposed to improve our lives, had once more become a worrying burden.

SIXTY-SIX

Seafield, which usually felt welcoming – after all, it had been our home base every winter for years – seemed strange and unfamiliar now. It was empty apart from the caretaker's trailer and a couple of wagons belonging to permanent residents.

The weather that week had been hot and the breeze drifting across the road from the sea was lifting miniature whirlwhinds up from the dusty ground. It was also delivering the most obnoxious smell, which the caretaker told us was from the broken pipes that spewed raw sewage into the sea. Never aware of this during the winter, we assumed that it must be a summer phenomenon and while it was a different stench from the one at Vinegarhill, it was just as sickening. This was no 'homecoming' – just another added stress to what had become a nightmarish day.

Having explained our difficulty to the caretaker, she agreed to our stopover, Dad assuring her that it would only be short-term. Richard and David headed off to the little corner shop for some milk and fresh bread, leaving Mam, Dad and I to discuss our predicament and any possible options.

How on earth could we manage to open at our grounds if we weren't legally allowed to tow the trailer? Failing to turn up at each of the scheduled fairs might mean we had forfeited our 'protected rights' to those pitches. We should already have been building up at the next West Lothian ground in readiness for the miner's gala that weekend.

Time was of the essence and in the absence of any ideas from either Dad or myself, Mam decided to take charge and, turning to Dad, said, 'Well, there's nothing else for it. You'll just have to go on without us.'

We looked at her, not sure what she meant or how this could be managed. We listened as she continued, her soft Geordie accent still noticeable as she spoke. Clearly, a plan was forming. She looked out the trailer window at our bus, which Dad had uncoupled and parked alongside.

'It's the only way, but obviously depends on the caretaker agreeing to let us keep the trailer here all summer.'

Dad still hadn't quite grasped what she was proposing and lit yet another cigarette. I sipped lukewarm tea, willing the boys to come home and bring some feeling of normality to the situation. Mam continued to look at the bus as she spoke.

'That alcove behind the cab will have to function now as a temporary 'wee wagon'. The bunk seat you made can be used as a bed, and we still have that little two-ring Calor gas cooker so you can at least heat up some food. You head off tomorrow and get the joints built up. We'll catch a bus and join you in time for opening at the weekend.'

Dad nodded, not saying anything but obviously thinking this might be workable, and now my imagination was in overdrive, picturing all the inconveniences of the plan.

'Mam, there are five of us. Surely we can't all sleep on that bunk?' I knew the answer almost as soon as I'd asked the question. Mam smiled at me.

'Your granny's wagon is at the next couple of grounds, and I'm sure your Aunt Rosie won't mind sharing her bed again. It will just be a temporary arrangement until your dad and I work out a better plan.'

I groaned silently, knowing what was ahead.

And so we spent the rest of that day turning the void behind the cab into a 'wee wagon'. Mam shared out the bedding, some towels, dishes and cutlery, a couple of pots and a few starter provisions. We gazed with little enthusiasm at the very hastily made accommodation. Even the boys, who tended to treat everything as an adventure, were silent, and Mam felt that something positive needed to be said.

'There now,' she said briskly, as she brushed her hair back and wiped her hands on her pinny. 'It's not ideal but it will at least get us started again.' She turned to Dad. 'You used to live in a wee wagon when you were young so you'll manage alright, and I'm sure Rosie will probably feed you during the week. You won't starve, will you?'

I felt this was more of an assertion rather than a question and Dad just nodded.

Waving our bus off the following morning was awful, made even worse by Dad's (very practical) decision to take Flash with him. He knew neither Mam nor I could cope with the two boys and luggage plus a large dog when we journeyed out at the weekend.

I wasn't too sure how Mam felt, but somehow losing Flash, our constant companion and protector, seemed worse to me than Dad's absence.

As promised, Mam packed enough clothes, toiletries and food to last us the weekend and we set off on the Friday for St Andrew Square bus station. To all outward apearances we probably looked like holidaymakers.

It took several frustrating hours to reach the fairground. Unfamiliar with bus timetables and routes, and then discovering services to that particular town were infrequent, meant we arrived late and just as shutters were being lifted. (Opening times were commonly 6pm on Fridays and 1pm on Saturdays.) We were tired and hungry and now expected to get on with the business of minding the joints. Mam was having none of it, and Dad didn't complain when she insisted that we had to eat first.

He stayed out front while we piled into the bus's small compartment and sat on the bunk, watching Mam as she boiled water for tea on the little stove and made us sandwiches. The bus smelled – a combination of engine oil and stale cigarette smoke, plus bodily odours of man and dog – but that did nothing to quell our appetites.

We sat like a little band of displaced persons and devoured our food, still feeling the motion of the journey on the Eastern Scottish bus and already dreading the return trip.

Friday and Saturday nights' sleeping arrangements were, to say the least, uncomfortable for everyone. Mam, Dad and David squeezed into the little bunk in our bus, while Richard and I shared Aunt Rosie's bed in Granny's wagon… along with the inevitable nocturnal visitors.

The weekend takings just about covered expenses, but at least we had managed to get there, open the joints and preserve our rights to the ground space for another year. It was clear that, no matter how difficult, we would be forced to maintain this routine for the rest of the summer.

The Seafield caretaker agreed to our trailer remaining on site, which, while a relief, also meant we would be paying rent and this was an additional financial burden when added to our travel costs.

We became very knowledgeable about the buses/trains to take that would get us to the various grounds. We also adjusted quickly to Dad's role of absentee parent, only seeing him at weekends.

I noticed that Dad never ever said he'd missed us, and often the greater welcome was from Flash, who turned into a great lolloping bundle of joyous, tail-wagging, fur-flying delight when we arrived.

SIXTY-SEVEN

While these weekends stressed Mam, the weekdays spent at Seafield were different. Life – at least for four days every week – seemed settled and had routine. She could use the wash-house in Portobello instead of pestering Dad to put up clothes lines or borrow Aunt Marie's washing machine.

She missed the company of her sisters-in-law, Marie and Charlotte, their companionship and support through the week no longer available and the weekends too busy for any real social interaction. But the compensation of being part-settled was enough for her.

She knew which shops in Leith to buy the best value groceries and also how to use the Easter Road Co-operative. Grocery orders could be placed mid-week and were delivered on Fridays just before we were due to leave, and payment was not required until the following Monday.

The Co-op used a horse and cart for deliveries and it was always a delight when this arrived, reminding Mam of her own mother's stories about the horse that always stopped at their house in Newcastle for a carrot.

Richard was attending Links Primary School again and was no longer classed as an itinerant scholar. David would soon be of school age and Mam hoped that he might never have to experience a peripatetic education.

Richard was shy and reserved and didn't enjoy the constant changes, so the stability of being at one school suited him. David, on the other hand, was a chatterbox and talked non-stop, once exasperating Old Teddy to the point where he shouted 'For God's sake… will somebody shut that laddie up?!' David would probably cope with different schools, but Mam hoped this would never happen, and was determined to grasp tightly to this sense of permanence in Edinburgh.

Television was our main source of entertainment through the week, Dad having arranged our power supply and set up the aerial before he left. The old, humongous TV, which had never worked properly, had long since been replaced by a smaller set called a PYE portable.

All through the previous summer we had tolerated a fault with the aerial socket, and Dad's improvised repair with a matchstick was no longer effective. Now we were based on Seafield, Mam arranged for an engineer to call and fix it. David watched as the engineer examined the set and the man felt duty-bound to say something.

'Well, m'lad… I'll have to see if I can fix this for you. Was it you that broke it?' he joked as he began to dismantle the set.

David was quite annoyed at the suggestion he might have misbehaved and quickly replied, 'No, it wasn't me, it was a horse! We were just watching the cowboys and wagon train and a horse broke loose and pulled the aerial out.'

The poor man must have thought David's imagination was out of control as he quickly completed the repair and left. Richard, Mam and I burst out laughing, knowing David had actually been telling the truth. The previous summer when we were at Innerleithen, we'd managed a tap on to a power supply which meant we could watch TV. The aerial was fastened to our bus roof and the cable stretched across to, and through, the trailer window.

Two horses owned by a relative of the Pinder family, probably ex-circus horses, were earning him money as children's rides. One evening when the fair was closed, the animals slipped their tether and wandered round the ground, enjoying the freedom.

One decided to graze in the space between our bus and trailer, but got tangled in the aerial wire and in its panic, yanked the cable out of the TV socket. We *were* actually watching 'Wagon Train', an American Western of the sixties, at the time.

The horse came to no harm but our TV was faulty for the remainder of the summer.

Hilariously true though David's account had been, there was no way we could share the story with the engineer and allowed him to leave convinced that our four-year-old was being exposed to too much American TV.

The four days away from fairgrounds each week felt like an escape. We had fallen into the settled life easily and Mam continued to tell us that this was how things could be if only Dad would stop travelling.

'Do you remember me telling you that I'd tried to put our names on the council waiting list?' she asked me, checking first that the boys weren't listening.

How could I forget? That was the day she had sold her engagement ring, and I wondered why she was mentioning it now. We were standing at the bus stop, about to set off to St Andrew Square for yet another journey to join Dad.

Richard and David were engrossed in patting the little donkey that was kept in a small grass enclosure next to the bus stop. The animal belonged to the Hunter family, who had a scrap metal business, filling station and bungalow on Seafield Road.

The donkey was a favourite with everyone and now a helpful distraction, Mam obviously not wanting the boys to hear us talking. She lowered her voice to an almost conspiratorial whisper.

'Well… I wasn't *exactly* telling the truth. We've been on the list for a while now.'

This was a revelation and I was confused. 'But Mam… I thought you said they wouldn't accept us because we didn't live permanently in Edinburgh?' I stared at her, wondering what she was about to say.

'Ehmm…' she looked slightly uncomfortable, as though some heinous crime was about to be revealed. 'When I filled in the form I claimed we were Edinburgh residents and I gave Seafield as our permanent address. I did worry for a while that someone from the council might check this, but either they were too busy or they just didn't bother. However – the way things have turned out, we're stuck here for the foreseeable future and it is our address, should anyone check, so it's alright after all.'

I struggled to know what to say. Mam had always talked of getting a house but somehow to me, it had seemed something other people did, just a pipe dream. Now I felt a bit fearful that it might actually happen and of what the consequences could be.

'Does Dad know what you have done?' I asked, thinking ahead to our weekend trip.

'No... and don't you say anything. I'll choose the moment but meantime, it's our secret… promise?'

I nodded, struggling with this new information as the bus arrived. I was now entrusted with two secrets: the ring and the housing application. I worried that she might have opened a Pandora's box resulting in all sorts of penalties and sanctions being imposed on us.

Somehow, we were surviving the summer with all its difficulties. The final trip was to the last ground of our season in Egremont. This was the most gruelling journey for us, requiring several different buses and a train journey. We inevitably arrived late, the fair already opened and Dad standing alone in the joints, scowling… but Mam didn't care.

It was the last fair of our summer. We would be heading back to Seafield in our own transport (the bus) and also with Flash, his showbiz duty done.

Life would start to feel manageable again and at some point, when Dad had emerged from his latest huff, Mam would tell him about the council list.

SIXTY-EIGHT

Seafield was back to its winter normality, as though someone had pressed a reset button. All the familiar wagons, trailers and lorries pitched exactly where they stood previously, everything where it should be… our little community reunited again.

Summer, despite all the difficulties, had been fairly profitable for us and Mam was managing to save a little money again. Dad found work quickly at the Henry Robb shipyards. The foreman Alf – a Norwegian – had employed Dad and also Uncle Tommy previously, knew they were good workers and had no hesitation in taking Dad on again.

I wasn't as fortunate. I scanned the 'situations vacant' columns of the Evening News, circling possibilities and phoning if a number was provided, or writing when this was requested. I was beginning to think I should just take the seasonal route to the chocolate or biscuit factories when I received an invitation to be interviewed.

This was one job I'd dismissed as beyond my reach even when completing the application form and I had completely forgotten about it. Yet here it was – a formal letter-headed notification acknowledging my interest in the civilian post of wireless/telephone operator with Edinburgh City Police.

'INTEREST! That was a massive understatement and I was sick with excitement as, hands shaking, I read and re-read the letter, not quite believing what I was seeing.

'You see,' Mam exclaimed as I shared the news. 'I *told* you that your office experience would pay dividends eventually.'

Before I could remind her that I didn't actually *have* the job yet, she dashed out the trailer to share the news with Dad and the boys, who were standing with a group of men. Word spread like wildfire around the ground, almost like a scandal. Dickie's lassie was joining the 'rozzers'!

It took some time for the recruitment and selection process to be completed. Criminal records had to be checked, including those of immediate family members.

This did not worry me unduly. My family might be considered unorthodox in their lifestyle but were not criminals. I did have a passing concern that Dad's earlier winter coal 'heists' might count, but he reassured me that he had never been caught so there would be no record.

I was eventually interviewed and must have been paralysed with fear because I could remember nothing of the process beyond being told that I would have to attend a medical. All boxes eventually ticked, I was offered the job and started in January 1964, based in the control room of police headquarters, Parliament Square.

There were only eleven operators in post, and just like the uniformed officers, the civilian staff were given ID numbers.

I was twelfth in line so I became WTO12 (Wireless/Telephone Operator 12).

The job involved shift work, including night shifts, but this did not worry me. I was young, fit (according to the medical referee) and was finding the job interesting and exciting. Mam did worry nevertheless, and was constantly trying to keep the trailer quiet during the day when I slept.

Aunt Rosie, who tried to describe my job to someone, told them, 'She's one of those… ehmm… you know, call girls, and she gets picked up by the police at the weekends.'

Although the basics of this were true (when there was no bus service on public holidays or weekends, a traffic car was sent to collect me), we very quickly had to ask my aunt to rephrase her description before my reputation was irreparably damaged.

I loved the job, my only initial difficulty being the twenty-four hour clock system (numbers again), which took a little longer to learn than the NATO phonetic alphabet, which I managed effortlessly.

I was not shy when broadcasting… perhaps my showbiz 'speil' when touting for punters had given me the required and necessary confidence.

I enjoyed getting to know my colleagues. One lady, probably nearing retirement, used to be an RAF radio operator during the war. Unfortunately, she had now developed a stammer, which became more pronounced when operating the police radio, especially if it involved something exciting such as a 999 call or high-speed car chase. The policemen cruelly joked that she must have brought more of our planes down during the war than the Germans.

Another lady, also quite 'mature' although never admitting her age, must have been an actress in a previous life. She kept a mirror propped in front of her on the desk, and seemed to apply lipstick every five minutes. She watched herself in the mirror when 'on air', and when she broadcast it was akin to a Shakespearean drama, every word drawn out in an exaggerated drawl, which she called her 'BBC voice'. While just a little intimidated by her, she fascinated me and took me under her wing, spending time teaching me the proper Home Office rules of wireless telephony and also the various call-signs of the district offices and patrol cars.

I grew to respect both her and the 'stammer lady'. They were unique individuals who had earned their places, and now it was my turn.

Me (on left) with my team, in the Charge office, Police HQs

On the days when the traffic cars 'picked me up' (as Aunt Rosie called it), I stood at the gate to wait for them rather than have them drive onto the ground.

The drivers were either extremely diplomatic or just not really interested, since at no point did they ever express any curiousity about why I lived there. I was accepted without question as one of the team and this delighted me.

My only – and *major* – concern, was that spring and our schedule of fairs would soon begin again, and I hadn't properly worked out what to do about my job.

SIXTY-NINE

We were fast approaching 'starting out' time again, the trailer problem had still not been resolved and my parents were beginning to panic.

During the winter, Dad had considered the possibility of somehow converting the trailer chassis to a four-wheel arrangement; unfortunately this was not only structurally but also financially impossible.

We were aware of other travellers getting ready to leave, lorries being checked, engines turned over after months of inactivity, and of women helping to wash the Seafield grime from their wagons' bodywork. Everyone was preparing to start out with clean, tidy loads. Our trailer certainly was clean and tidy, just not mobile.

We had survived the previous summer by roughing it in the front of our bus and if necessary we would have to do this again. However, I had now become the main cause for concern.

Mam, Dad and I sat round the little red formica table having just finished dinner, and the boys had gone off to explore somewhere with Flash. The trailer was warm and I was half asleep, still adjusting to my shift patterns.

'We've been thinking.' Mam looked at me to make sure she had my attention. 'We're obviously having to start out again but we don't want you to give up your job.' Dad nodded in agreement but remained silent, leaving Mam to do the talking.

'So your dad and I have decided that you keep working and just come out to help us on your days off. The trailer will still be here so you will at least have some peace and quiet to sleep when we are away.'

Suddenly I was wide awake. While delighted that I would not have to resign from my police job, I could not imagine how my folks would cope during the summer without me.

I considered myself the family 'mainstay', indispensable to their financial and practical support. I had a sense of abandonment momentarily, and as though reading my thoughts and sensing my apprehension, Mam kept talking – partly, I suspected, to convince herself the plan was workable.

'Your dad will go out to each ground with the bus, just like last summer, and he'll build up the stuff ready to open. I'll be here with the boys through the week so you won't be on your own.' She paused, trying to think of something that did not seem to be replicating last season's misery. 'And don't forget, you not only will be a great help when you manage to join us at the weekends, but you are earning a good wage now and your contribution to the 'pot' is going to give us a wee bit more security, especially when the takings are poor.'

My sense of importance was restored. The plan, although not ideal, was at least workable, allowing me to keep my job and Richard to continue attending Links school.

And so it began again, Mam packing clothes and provisions, then heading off every Friday to work the weekend fairs with my two young brothers. Most times I managed to join them, either by swapping shifts or using holidays and lieu days.

On one occasion, heading straight out after a night shift, I fell asleep on the bus, waking up with a start as the bus jolted, completely disorientated and not remembering for a moment *which* fair I was supposed to be heading for. After this fright, I always ensured that I went home to the trailer and had at least four hours sleep before setting off.

Once more, this became the pattern of yet another summer fairground treadmill. My work colleagues never questioned why I needed to change or swap shifts so often. I think they were of the impression that I must have been leading a wonderfully chaotic but secretive social life. I did nothing to dispel this belief!

SEVENTY

'I've just come back from those council offices again,' Mam announced as she tossed her shopping bag and coat on the couch and sat down, obviously upset about something. 'A wee lass, about the same age as you, informed me that we weren't considered a priority and we were low on the waiting list. So I asked her how their waiting list actually worked and she told me it was a points system. Apparently, we don't have enough points.'

This was mid-week. It was my day off and Dad had moved on to the next scheduled fair. Mam had at some point told him about her applying for a council house, but my impression was that he didn't believe it would ever happen, and never discussed the possibility. I was relieved that at least that was one less secret for me to keep.

Now clutching the cup of tea I'd made for her, she continued, 'So, do you KNOW what that wee flibbertijibbet told me?'

I shook my head, picturing the scene in the council office, a queue behind Mam as she stood her ground demanding answers.

'She said, in a really patronising voice, that we weren't homeless or destitute or living in overcrowded sub-standard conditions and other people got the points because they met that criteria. I tried to tell her we lived on a rat-infested, unsanitary caravan site, and that you shared a bedroom with your young brother, and David didn't even have a bed and slept on this couch. She wouldn't listen, just kept repeating that we *were* on the list, but other people with greater needs gained more points and kept overtaking us.'

Mam turned to gaze out the trailer window and sipped her tea.

'I'm not going to stop. I'll keep going up to that office until someone properly listens to me and increases our points.'

I could understand her frustration and disappointment. She thought, when first having her application accepted, that the offer of a house would soon follow. Now she was forced to realise that we might always be at the bottom of the list, other families continually being deemed higher priority.

As I listened, nodding sympathetically, I felt just a little relieved. I had always supported her dream of having a house and settling down, but I just could not picture myself as a 'flattie'. I was nineteen and had only ever known the fairground community and lifestyle. While integrating, up to a point, with my police colleagues, I still managed to maintain a certain distance, just as I had done at my various schools and jobs. I always avoided questions such as where I spent my holidays, what I might be doing at weekends etc. My quietness and reluctance to talk about my private life was just accepted as shyness.

I quite enjoyed the 'air of mystery'. I was a traveller masquerading as a flattie when at work, and somehow managing to strike a balance between the two worlds.

Dad probably shared my qualms about 'settling down'. When we all joined him that weekend and mam repeated the saga of the points system, I sensed that he was also relieved. His only comment was 'never mind' and he quickly changed the subject. We finished our usual makeshift snack in the bus then went out to the joints.

It was opening time Friday, time for the shutters to be lifted, for my goldfish to be set out in the wheel-'em-in – and life, for Dad, with his family around him, was running as normal. Houses were just some fantasy, but this was his comforting and safe reality.

Those summer weeks, although still stressful, brought some happiness for Mam. Her father, who continued to keep in touch, suggested we might like to visit him. He had previously paid a flying visit to us during the winter, using the travel concession he was entitled to as an ex-railwayman to book a day trip.

We picked a time when there was a gap between fairs, Dad hired a little Ford Prefect, which had seen better days but was cheap, and we drove to Newcastle.

Granda now lived in a little, one-bedroom house, one of a row of pensioner's cottages. We arrived around lunchtime and after the hugs and welcomes, Mam set about making us all something to eat, having packed rolls, fillings and a variety of cakes, biscuits and fruit. She was loving the visit, especially enjoying our difficulty in trying to follow her dad's broad Geordie accent, which she suspected he was exaggerating for effect.

The conversation eventually turned to the aunts Edith and Hilda, and Granda confessed that he hadn't seen them or Fred for years, although he did write.

Mam looked at Dad, who as usual scarcely spoke during the visit, preferring to just be an observer, and nothing daunted, she announced, 'RIGHT. Enough's enough, this will never do. Too much time has passed and I think, since we are all here, we should take my dad to see his sisters.'

With no further ado, we all squeezed into the little Ford and headed for Barnard Castle. This was a journey of just over fifty miles. I sat squashed with Mam and the two boys in the back seat – Granda in the front, giving Dad directions.

I could see Dad's face in the small driving mirror and knew from his expression that he was not happy with this unforseen side trip. I wondered which might be the greater cause for his concern – the old Ford, which creaked and protested at the overloaded springs, or the prospect of meeting the aunts.

After all, he had been the cause of the acrimony and twenty years' estrangement.

SEVENTY-ONE

Bumping along the road in the old Ford, I glanced at Mam and was worried for her. From initially being full of happy chatter and enthusiasm, she was noticeably quiet, and I sensed that she was now regretting suggesting the visit.

As we drove through Barnard Castle the boys were becoming excited, noticing the quaintness of the market town and the ancient octagon-shaped Market Cross that was not only a tourist attraction but also a roundabout.

We had only just passed this when Granda pointed to some buildings on our left.

'Right, we're here. There's the shop, Dick, and you can park outside, but make sure the brake is on.'

This hardly needed saying. The aunts' shop was at the top of an exceptionally steep hill aptly named The Bank. Dad slowed the Ford to a stop, front wheels braced against the kerb, handbrake hauled on, every ratchet complaining, and the car left in gear. He still looked at it anxiously as we all piled out, and had any bricks been handy I'm sure he would have used them as wheel chocks.

The shop was closed and 'for sale' notices were on the windows. I couldn't help thinking how impulsive and foolhardy this trip had been. We weren't expected and there might not be anyone at home. We all stood at the side door, which was still on the main street, and waited for someone to answer Granda's knock, then Hilda opened the door. At first it seemed she could not fathom who this little group of people were.

Then she gasped and clutched her throat as realisation slowly dawned.

'Oh my goodness! My goodness gracious! Eadie, you'll never guess who is here,' she called out as, arms outstretched in welcome, she beckoned us to come in.

Eadie, who was now crippled with arthritis, sat in the corner of the little room, her chair positioned next to a window that overlooked the busy main street. I guessed this was where she stayed for most of the day, since a little table next to her held a box of tissues, magazines and various pill bottles. She recognised Mam immediately and gave a little sob.

'Oh, Winnie lass… we've missed you so much!'

Mam, who'd already hugged Hilda as we walked in, hurried across and cuddled Eadie for what seemed like ages, both becoming tearful. Granda and Dad stood in the doorway, not speaking, just watching this reunion between neice and aunts while I waited with the boys, none of us sure what to do next. Then Hilda took charge.

'Right… you must all be gagging for a cup of tea, or maybe the boys would prefer some juice?' She looked at them, both too shy to answer. 'Now which one is which? You must be Richard because you're bigger.' Richard smiled and looked at the floor.

She turned to David who, needing no prompting, solemnly announced, 'Yes, and I'm David… and I've lost a butting off my cardiging.' He pointed to the woolly thread that once held a button.

This was a real ice-breaker and everyone laughed at the youngster's idea that speaking politely required the addition of 'ing' to each word. Any fears we might have had that we might not be welcome had gone, and as we sat enjoying the tea, sandwiches and home baking Hilda seemed to produce from nowhere, I felt as though I had known these people all my life.

The conversation was easy and I noticed that the past was never mentioned. Neither were any questions asked of Mam about our living arrangements or lifestyle. Eadie was delighting in David's constant chatter, while Richard's shy smile and quiet manner had captivated Hilda.

Dad, now relaxed and no longer fearing a cool reception, sat near the door with Granda, occasionally glancing outside to make sure the car hadn't rolled down the hill. The aunts had been welcoming and at one point I overheard Hilda telling him he had a 'family to be proud of'. He blushed and I was not sure whether this was embarrassment or pride.

The conversation turned to the shop and the 'for sale' notice, Hilda explaining that both the business and the house were being sold, the plan being that they would move to something more practical for Eadie.

Their home was anything but practical. There were many rooms alongside and above the shop, all of which seemed to be on different levels and with stairs to negotiate. They needed something that was hopefully on one level and thought they might find a property somewhere near Cotherstone, where Fred now lived.

'When did you last see Fred?' Hilda asked Granda and he thought for some time, then had to admit that he couldn't remember, but did write 'now and again'.

As they were talking, Dad was pointing to his watch, trying to discreetly signal to Mam that we should be leaving. It was late afternoon and we faced a long drive home, but Hilda noticed what was happening.

'Oh, you can't come all this way without seeing Fred. It's only four miles away and he'd love to see you all.'

Mam knew that Dad would not be happy at the prospect of yet another detour. He stood silently at the door, car keys in hand and showing no sign of enthusiasm for the visit. Nevertheless, she wasn't going to miss this chance to see her uncle and his wife Mary and was happy to let her aunt keep talking. Hilda patted Dad's arm reassuringly.

'The boys can stay here and keep Eadie company. I'll sit in the front with you and show you where the house is.'

Before Dad could think of any excuse not to go, he found himself chauffeuring Hilda, Granda, Mam and me down the steep bank and on the road to Cotherstone.

Again, we received the same shocked welcome and then emotional reunion, not only for uncle and neice, but also the two brothers – Fred and John.

After many hugs, promises not to lose touch, and tearful farewells to Fred, Hilda and Eadie, we set off again for Newcastle.

Our planned day trip had turned into an expedition. The two additional visits meant it was too late to travel back to Edinburgh and everyone was tired. Granda suggested we just stay overnight at his house, which had only one bedroom so we camped on his living room floor, utilising his cushions, spare pillows and blankets.

Granda apologised continually for the lack of comfortable bedding. Little did he know that this was luxury compared to our various experiences of roughing it in the front of our bus, and Granny's wagon.

The following morning there were more tearful farewells, Mam hugging Granda, then as we drove away, my abiding memory was of him standing at his door waving to us, and Mam silently weeping.

That journey back to Edinburgh was miserable. Dad was in 'silent mode', apart from snapping at the boys when they became boisterous. Mam and I recognised all the signs of another huff brewing.On the visit to Cotherstone he'd hardly spoken and even when returning to Granda's, he added nothing to the conversation, leading Granda to ask Mam if he was alright.

To my shame, I was relieved when Dad left Seafield the following day to return the hire car and then head off to the next ground. The atmosphere at home was happy again, all tensions gone and Mam enjoying talking over and replaying the visits. She had reconnected with her beloved aunts and bridges, long-broken, were rebuilt.

When we rejoined Dad again at the next fair, he was back to 'normal', his black mood or the cause forgotten. Showbusiness took precedence over everything and was probably his refuge and therapy. He had tasks and routines that had to be maintained – swag to set out, dynamo to check, goldfish to attend to etc etc.

He never mentioned the trip, and I wondered whether he felt a little guilty at his churlish behaviour.

Sadly, in October 1965 and only a few months after our visit, Granda died, and the following year his sister, Mam's Aunt Eadie, also passed away.

While Mam grieved for both, she took solace from knowing that they had met her children, and although not realising she was bidding her dad and aunt a final farewell, she was comforted in the memory of a trip that – finally – had reunited and repaired what had been a broken family circle.

SEVENTY-TWO

Reunions did not end with our trip to Newcastle, but with one unexpected event.

I had just finished an early shift and my bus home was not due for ten minutes. It was raining so I sheltered in the doorway of a jeweller's shop, gazing idly in the window as I waited.

And then I spotted it – displayed in a tray of second-hand rings was Mam's engagement ring! I rubbed my eyes, fearing tiredness was just playing tricks with me, and looked again. A small label described it as white gold with a claw-set diamond and just confirmed what I already knew. This was the long lost ring and I had to see it.

There were no customers in the shop, just an elderly man sitting behind the counter, gold-rimmed glasses pushed back on his head while he closely examined a piece of jewellery through a small loupe.

'Excuse me,' I ventured. 'Could I possibly see the ring in that tray?'

I pointed out which one and he sighed as though this was a great inconvenience, then produced a key from his waistcoat, unlocked the window and removed the tray, placing it on the glass counter in front of me. He looked at me, and then at the little display.

'Which ring are you interested in?'

He sounded a little impatient and I wondered whether he just considered me a time-waster, sheltering from the rain. I pointed to it and watched, scarcely able to contain my excitement as he removed it from the tray. I was already picturing Mam's delight when I triumphantly returned it to her. The man looked at the label, then examined the ring through the little loupe. By now, my heart was beating through my chest.

'Yes… it's as described on the label and it has the Newcastle assay hallmark, though it's not white gold but actually platinum… which is more expensive.'

There was no price on the label and I wondered whether the man was trying to over-promote it to beef up the price. I wished Aunt Charlotte was there. She was an expert haggler and could spot any hustle instantly.

'Do you not want to see any others? There are some prettier ones here.' He pointed to the tray again, waiting for some response from me.

I could scarcely speak. There was absolutely no doubt that this was the same ring, but now I had a problem. It would be two days before my salary was paid into the bank and I only had two pounds plus my bus fare in my purse.

I looked at the man, trying to gauge how sympathetic he might be.

'No… that's the ring I want. You see, it was my Mam's ring and she had to sell it a few years ago. It broke her heart at the time, thinking she would never see it again.'

The man's face was expressionless and I cursed myself for revealing how desperate I was to get the ring back. He would probably ask a ridiculous price for it now, but whatever that was, I knew that somehow I had to buy it – but I must have visibly gulped when he told me how much it cost. This was half my month's salary.

'Would you keep it for me if I leave a deposit and pay the balance in a couple of days?'

The man nodded, took my two pounds and wrote out a receipt, and I watched to make sure the ring was removed from the tray before the display was placed back in the window. He put the ring in an envelope and locked it in a drawer, with the warning that if I didn't return in two days it would be back on sale and my deposit was non-refundable.

Despite his gloomy warnings, I stepped out of the shop with a feeling of absolute joy at my find and a determination to complete the purchase and bring the ring 'home'.

Two days later, cash in hand and accompanied by Richard and David, both having been sworn to secrecy, we headed back to the shop. Mam did not question our departure, just accepting my excuse that we were heading for the museum in Chambers Street. This was not unusual for us as the boys and I had often visited when there were new exhibitions, and admission was free.

The same man sat behind the counter, still peering through the loupe at some minute object, as we entered the shop. I approached the counter, the boys on either side of me, hoping the sight of my two little brothers and the story of our mother's sacrifice might soften the man's heart and result in a discount. He looked up.

'Yes, can I help you?'

I was alarmed. It seemed he did not remember me. Had he already sold it?

'I've come to pay the balance on this.' I handed him the receipt.

He put down the loupe, wiped his spectacles then closely examined the piece of paper.

'Ah… yes, the ring.' He looked at the two boys as he opened the drawer, brought out the envelope and tipped the ring onto the counter. 'And it was your mother's, I'm told?' He watched as they gazed at it, nodding their heads to confirm the fact, both looking suitably well-scrubbed and angelic.

I was sure our little ploy would melt the man's heart until he handed me the bill and I realised it was for the full amount.

We left the shop with our purchase, which was not even in a box but back in the envelope, along with a receipt and another warning from the man that he did not give refunds. We didn't care. We were just delighted to have 'rescued' the ring, although it did feel to me that I'd paid a fairly hefty ransom for it.

Making sure Dad was not at home before revealing our surprise, we sat Mam down and made her a cup of tea, worried that she might be shocked. Richard and David could scarcely control their excitement and it was obvious to Mam that we'd been up to something.

I handed her the envelope and at first she thought it was empty. For a moment I worried that I'd lost it. Puzzled, and urged on by us, she shook the envelope then gasped as the little ring tumbled out and into her hand.

We watched as she held it, her look of disbelief turning to shock then tearful delight when she realised what she was holding. I described how I had found the ring and she loved the story, especially our attempt to 'hustle' the man by trying for a sympathy vote, and insisted on hearing it several more times.

I avoided telling her how much I'd paid, and she refrained from asking, unwilling to spoil the moment for us. Unfortunately, a few days later she found the receipt and was horrified to discover that not only was this three times more than she had previously been given for it, but it was also the same shop.

Without telling us, and furious at the thought of her children being grossly overcharged, she took the ring and receipt back, primed and prepared to confront the jeweller.

This was the Edinburgh Festival month. The High Street and Royal Mile thronged with visitors, Mam having to side-step and dodge people who seemed to constantly get in her way, adding to her irritation. By the time she reached the shop she was ready for battle.

She recognised the man immediately as the one who had bought her ring.

'Can I help you, madam?' he asked, obviously anticipating a sale.

'Do you recognise this?' Mam demanded, holding out the ring and throwing the receipt onto the counter. The man looked bewildered and shook his head.

'Well… *you* bought it from me, and now you've charged my kids *three times* what you paid me, for them to buy it *back*!'

Now realisation was beginning to dawn, the man smirked slightly and asked her, 'And your point is?'

This response only served to infuriate Mam further and she was determined to shame him, especially now that a group of American tourists had come into the shop.

'My *point* is that this is gross profiteering, made all the worse by you overcharging kids. Have you no conscience or moral compass?'

Arms wide open as though he was about to embrace someone, he shrugged again. 'Well, my dear… *that's business*!'

She realised that her words were having no impact on the man and was aware that the Americans had been listening. As she was leaving , she turned to them and said, 'There are *some* businesses that don't *deserve* customers,' and then stomped out of the shop, noting with satisfaction that the Americans had also decided to leave.

Calmer now on the bus home, she looked at the ring, remembering the day in Newcastle when Dad proposed, and his insistence that they chose the ring that same day; the number of times over the years that, watched by her children, she'd taken it from its box, polished it and replaced it, ready to be worn

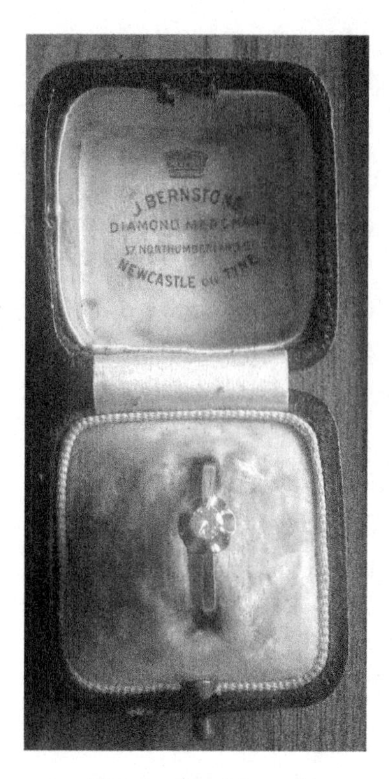

The ring 'back home'

on special occasions, which were few and far between; and then the agony of having to sell it, the memory still painful.

Once home, she replaced it back in the little box she'd kept, delighted that another piece of her life had been found and returned home.

She recalled the scenario in the jeweller's, pleased that while she hadn't managed to shame him, she had at least lost him the custom and spend potential of the Americans.

Mam insisted, despite my protestations, on repaying me and that I put the money back into my bank account.

We often talked about the ring, wondering who, if anyone, had worn it after Mam, and whether some similar misfortune had required *them* to sell it back. We also considered the very real possibility that it was not resold and had just remained, forgotten, in the back of the jeweller's cabinet until he'd gathered enough second-hand rings to justify a display.

Either way, we didn't care and had managed the situation from start to finish without Dad knowing.

The boys were reminded to keep shtum about our trip to the jeweller's, and I was also relieved that I was no longer required to keep the secret of the original sale.

SEVENTY-THREE

It was now 1966 and we were still coping with our 'homeless' nomadic summers – the trailer, in the absence of any solution, becoming a permanent fixture on Seafield.

Although not well off, we at least were debt-free and somehow coping financially. However, we still dreaded the weekends, not just for the often torturous journeys out to help Dad at the weekends, but also wondering what our reception would be when we arrived.

We never knew what to expect, and although we accepted that these summer months were just as difficult for him, it was hard to make allowances when we were on the receiving end. Whether it was the stress of travelling without his home or only seeing us at the weekends, his mood swings seemed much worse. Mam, Richard and I had experienced this for years, and while David was probably still too young to notice, for us it was tantamount to mental cruelty. Dad could change within hours and for no apparent reason, often brooding head in hands, not speaking and just gazing at the floor.

Whenever Mam tried to ask him what was wrong, he just scowled, refused to talk and walked out… usually to sit in Granny's wagon, still silent and making their lives equally miserable.

Mam remembered Granny's comment years earlier – that he had 'always been a moody bugger, just like his father', and worried that he might be morphing into a clone of Old Teddy, who she had never liked.

In more enlightened times, Dad might have been diagnosed as bi-polar, but this was still the sixties, and mood swings were generally considered to be personality flaws rather than signs of depressive illnesses.

As a young adult I sometimes challenged his behaviour, using humour to jolt him out of the mood, even calling him 'old torn face', which often worked.

During our many conversations, I once asked Mam why she had tolerated the lifestylea and also Dad's moods for so many years. She did not hesitate in her response.

'You must remember that although your dad never actually *says* so, he loves us, and has always tried his best to look after us. He doesn't drink, he is a hard worker… and some of the jobs he's taken during the winters have been awful. He has fretted and worried along with me whenever any of you have been ill, enjoyed boasting about the various skills you all have, and is so proud of you. Yes, he has flaws… but haven't we all? And as for the lifestyle… Well, admittedly not one I originally expected when we married, but I was accepted into the community by the showmen/women, treated with nothing but kindness, and I grew to respect them.' She thought for a moment, considering what else to add. 'Nonetheless, this has never been the life I wanted for any of you and my agenda remains unchanged. We *will* settle down!'

My birthdays always coincided with the July fair at Burntisland, where we opened to catch the Glasgow Fair holidaymakers every summer.

This year's birthday was my twenty-first and Aunt Marie declared that a party must be held. Since we were still 'homeless' (i.e. camping in the front of our bus), she insisted that it be held in her trailer. I never enjoyed 'fuss' or being the centre of attention, and hadn't even told my work colleagues that I would be twenty-one, but everyone insisted that this was a special day and must be celebrated.

I'd already received my gift of a gold bracelet watch from Mam and Dad, and Uncle Leslie had sent me a gold locket, so I was quite happy just to let the day pass without any further acknowledgement, but Marie would not give up and a party was arranged to take place once we'd closed.

I received several small gifts and cards from my aunts, and when I opened Aunt Rosie's card I found she had enclosed the five £1 premium bonds I'd given her as 'surety' years previously. I was so touched that she'd kept them for me and couldn't help feeling that this, just like Mam's family and then the ring, was yet another 'reunion'.

I don't know how everyone managed to squeeze into Marie's trailer that night. Every available bit of space and seating was taken – aunts, uncles, cousins, various travellers from the ground, and of course my own family, all determined that I would enjoy the event. I was most embarrassed and uncomfortable, wishing the whole thing was over. However, once the 'birthday bit' was done, it just evolved into one of Marie's usual parties. Relieved that I was no longer the main event, I was able to relax and enjoy the family get-together.

As the evening progressed and drink flowed, the music began. Dad played the accordion, trying to accompany those who wanted to sing, and I realised, having heard all these songs countless times before, that everyone had a favourite, a signature tune that was trotted out at every event.

I watched and listened, and suddenly understood – almost as a eureka moment – that these 'party pieces', which as a youngster I'd always considered to be embarrassingly sentimental schmaltz, were actually forms of communication… apologies for harms caused, or reaffirmations of love.

I noted that Aunt Marie and Uncle John weren't singing to us, but to each other, and when it was Dad's turn, he gazed at Mam as he sang 'Do I Worry', a 1941 song by the 'Ink Spots', the lyrics all about the man's fear of losing his woman and agonising over the many ways this might happen. Dad was quite emotional at the end and everyone blamed the drink, but I felt that this was his way of telling Mam that he always feared she would leave.

Mam's song was 'Can't Help Lovin' That Man of Mine' from the film 'Showboat', where the woman declares forgiveness and undying love for the man, no matter how badly he might treat her. Everyone was silent as Mam sang, listening as though hearing the song for the first time. She sang with such hearfelt emotion it was almost as though she was re-living the heartache of the broken promises, hardships and happiness of her married life. When she finished there was a round of applause, quickly followed by Aunt Marie topping up everyone's drinks, and the party continued.

I began to understand that relationships were a bit like a mirror – initially perfect and a reflection of what should be, but if later cracked or broken, the shards and pieces remained, still reflecting something precious and to be cherished… perhaps not as perfect… just different.

I declined my aunt's offer of another drink, wondering whether that was causing my psychoanalysis of the songs, and decided I needed to go to bed.

Gathering up my cards, gifts and some remaining pieces of birthday cake, I thanked everyone for my day and headed off to Granny's wagon, a feeling of great euphoria at my twenty-one-year-old maturity as I staggered up the wooden steps… or perhaps it was just the drink!

SEVENTY-FOUR

Back home to Seafield again. Mam, the boys and I dumped our various bags on the trailer floor, thankful that fairs and long journeys were over for another week.

Richard, who had become the family tease, was tormenting David, both boys still a bit fractious after the trip. The settled part of our week, minus Dad, was beginning again. Mam filled the kettle, tea always first on the agenda.

'Right, you lot. I'm going round to Mrs C's to check whether we have any letters.'

'Mrs C' and her husband were the caretakers, and with their trailer positioned at the yard entrance, it was convenient for the postman to leave everyone's mail with them.

During our 'Bowmaker period', when the red-letter, final demand notices arrived, this collection arrangement had been quite embarrassing for Mam, but Mrs C refrained discreetly from commenting.

The kettle boiled, I made the tea, and a few minutes later Mam returned and sat down, hands shaking – gazing fearfully at the as yet unopened letter.

'Are you alright, Mam?' I asked, afraid that this was going to be bad news.

The boys were quiet now and we all sat next to her, watching as she slowly and carefully opened the envelope as though it contained some terrible contaminant.

By now, the tea was starting to stew on the cooker, but this was the least of our worries.

She unfolded the letter, every transaction seeming agonisingly slow, and then she read and re-read the contents, clearly not believing what she was seeing.

Then she looked at us, her cheeks flushed with excitement.

'OH MY GOD! It's actually going to happen… the council are offering us a house!'

'FINALE'

So, was this to be the fairytale ending she'd dreamt of for over twenty years?

Well, as our Mam would say…

'That's *another* story!'

POSTSCRIPT

VINEGARHILL

While doing a little bit of research about Vinegarhill, I came across a whole variety of articles by the Parkhead Historical Society, which also included the story of Vinegarhill.

I had only ever known the yard as a temporary 'stopover' for us when we needed a 'pull on' during gaps in our round of fairs. I never liked the place – especially the awful smell, which we were told was from the nearby gutworks – and was always glad to leave.

However, it was home to several members of my dad's family. His brother Harry and sister Becky were permanent residents, while others, such as his brothers Edward and John, spent their winters there. They regarded Vinegarhill and Glasgow as their home, just as we viewed our base in Edinburgh, on the Seafield yard.

I was unaware that travelling showmen and fairs had such a deep-rooted history in Vinegarhill until I read the article, and am indebted to the Society for allowing me to add it to 'my' story.

For anyone interested in learning more about the life and culture of travelling showpeople, The National Fairground Archive, which is based in Sheffield University Main Library, houses a huge and unique collection of material – photographic, audiovisual and printed.

Email: fairground@sheffield.ac.uk ***Web page: http://www.shef.ac.uk/nfa***

Printed in Great Britain
by Amazon